FORGIVING
OUR PARENTS
FORGIVING
OUR SELVES

FORGIVING
OUR PARENTS
FORGIVING
OUR SELVES

Healing Adult Children of
Dysfunctional Families

Dr. David Stoop
and
Dr. James Masteller

Regal

From Gospel Light
Ventura, California, U.S.A.

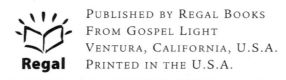

PUBLISHED BY REGAL BOOKS
FROM GOSPEL LIGHT
VENTURA, CALIFORNIA, U.S.A.
PRINTED IN THE U.S.A.

Regal Books is a ministry of Gospel Light, a Christian publisher dedicated to serving the local church. We believe God's vision for Gospel Light is to provide church leaders with biblical, user-friendly materials that will help them evangelize, disciple and minister to children, youth and families.

It is our prayer that this Regal book will help you discover biblical truth for your own life and help you meet the needs of others. May God richly bless you.

For a free catalog of resources from Regal Books/Gospel Light, please call your Christian supplier or contact us at 1-800-4-GOSPEL *or* www.regalbooks.com.

Originally published by Servant Publications in 1991.

Published in association with the literary agency of Alive Communications, Inc., 7680 Goddard Street, Suite 200, Colorado Springs, CO 80920.

All Scripture quotations, unless otherwise indicated, are taken from the *Holy Bible, New International Version®. NIV®.* Copyright © 1973, 1978, 1984 by International Bible Society. Used by permission of Zondervan Publishing House. All rights reserved.

© 1991, 1996 Dr. David Stoop
All rights reserved.

Library of Congress Cataloging-in-Publication Data
Stoop, David A.
  Forgiving our parents, forgiving ourselves : healing adult children of dysfunctional families / David Stoop and James Masteller.
    p. cm.
  ISBN 0-8307-3423-6
  1. Adult children of dysfunctional families—Psychology. 2. Problem families—Psychological aspects. 3. Forgiveness. I. Masteller, James, 1943- II. Title.
RC455.4.F3S785 2004
362.82'4—dc22   2003028052

        6 7 8 9 10 11 12 13 14 15 / 14 13 12 11 10

Rights for publishing this book in other languages are contracted by Gospel Light Worldwide, the international nonprofit ministry of Gospel Light. Gospel Light Worldwide also provides publishing and technical assistance to international publishers dedicated to producing Sunday School and Vacation Bible School curricula and books in the languages of the world. For additional information, visit www.gospellightworldwide.org; write to Gospel Light Worldwide, P.O. Box 3875, Ventura, CA 93006; or send an e-mail to info@gospellightworldwide.org.

CONTENTS

ACKNOWLEDGMENTS

MY SINCERE THANKS to Ann Spangler, Beth Feia, John Blattner, and Cec Murphey for their expertise and help in bringing this book together. The staff at Servant Publications has been the best!

And to my colleagues—Dr. Henry Cloud, Dr. John Townsend, and Dr. Paul Meier—my gratitude for their role as we worked through many of the ideas on forgiveness both in our seminars and in our work at the clinic.

INTRODUCTION

MORE AND MORE the family is being seen as it really is—the primary influence in our lives that not only builds us and shapes us, but also sets in motion the disorders that limit and frustrate us as adults. The child who was physically or emotionally abused, for example, usually becomes an adult who will also tend to abuse his or her own children, or else will marry someone who does. All too many of us find ourselves behaving like our parents in ways that we vowed we would never repeat, even though we don't have to follow that pattern.

I remember the pain of a young man whose wife had left him for another man. As he talked to me about it, he mentioned in passing that she was at the same age as her mother was when her mother left her father for another man. I asked him about what he had just said. He didn't answer. He just sat there shaking his head, tears filling his eyes. Finally he said, "I can't understand it. She talked often of the pain her mother had caused by leaving. She was still angry at her mother for it. Now she's gone and done the same thing. Why?"

There is no simple answer to the pain of these patterns. Usually, these problems serve a function within the extended family that is beyond our awareness. That is why we get stuck behaving in ways we swore we never would. In some cases, the function that is served by our problem within the family will literally drive us mad.

Many people, in trying to break patterns like these, decide they are better off to try to go on without their family. They move away—even across the country. They stop writing or calling, and start acting like they have no family. But so many times they keep finding themselves drawn back home.

Others try to confront their family, thinking that if they express their hurt and anger directly, things will be resolved. There seems to be a movement today encouraging people to confront their parents, often with devastating results for everyone. Many times, the confrontation alienates the family members even more. People are separated and nothing is resolved.

Deep down inside each of us is a longing for a satisfying and lasting family relationship. The task for each of us is to somehow come to grips with our family and to resolve the basic issues we have with the individuals within our family. The only way I know to resolve the issues of the past in our families is through forgiveness. The alternative is to hold onto grudges, and we pay a tremendous price for doing that.

As a physician and psychiatrist, I can attest to the vast medical and physiological consequences that take place when we don't get our home in order. Dr. C. Everett Koop, our former U.S. Surgeon General, has told me personally that about 80 percent of all the medical illness seen in a doctor's office are either caused by emotional stress, or will be significantly worsened by stressors.

Ongoing, unresolved family issues, along with other stressors, cause ACTHRF (adrenocorticotrophic hormone releasing factor) to be released from the hypothalamus, causing ACTH to be released from the pituitary gland. This causes stress hormones to flow out of the adrenal glands, causing decreased lymphocytes (white blood cells), decreased antibodies, and increased vulnerability to all kinds of infectious diseases, including viral-induced cancers.

The physical, emotional, and spiritual aspects of a human being are all intricately intertwined. Repressed injuries that we experienced in our families can cause migraine headaches, ulcers, colitis, muscle aches, and other disorders. But we often forget that they can also be the indirect cause of bronchitis, pneumonia, strokes, cardiovascular disease, mental illness, and death. Taking the effort to analyze and understand the dynamics of our families of origin will help us to take control of our lives, and to move in new and healthier directions. Unless forgiveness is part of the equation, our analysis and understanding will leave us still caught in the family dysfunction.

I have known Dr. Stoop for many years, both as a colleague and as a personal friend. There is no one I trust more to guide me personally into an understanding of my family and its issues. His gifted abilities and experiences, as well as his extensive psychological and theological training, have all contributed to this important book. All too often the process of forgiveness is either left out or distorted. I'm thrilled that Dr. Stoop and Dr. Masteller have restored it to its central role in the process of our healing.

Paul D. Meier, M.D.

"If dad were around today, he'd be charged with child abuse."

"No way!" I cried. "Not *our* dad!"

"Think about it," my sister replied. Then she hung up.

This terse conversation took place more than ten years ago. But I remember it as though it had happened yesterday. The moment my sister slammed down her receiver was the moment my bubble burst. For years I had thought my dad was the ideal father. Now suddenly I found I could do so no longer.

He had been dead for twenty years at the time of our angry conversation. I did not particularly like to talk about him, for I had very little of him to hold onto in my memory. So I was not about to let anyone—not even my sister—destroy what little I had left.

Her remark about child abuse had to do with the way Dad used a belt when he spanked us—or at least when he spanked *me*. I never believed that he spanked *her* at all; according to my recollection, I took the blame for everything she did. I'm sure she remembers it differently. Dad believed in spanking. The only problem was that the spankings always came with a heavy overlay of anger and a lot of physical abuse.

Getting spanked by my father always followed a familiar pattern—almost a sort of ritual. Something would go wrong, and he'd look at me with that stern glare and snap, "Get down to the basement." I knew what *that* meant. There was no way to talk him out of it. Begging didn't work. I know; I tried it many times. Even offering an explanation was useless.

I can still remember how I felt, slouching down the

basement stairs with him close behind me. First, he'd take off his belt; then he'd sit on a chair in the middle of the room. I'd bend over. Then I'd get the belt across my backside.

My dad would remain silent through all this. If I cried too much, I'd get more. If I didn't cry *enough*, I'd get more. I remember working out a system for knowing how much crying was "enough." I'd wail away until he warned me to stop "before he gave me something to cry *about.*" That was my cue to quit, perhaps with a few final sniffles thrown in for good measure.

Once or twice I tried to stuff a book or magazine down my pants before heading downstairs. Despite the fact that our family went to church every Sunday, I wasn't exactly what you'd call a "praying man." But at those moments I'd pray earnestly that Dad wouldn't notice. One time he didn't notice until he was almost finished whipping me. He icily ordered me to take the book out. Then he spanked me for that infraction as well.

Up until that conversation with my sister, I never gave much thought to those incidents. Actually, compared to what some of my friends reported about the way they got disciplined, I didn't think the treatment I got was all that awful. *Everybody* got spanked by their parents in those days. And I don't suppose I really wanted to spend much time recalling the sick, scared feeling in my stomach when the time came to "go downstairs."

Still, when I was getting spanked, at least I had my dad's attention. For the most part, he always seemed too tired or distracted to notice me, or to care about anything that interested me. He worked long hours in a factory. When he came home at night, he was extremely tired. On the weekends he spent most of his time keeping the house up, working until he was exhausted.

The rest of his time—what little there was—was spent in "Porchville." We lived in Cleveland, Ohio, in a small house with a porch across the front and a swing at one end of the porch. I can remember Dad sitting on that swing, reading the newspaper or just staring out across the lawn. When he was finished with the paper, he would go out to the garage to work on something. We never talked about much of anything. Dad never took time to play catch with me, or to notice how I threw a ball or fielded a grounder. He was emotionally absent—except when the time came to "go downstairs."

The interesting thing is that for years, if you had asked me whether I'd had a happy childhood, I would have said yes without giving it a second thought. Were we close as a family? "Of course," would have been my answer. My parents took good care of us. We never lacked for anything important. We were a good family.

Or were we? My sister's words on the phone suddenly made me feel less confident that we really *were* all that close, or that everything had really been all that wonderful. I did not like these new thoughts. They felt dangerous.

Like all people who have idealized a parent, I had let my dad off the hook in a number of ways. I had carefully created a picture of my family as a happy place, one where anything unpleasant could be readily explained away. I focused on remembering the good parts.

For example, because we were all so emotionally distant, I enjoyed a great deal of freedom and independence. I had newspaper routes from an early age, so I always had money. In summer, when school was out, I could hop on my bike in the morning and not come home until dinner time. One of my special pleasures was going to symphony concerts all by myself, even in grade school. I'd ride the streetcar there and back.

It wasn't until years later—when I realized that I never allowed *my* kids that kind of freedom—that I began to have second thoughts about my family. I came to see that the reason why I didn't grant my kids that kind of latitude was not simply because "times are different now." It had to do with the fact that in my mind, all that freedom was linked to a sense of emotional abandonment. I just knew I wanted my family to be *different.*

I worked hard at earning Dad's approval. One summer, when I was still in grade school, his major project was repainting our wood frame house. I found it fascinating. I wanted to do what my dad was doing, so I pestered him to let me help. I could paint the bottom rows of siding, I said. He wasn't interested. "You don't know anything about painting," he said. "Go play with your friends. I've got work to do."

Several weeks later I was attending a Vacation Bible School at church. The craft project was to build a birdhouse. If we finished it in time, we would get to paint it. I felt so proud when the teacher commented on how well I had painted my birdhouse. "You're an excellent painter," she said. "You even know how to hold the brush."

I couldn't wait to show the finished project to my dad. When I told him what the teacher had said, he responded with a quick glance and a barely-audible, "Hmmm." Then he went back to reading his paper.

I can still remember the hot shame on my cheeks. Why did I have to have such an old father, one who was always too tired to care about what I did?

As I grew to adulthood, I searched for answers, for some way to understand why my father was the way he was. I wanted to find out what he was like, and where he had come from.

He had come to the United States from Northern Ireland, I knew that much. I had always been proud of the fact that my dad was Irish, and my mom *mostly* Irish. But when I asked him about it, he would brush me off with a gruff, "I don't want to talk about it." I dreamt of someday going to Ireland. I once asked him if he ever wanted to go back. "Never!" was his standard reply.

Dad lived in Northern Ireland during the tumultuous era that Leon Uris wrote about in his novel, *Trinity*. It was a cruel, terrifying period of history. The few things Dad did say about Ireland were beyond my comprehension. He would talk about "the troubles," and about truckloads of bodies being dumped into the river. Then he would become silent, and nothing could get him talking again. He acted as though he wanted to forget his roots.

But other things he did seemed to belie his disinterest in his heritage. Sometimes I would find him sitting in the living room, next to the radio, listening to the Queen of England speaking on a Canadian station. I remember thinking to myself, "Why is he so interested in what the Queen is saying if he won't even talk about where he grew up?"

I dug around, asked questions, and pried loose whatever scraps of information I could. I learned that my father's father had died when Dad was only thirteen (though I could never learn *how* he died). It became Dad's job to take care of his mother at that point. When the family came to America years later, it was still his job to look after her. It was through reading Uris' book that I learned of the old Irish tradition of the youngest son taking care of the widowed mother. Dad had no life of his own until he was thirty-three. That was when his mother died. He met and married my mother when he was thirty-five.

I worked hard at maintaining my idealized picture of my father. I started at an early age, and kept at it long after he died. Now, even after talking with my sister, as I struggled with my hurt and anger toward this man who had passed away so many years before, I found I still wanted to let him off the hook. I could still explain away most of what I remembered.

My studies in developmental psychology only reinforced my rationalizations. It was clear to me that my dad had lived a painful childhood. He knew little of intimacy or closeness in his family. His mother, I learned, had been a large, domineering woman who had controlled his life for thirty-three years. His brothers and sisters had gone off and built lives of their own. But not him. How, then, could I expect him to know how to relate any better to me?

But after the conversation with my sister, it suddenly became more difficult to believe the things I told myself about Dad. I finally had to admit it; he had failed me and injured me in many ways. Yes, there were reasons. Yes, it may not have been "all his fault." But it still hurt!

I began having angry confrontations with him in my mind as I was driving, or lying awake in the middle of the night. I told him all the things I had wanted from him that he never gave me. I let him know how afraid I was of him, how I tried to stay out of his way in order to avoid his temper. I told him how much I missed having a father who was interested in me and in what I was doing. I found myself, twenty years later, grieving over his death—something I had been unable to do at the time.

I wrote down some of the conversations that coursed through my mind, and related them to some people I trusted. As I did, the burden of pain and anger seemed to lift. I was surprised to discover that the image I held of my father did not disappear. If anything, he became more real, more complete. I still saw a father who had disappointed and injured me. But I also saw a man with strength and goodness in him. My new image, I felt certain, was much closer to reality.

But even though I had worked through my "father issues," the process still felt incomplete somehow. The bubble of idealization had burst. But I didn't feel settled. There was one more step needed to complete the process. I needed to *forgive* my father.

Why? Wasn't he dead and gone? What would be the point of

forgiveness in such a situation? What was to be gained? The answers to these questions helped me come to a whole new understanding of what forgiveness is all about. Working through the issues raised by my own experience laid the foundation for much of the work I now do with patients in the clinic, for my workshops and seminars, and for this book. *Forgiveness,* I have learned, *is the key to resolving the pain of the past.* Without it, nothing is ever laid to rest.

My own time of grappling with these issues came just as I was starting in practice as a psychologist. I was bothered by the fact that despite my best and most determined efforts to have things be "different," I was noticing in myself the same kind of detachment toward my children that my father had shown towards me. I became intensely interested in how families worked, and why patterns of relating that were hated and despised nevertheless got passed along from generation to generation. The study of Family Therapy provided a framework for solving these riddles, not only in my life, but in the lives of the people I worked with.

The issues you face regarding your parents will be different than mine. They may be far more painful and damaging. But as you read this book, I want you to know that I have walked the path of hurt, confusion, and pain that you now walk—and that I also know the release that will come as you follow the path of forgiveness. It was not until I worked through the process of forgiving my father, both for what he did and for what he did not do, that I felt our relationship was settled. And when that happened, I found that some other important relationship issues got settled for me as well, including a new openness to my own family.

A word of encouragement: many people are put off by the word, "forgiveness." Don't be. The purpose of this book is to explain what forgiveness is really all about. We'll see that its greatest value lies in what it does *within us,* and that forgiveness need not have anything at all to do with those who have hurt us until later—if, indeed, it needs to involve them at all. Forgiveness is for *us.* It sets us free.

PART ONE

Unpacking Family Baggage

1

*The pain and heartache
you may have suffered in your family
may tempt you to put your family
behind you once and for all.
But "leaving home" is not that easy—
and may not be the healthiest
course of action, anyway.*

Family: Who Needs It?

BRIAN WAS CLEARLY in a bad way.

By the time he came to see me, he had been hospitalized four separate times for the same set of problems: severe depression, alienation, thoughts of suicide. The hospitals and clinics he had attended had all done their best, applying every conceivable form of individual treatment and therapy. Brian would get better for a while, improved enough to be released and sent home. But before long his symptoms would reappear and he would be right back where he started.

We talked for a long time. I* asked him a lot of questions about himself, his feelings, his problems. I also asked him about his family. Much experience has taught me that family patterns can sometimes unlock mysteries that have yielded to no other attempts at understanding. One of the things he told me was that several years before—just prior to his first hospitalization—his cousin Sheila had tried to commit suicide. The attempt had failed, and she had been left permanently handicapped as a result.

---

* Throughout the book, when a single individual is speaking, the "I" refers to David Stoop. When both of us are speaking, the "we" refers to David Stoop and Jim Masteller.

Brian spoke bitterly about the way his family blamed *him* for what had happened to his cousin. It seems that a week before she tried to kill herself, Sheila had talked to Brian about how hopeless she felt, how alone and depressed. Brian had been alarmed. He had asked her if she was contemplating suicide. She had insisted vehemently that she was not. Then, a week later, she made her futile but destructive attempt.

Family patterns can sometimes unlock mysteries that have yielded to no other attempts at understanding.

When the family heard about Brian's conversation with Sheila, they were outraged. Surely he should have seen what was coming! Surely he should have insisted that Sheila seek help! Surely he should have *told* someone what was going on! The fact that Sheila had specifically denied that she was thinking of suicide meant nothing. It was all his fault—or so the family seemed to think.

And so, in time, did Brian. He was only fifteen years old at the time, and could not possibly have been expected to recognize his cousin's cry for help. But he felt responsible for what had happened. His parents, his aunts and uncles—they were right. It *was* his fault. He *was* to blame for Sheila's tragic condition. The feelings of remorse and guilt were almost enough to—quite literally—drive him crazy.

Over the course of our time together, I was able to point out to Brian the pattern that seemed to have developed regarding his problems. When he went into the hospital— where, of course, he was away from his family—he got better. But when he got out, and went back home to live, it was only a matter of months until his trouble resurfaced.

I talked to Brian about *dysfunctional family systems*—about patterns of behavior and relationships within families that work to make us unhealthy rather than healthy. I talked to him about the roles that members of such families take on, and the effects those roles can have on them. In particular, I talked to him about the role of scapegoat—the one onto whom all the others project their own feelings of guilt and shame. The more we talked, the clearer it became to Brian and to me that his problems stemmed, at least in part, from his participation in a highly dysfunctional family. In time we were able to identify a number of family patterns and dynamics that had to change if Brian were to remain healthy. There were other factors, of course: the treatment and therapy provided in the hospital played an important role. But in Brian's case, family issues were the key. As we worked to resolve them, his other problems became more manageable and his life became more stable.

Children don't know what causes their misery. In fact, children don't realize their dysfunctional home is abnormal. Even physically abused kids don't realize, while young, that normal parents don't beat their kids; they think that there is no other way to live.
—Nancy Curtis, *Beyond Survival,*
(Lake Mary, FL: Strang Communications,
1990) pp. 27- 28.

THE DAUGHTER WHO DIDN'T UNDERSTAND

Julie came from what most people would consider a perfectly "normal" family. On the outside, her parents looked like the classic "Ozzie and Harriet" couple. Her mother and father were still faithfully married to each other. Her father provided well for the family. Her mother never worked, preferring to stay home and care for the children. But on the inside, there were subtle dynamics at work in Julie's family that made it a difficult place to live.

One day Julie poured out her pain over one especially vivid memory. She was about four years old, and she was walking somewhere with her parents. They were arguing about something—Julie never knew about what—and all at once her mother simply started walking away. Julie's father suddenly turned and yelled at *Julie.* He grabbed her by the shoulders, shook her, and threw her down on the sidewalk. Then he stomped away.

Julie's mother froze in her tracks. For what seemed like forever, she simply stood there, staring at Julie, then at Julie's father. Finally she motioned for Julie to come to her. Julie ran to her mother in tears and clung to her, sobbing.

A few minutes later, Julie and her mother came around a corner and found her father standing there, about twenty feet away, his hands in his pockets, his head down, shuffling his feet awkwardly. "He looked like a hurt little boy," Julie said. "Like a little boy who knew he had done a bad thing and didn't know what to do about it."

Neither Julie's mother nor her father said a word. They just *silently* fell in and started walking again. Julie remembers her father reaching out to tousle her hair. She drew back, still trembling with fear from his recent outburst. But her mother seemed to have forgotten all about it. The three of them walked along together, her mother holding hands with Julie's father on one side and with Julie on the other. Years later, Julie could still remember the confusion she felt, the empty, hurt feeling inside. How could her father treat her like that? How could her mother *let* him? And how could both of them simply go on *as if nothing had happened?*

As I listened to Julie talk, I wondered to myself how many other times that scene had been played out. How many times was she angrily shoved aside, bearing the brunt of a parent's pent-up anger? How many times, I wondered, had her *father* been similarly shoved aside, his fears and hurts ignored, when *he* was a child? Julie had described him as looking like "a hurt little boy." I suspected there was more truth to that characterization than she knew.

And what about Julie's mother? What did her behavior say about the way she had learned to deal with conflict? Evidently she had learned not to confront, but to simply stand back, stay silent, and wait for the storm to pass. Julie described her as literally caught between the two people who were the most important to her, silently enduring their crises, hoping for the best.

In time Julie and I were able to learn more about both her own family and about her parents' families. We could see how patterns of behavior had been passed *cross-generationally* to both parents, and then on to her. She came to understand how her mother's *peacemaker* role prevented clean, clear resolution of problems. She came to recognize how *unspoken rules* in her family prevented everyone from talking about what they were experiencing, and from dealing with unpleasant realities. As Julie worked through the pain of her new awareness, she gradually discovered a wonderful freedom from unhealthy self-concepts and destructive emotions that had plagued her all her life.

THE LITTLE GIRL NOBODY BELIEVED AND THE PARENTS WHO WOULDN'T REMEMBER

Mary's story was more traumatic. Her depression was so severe and so long-standing that it was hard for her to dig

27

through the layers of emotional callouses she had built up, and to come to grips with her family background.

That background was a nightmare. Her father was an alcoholic. Her mother was physically abusive; Mary told how she had once beaten her with a metal towel rack. Both parents were verbally abusive. Mary told of the relief she felt when they would go out and leave her and her older brother home alone. But even that soon led to other problems.

When Mary was eight years old, her brother raped her. Later, when her mother came home, Mary sobbed as she told her what had happened. Her mother never even checked Mary's physical condition. When the brother denied having done anything wrong, Mary's mother called *her* a liar and sent her to her room. Both Mary and her brother learned the *lesson* of this incident: that the sexual abuse could continue and that Mary would endure in silence.

It took Mary a long time even to be able to remember all this. When she first came for help, she was not even aware that sexual abuse was part of her problem. Once this issue came to light, however, it was easy for Mary to see how the *law of silence* had held her prisoner all her life.

Lydia, by contrast, came into the clinic knowing full well that she needed to deal with issues of sexual abuse. Her stepfather had molested her from the time she was twelve until she left home at age sixteen. Her mother knew what was happening but did nothing about it. She simply waited in another room until it was over. Sometimes she even watched it occur.

After spending several weeks working through this issue, Lydia's therapist arranged for her mother and stepfather to come to the hospital for a combined session. Lydia had written down what she wanted to say to them. She had even practiced with other patients how she would say it. There would be no hysterical name-calling or exaggerated accusation, just a straightforward recitation of what had happened and how it had made her feel. Lydia and her therapist felt that taking this step was important if Lydia was to let go of her bitterness and get free of her past.

Lydia's parents sat silently through her presentation. When she finished, they stoically denied everything—both of them! They were quite calm and matter-of-fact about it. The only emotion they showed was irritation that Lydia had accused them of "such terrible things" in front of a stranger. In some ways, Lydia had run into a brick wall. She went back to the group and was talking through her disappointment at her parents' denial. As she worked through her feelings, she was also able to see why she had been held hostage by her past for so long.

Larry spent most of the five years of his life waiting. Usually, he was sitting in the back seat of a car, waiting for his parents to emerge, thoroughly drunk, from some bar. He became accustomed to being left behind. One day he stood on his aunt's front porch and watched his parents drive away and leave him yet again. But this time was different: this time they never came back.

As bad as those first five years had been, they were overshadowed by the questions that haunted him into adulthood. Where did his parents go? Why did they leave him? Where were they now? No one in Larry's family knows the answer to those questions. Larry has had to learn how to deal with the gaping hole left by his parents' *abandonment* of him. When he came to the clinic he was burned out from trying so hard to win everyone's approval. Slowly he started to see that his present lifestyle was directly connected to his fear of being abandoned and the experiences of his childhood.

ADULT CHILDREN OF DYSFUNCTIONAL FAMILIES

The people we have just described—and many others whose stories we could recount—are unique individuals with distinctly different backgrounds and life circumstances. No two are alike in every respect. But they are all alike in one very important respect: they are all products of families whose dynamics and relational patterns were sufficiently disordered that they can be considered *dysfunctional.*

Once we know what to look for and how to interpret it, we can all gain from understanding the dysfunctional dynamics of our own families—whether or not our pasts are scarred by such obvious forms of dysfunction as physical and sexual abuse, divorce, and the like.

To use a more convenient label, they are all *adult children of dysfunctional families.* They are grown men and women who, after years of struggling with a variety of emotional, psychological, and relational problems, have come to realize that part of the reason they "are the way they are" is because something in their family background made them that way. Usually there are other factors involved as well. But in all these cases, and in many others besides, family dynamics wound up holding the key to recovery. As these men and women have come to understand more clearly the way these dynamics have affected them, they have been able to cut themselves loose from their effects and go on to live happier, more fruitful lives.

The stories we have cited here are drawn from our experience as professional counselors. Some are obviously more dramatic and traumatic than others. But some—like the story of Julie, the little girl whose father shoved her in a fit of anger—

do not seem dramatic at all. There the family dysfunction was less extreme, less outwardly visible. *But it was no less real.* We are convinced that a great many of us, once we know what to look for and how to interpret it, can gain from understanding the dysfunctional dynamics of our own families—whether or not our pasts are scarred by such obvious forms of dysfunction as physical and sexual abuse, divorce, and the like.

It is here that we need to make some important comments. Both the "adult child" and the "dysfunctional family" concepts have become quite familiar in recent years. As that has happened, they have—frankly—become "trendy." It seems that almost everyone is labeling himself an "adult child of (fill in the blank)," and learning to explain—and often to excuse—his behavior in terms of parents who were in some way deficient and/or a family that was in some way "dysfunctional."

As children, we tend to mold our personalities to adapt to our environment. If our environment is supportive, nurturing, and flexible, we are freed to express our own individuality. If our environment is rigid, demanding, and conditional, however, we are forced to shape our behavior to fit the needs of others. We substitute our true self for a false self that is more acceptable to our parents, whose love and approval we need desperately. In essence we compromise who we really are, and become what our parents need us to be.

—Laurie Ashner and Mitch Meyerson,
When Parents Love Too Much,
(New York, NY: Avon Books, 1990) p. 53.

The problem, of course, is that we live in an imperfect world. We were *all* raised by imperfect parents in imperfect families. And, if we are honest, we recognize that we have all grown up to be imperfect adults. There is thus a sense in which we can *all* justifiably see ourselves as "adult children of dysfunctional families."

You may feel that your family of origin wasn't dysfunctional since your father wasn't an alcoholic.... The truth is, however, that, due to the fallen nature of all parents (and children), all families are flawed and therefore dysfunctional to a certain degree. Addictive and compulsive behaviors (addictions to food, sex, work, and so on) are extremely common in even "the best of families," and such behavior is almost always linked to some form of dysfunctional family background.

> — Dave Carder, et al.,
> *Secrets of Your Family Tree,*
> (Chicago, IL: Moody Press, 1991) p. 15.

But a definition that includes everything and excludes nothing is not a very helpful definition. Let's recognize, then, that we are talking about a problem with a range of expressions. Some of us will consider ourselves products of what one man we know calls "your basic, everyday, garden-variety dysfunctional family." We recognize that our parents had their flaws and our family its weaknesses, but we have never felt that our adult lives have been negatively affected by them in a major way. Most people who place themselves in this category are surprised when they discover how big the "little" hurts they endured are, and the effects they have had on their lives. If you place yourself in this category, we encourage you to read this book for the insights you can gain into how to make your own life even more fruitful, and how to make your family life even more satisfying.

Others will have already recognized that this is a book about *them*. As you read the stories of Brian, Mary, Lydia, and the others, you "heard bells go off" inside your head, and something inside you said, "That's *me* they're talking about. That's *my* life they're describing." If you are in this category, we believe this book can help you begin a wonderful process of growth and recovery.

Still others will be unsure at this point. You may never have heard the phrase "dysfunctional family" before, let alone understand what it means or how it may apply to you. All you know is that "something's not right" in your life. It may be anything from a lingering depression, to a problem with anger, to bouts of extreme anxiety, to inexplicable difficulties trusting others and getting close to them in relationships. You may have tried a number of things to deal with your problem, with varying degrees of success. You may be a deeply religious person whose commitment to spiritual truth has provided a great deal of comfort—but still you find yourself groping for the key to some personal difficulties that continues to elude you. If you place yourself in this category, we urge you to read this book carefully. It may well mark the beginning of an exciting time of self-discovery and growth for you.

✦ FAMILY: WHO NEEDS IT?

Let's get back to the men and women whose stories opened this chapter. Given the amount of pain and anguish their parents caused them, why don't they just "put it all behind them"? That's really the big question. Many of us, when we look at the problems we experience because of our imperfect backgrounds, are tempted to feel this way. Aren't we grown-ups now? Aren't we able to think and act and decide for ourselves? Why not just leave our families behind? Why not just forget about them and get on with life? We don't want to open up problem areas. So why think about them?

---

*We can't just walk away and pretend
that our family never happened. Indeed, trying to
"walk away and pretend it never happened"
is one of the worst things we can do.*

And yet... there is something in us that simply can't do it. We *can't* just walk away and pretend that our family never happened. (Indeed, as we go on, we will see that *trying* to "walk away and pretend it never happened" is one of the *worst* things we can do.) Every person I have met from a dysfunctional family goes through a period when they are so grieved and angry about what has happened to them, that they feel they never want anything to do with their parents again. Yet they constantly find themselves drawn back. Deep inside, they find they still want something, still *need* something from their families. The question is, why? Why does our family still exert such a strong grip on us even as adults?

To answer that question, we need to look back on our original experience of family. In the beginning of our lives, family is indispensable, for two reasons: first, for our sheer survival; second, for our early development and socialization.

It takes only a brief glance at an infant to recognize the survival aspect. Unlike most species in the animal kingdom, which shove their offspring out of the nest within a matter of weeks or months, human beings are so created that they are dependent on their parents (or some other adult member of the species) for their survival for many years.

But even as we grow older, our "family ties" continue. Because we are so needy at such a young age, we develop extraordinarily tight bonds to our family, even in those cases when it was harmful to us. Our neediness continues when we become adults, even though it usually takes different forms. This is a constant reminder of our original dependence on our family.

Many of us left home, defiantly vowing, "I'll never do it like my parents." Unfortunately, we are what we learn, and eventually, somehow, our parents manage to take up residence inside us. Only later as adults do we discover that we have never truly left home. In fact, in many ways we are just like our parents, who played the same game, different name—yet all products of a codependent heritage, "Lost in the shuffle."

—Robert Subby, *Lost in the Shuffle,*
(Deerfield Beach, FL: Health Communications, Inc., 1987) p. 92.

As hard as we may try to deny our neediness as adults, it is still there, exerting its tug on our psyche, always drawing us back to our original tie to the family. Consider the familiar case of the young adult who cannot wait to get away from his parents—but who, once he has done so, is forever coming back for home-cooked meals, for money, and (though he would never admit it) for parenting.

The longing for family is incredibly powerful, even in those cases where it might seem least warranted. Lydia, for example, knew full well what her mother and stepfather were like. She knew the pain she had experienced at their hands. Deep down, I think she knew how unlikely it was that they would ever acknowledge the damage that had been done to her, let alone take any responsibility for it. Yet she longed for their love and affection. The longing never went away, even after the disastrous session in which they blandly denied the shocking behavior she knew to be true.

THE SON WHO WANTED TO KILL HIS FATHER

If these longings for family exist in us as children toward our parents, surely they must also exist in parents toward their children. The overwhelmingly powerful instinct of mother love is familiar to all of us. I have never met a parent who, at some level, did not want to love his offspring. I have met some who did not *know how* to do it, many who simply *failed* to do it, and many who had lost heart and felt they no longer wanted to make the effort. But I have never met one who would not acknowledge a deep—sometimes almost desperate—desire to be "a good mom or dad."

If parents feel this way, if they long for closeness with their children this much, then why do they do so many destructive things to them? Part of the answer may lie in the parents' own early experience in their families.

Ray, for example, told me of the rage and hatred he felt toward his father during his late teenage years. Once when he was eighteen, he invited his father to go for a walk with him. He was planning, quite literally, to kill his father. As he contemplated what he was about to do, he asked his father for the first time why he had been so brutally abusive toward him.

"Tears welled up in his eyes when I asked him that," Ray remembered. "I was shocked. I'd never picked up the slightest trace of softness or sentiment in him before. He told me that his father—my grandfather—had done the very same things to him when he was a boy. His father would beat him with a horsewhip. Grandpa even whipped Grandma once, when she tried to stop him from hurting my dad."

Ray and his father walked along in silence for a few moments. Then his father turned to him and said, "You know, Ray, there were times when I just wanted to kill him."

Ray's murderous rage subsided after that. But his confusion grew. He felt sorrow for what his father had been through, even as he continued to feel anger toward him. Most of all, he grappled with understanding his father's behavior. "Why would he do the very same things to me that his father did to him?" Ray asked. (A good question, and one we will try to answer as we go along.)

THE FRACTURED FAMILY

It is not news that the family is changing. Instead of the proverbial large, extended family living together on the family farm—or at least close by each other—most families now live in urban or suburban settings with only the immediate family close by. An increasing number of these are single-parent families. In almost all cases, the support and care once provided by the extended family now comes from friends and acquaintances—if it is to be found at all.

As the family has been changing, it also has increasingly become the object of study and concern. Scholars have generated vast piles of statistics to describe *what* is happening. But their figures, charts, and graphs offer us little help in understanding *why* it is happening or what we can do about it. We know in excruciating detail how the divorce rate has skyrocketed, only recently showing signs of slowing down. We know how many more children are suffering the trauma of family collapse. But we don't know very much about how to change the trends, or about how to help the survivors recover.

Added to these changes is the changing place of women in our culture. Women have won some equality concerning their economic and social standing. But the effects of these changes have yet to be integrated into the family. Researchers still vigorously debate how—or even whether—the New Woman can be part of the Traditional Family.

Whether all these changes are good or bad is beside the point of our present consideration. The fact is that the changes *are* happening at such a dizzying pace that the family has not been able to keep up with them.

That the family is in trouble requires no proof. We have only to listen to friends and co-workers, or even to examine our own concerns and struggles, to know that the family as we have known and understood it is under attack. Young people increasingly are afraid to get married; they do not want to risk repeating the patterns of disillusionment and despair they have seen in their parents' generation. Or, if they do marry, many decide not to have children for the same reasons.

Clearly, something is wrong. But how do we define what is right?

THE NORMAL FAMILY

What is a "normal" family? Is it the two-parent, 2.3-child unit that came to seem so common in the "Baby Boom" years of the late 1940s and 1950s? Or the extended clan immortalized by such television programs as "The Waltons"?

It is harder to answer these questions than it might seem at first. The birth of the family predates recorded history. Even in Genesis, the first book in the Bible, the family is more *assumed* than *explained*. Indeed, Genesis offers examples of many different types of families throughout its pages. Anthropology offers a similarly varied picture. There seem to be as many different patterns of "the family" as there are different human cultures.

Nevertheless, there *are* some elements that all these family types have in common. By focusing on them, we can at least arrive at an understanding of "family" that can serve as a basis for our discussion in this book.

One common element is the bonding of a particular man and woman in a relationship that is understood, at some level, to be stable and exclusive. In most cultures with which we are familiar—especially in those built on the foundation of a Christian world view—this takes the form of marriage.

The other common element is the parent-child relationship. There is an understanding that the offspring produced by the union of a particular man and woman "belong" to them in some unique sense, and are their specific responsibility to care for and raise.

There are, of course, variations on these patterns. In our own day we are quite familiar with the single-parent family. But even this pattern, common as it is, is almost universally regarded as a departure from the ideal. Almost no one proposes that single-parent families ought to be the norm for everyone. Other variations—communal families, for example, with a large group of adults accepting equal responsibility for a large group of children—have also been attempted, usually with little success. Again, few would propose them as a universal norm.

Thus we seem to arrive at a very basic concept of what constitutes a "normal" family. Indeed, the almost instinctive tendency of human beings to gravitate toward a two-parent-plus-children model of the family—augmented in various ways by the presence of extended-family members ranging from grandparents to uncles, aunts, and cousins—suggests that such an arrangement has been "designed into" the human race by a wise and loving God. Since our aim is to examine the effects that family dynamics have on children, especially when those children have themselves grown to adulthood, we will focus on the parent-child component of the "normal" family. By understanding the basic goals of parenting, we can refine our understanding of what the "normal" family looks like.

Our first task in life—the first job we set out upon, even before we are old enough to consciously know what we are doing—is to form an attachment with a figure who will make the world a safe and reliable place for us. Ordinarily, of course, this is the mother, though the father also plays a crucial role. So we can say that one norm for a healthy family is that it provides a loving environment in which the child can learn to trust.

The almost instinctive tendency of human beings to gravitate toward a two-parent-plus-children model of the family suggests that such an arrangement has been "designed into" the human race by a wise and loving God.

Our second task in life is to define ourselves as separate, unique individuals within this context of love and trust. This is sometimes referred to as "individuation," the process of discovering what it is that "makes me, *me.*" Our ability to accomplish this second task will be directly related to how much love and security we have experienced in the earlier process of bonding with our parents and our environment.

Since unconditional love is the basis for all that occurs at later stages, we can round out our definition of the normal family by saying that it is a place where we can experience an unconditional love that gives us both the security and the freedom to successfully become autonomous individuals.

THE FAMILY COVENANT

An example of this kind of relationship can be found in the ancient concept of *covenant*. A covenant was a type of relationship in which the parties each committed themselves, totally and unilaterally, to faithfulness.

The word "unilaterally" is important. In most relationships and agreements, each party feels bound to the relationship only so long as the other party "holds up his end of the deal." If the other person fails to live up to his or her part of the bargain, then I (the first party) am excused from living up to my part. (In our society, this is the way contracts work.) Not so in a covenant. In a covenant relationship, each party has certain duties and obligations which he or she is obligated to fulfill *even if the other party fails to come through.*

The place from which most of the western world draws its understanding of covenant is the Bible, which speaks of two kinds of covenants. The first is a covenant between two (or more) people who are on an equal footing with one another. A business agreement, for example, could be in the form of a covenant. The most obvious instance of this kind of covenant, of course, is marriage.

A second kind of covenant involved an unconditional offer from a lord to a vassal, in which the lord promises to protect and care for the vassal. A king might make such a covenant with his subjects. Another example of this kind of covenant relationship was between God and the Jews. It is easy to see how this kind of covenant exemplifies what is supposed to happen between parents and children.

Thus we can say that the family is meant to be an intersection of two covenants: a "horizontal" covenant between husband and wife, and a "vertical" covenant between parents and children. Again, we will be focusing on the parent-child dimension in this book. But both dimensions are important, for without them it is impossible to create the environment of unconditional love—some would call it a community—in which human beings can grow as autonomous individuals.

> *The family is meant to be an intersection
> of two covenants: a "horizontal" covenant
> between husband and wife, and a "vertical" covenant
> between parents and children.*

It is important to note that the existence of a covenant does not mean that a relationship will be free of discord. Quite the opposite. As in any human relationship, the parties to a covenant will have their ups and downs, their trials and struggles. The difference is that they are committed to working through these difficulties, and to trying to resolve them. The bonds of covenant are often tested. They can be broken. But they can also be restored.

It is also important to understand that the bonds of covenant love, and the effects of their being broken, can extend across generations. Each individual family, each parent-child bond, is but one link in a chain that extends both backwards and forwards in time. As we examine the effects of growing up in a dysfunctional family, we will need to trace the ways in which our parents may have been similarly impacted by *their* families. And we will want to understand how we, in turn, can avoid handing on a legacy of family dysfunction to our own children.

When we talk about dysfunctional families then, this is what we mean: situations in which the bonds of covenant love, especially between parents and children, have been strained or broken. How those breakdowns occurred, and how the bonds can be restored (and the ill effects of the breakdown reversed) is the main topic of this book.

When we talk about dysfunctional families,
we mean situations in which the bonds of
covenant love, especially between parents and children,
have been strained or broken.

FREEDOM AND CHANGE

Let's summarize what we have said so far. All of us are deeply influenced by our families. All of our families are imperfect—perhaps more so today than ever, as the institution of the family has gone through unprecedented change and upheaval in recent decades. Some of us have come from families where the "imperfections" were significant enough to cause us noticeable difficulty in our adult lives. We are "adult children of dysfunctional families."

As much as we may try to cut ourselves free from our "family ties," their attachment runs too deep. Freedom lies in facing our problems squarely, in understanding as concretely as possible how our family fell short of the norm—how it failed to provide us with a community of unconditional love in which we could grow up healthy and strong. The goal of this is not to reinforce our self-pity or prompt us to hold our parents in contempt. As we shall see, clearer understanding enables us to take steps that will release us from the bondage of our past by enabling us to forgive those who have hurt us.

> A necessary part of recovery is for us to gain a balanced perspective of those who raised us. We need to lift the veils of denial from our eyes and see the past as it was, not as we wish it might have been.
> —Robert Subby, *Lost in the Shuffle,*
> (Deerfield Beach, FL: Health
> Communications, Inc., 1987) p. 89.

The kind of family we come from can have a profound effect on a number of important dynamics in our personal lives—even as adults. We sometimes talk of "growing up and leaving home." But as we have seen, in many respects, "leaving home" is hard to do. Our families continue to exert influence on us long after we think we have left them behind. To the degree that our family was healthy, it is good news. To the degree that our family was dysfunctional, it can be bad news.

Even so, freedom and change *are* possible. The key lies in understanding more thoroughly the dynamics of family life and how they have affected us. The next step in gaining this understanding is to learn to look at the family in a new way: as a *system.*

In the next chapter, we hear about Traci, a teenage runaway, whose problem became the key to unlocking the dynamics of a dysfunctional family system. Only when Traci and her parents understood the role she had been playing in the family as a system could the root problem be identified. Only then was real freedom and change possible.

2

A family is more than a group of individuals who happen to share the same address and the same last name. Many of the riddles of "why you are the way you are" can be unlocked by looking at the family as a system of relationships and interpersonal dynamics.

The Family System

T RACI'S PARENTS were dis-
traught.

They had come for counseling because their sixteen-year-old daughter had run away from home several times, and had been gone for several weeks each time. Their worry was justifiable.

One traditional way of looking at the situation would have been to say that Traci herself had a problem and needed help. That was certainly the way her parents saw it. What was wrong with their daughter? Why did she take it into her head to act like this? What could be done to change her behavior? Their focus—again, understandably—was on her problems as an individual.

But their counselor was looking at the situation through different eyes. He saw Traci not just as an individual, but as part of a family, as one part of a larger picture. He knew that whatever personal difficulties Traci might have—and there was no reason to doubt that she had them—it was likely that her behavior was also influenced by some dynamic in her family experience.

From hours of conversation with Traci, her two younger sisters, and her parents, a pattern began to emerge. The parents' marriage was on thin ice. They fought a lot, and had talked more than once about divorce. About two years before, they had separated for a few months; it was just after her father came back from that first separation that Traci ran away for the first time. The parents, while obviously aware of the difficulties they were experiencing in their own relationship, saw no correlation between that and Traci's troubling behavior.

It was during a joint counseling session, with both Traci and her parents present, that the lid came off.

It began innocently enough. The counselor complimented Traci: "It's out of *loyalty* to your family that you keep running away, isn't it?" he said. "You're so concerned for their welfare that you're even willing to sacrifice your own safety." Traci blushed a bit and smiled, nodding her head ever so slightly. She seemed to understand what the counselor was saying.

Her parents, however, did not. They erupted in anger. "Loyalty?" they cried. "What has that got to do with anything? Why are you applauding her for running away from home?"

The counselor waited for the explosion to subside. "Well," he said, "during our discussions together, it has seemed clear to me that the only thing you two agree on is that Traci is a problem. In fact, it seems as though working on her problems is practically the only thing that holds you together.

"What I think is happening is this: Traci has somehow picked up that when she's doing okay, the two of you begin to experience and express your problems more vigorously. I think she's concluded that the only way to hold the family together is for her to create a crisis that will force you to stick together. The fact is that your marriage problem has cast her in the role of 'family scapegoat.' When she runs away and causes you grief, she's just acting out the role she's been conditioned to play."

From that point, the theme of the counseling sessions shifted from *Traci* having a problem to the *family* having a problem. The parents came back for several sessions by themselves, without the kids. They began the arduous process of addressing their own relationship and the way it impacted their children. As we write, they have made good progress, though they still have a long way to go. But they have learned an important lesson: they have learned how helpful it can be to view their family as a *system*.

THE FAMILY ORGANISM

It was in the 1950s that psychologists made a remarkable discovery about families. That was not what they set out to do, which was to study the behavior of patients who had been diagnosed as being schizophrenic. Among the things they did was to observe the patients interacting with their families.

Much of the patients' behavior could be seen as perfectly reasonable and orderly in the context of the family. In other words, it was the family, not just the individual, that was dysfunctional.

What they saw astonished them. In many cases, what they had thought was a mental illness was not an illness at all. Much of the patients' behavior, when looked at by itself, seemed clearly disordered. But it could actually be seen as perfectly reasonable and orderly *in the context of the family*. In other words, it was the *family*, not just the individual, that was dysfunctional. To some degree, these apparently sick individuals acted the way they did because their role in the family prompted them to do so—much as Traci's role prompted her

49

to become a chronic runaway. Thus arose the notion of seeing and assessing the family as a system.

A family is not merely a collection of separate individuals who simply happen to share the same last name and street address. It is an organism, in which the attitudes, values, and actions of each member interact with those of all the other members.

A family is not merely a collection of separate individuals who simply happen to share the same last name and street address. It is an organism, in which the attitudes, values, and actions of each member interact with those of all the other members. Each one shapes, and is shaped by, the others. Each one is the way he is, in part, because of the way he fits into the overall scheme of things, the system. Many of our behavior patterns—both the healthy ones and the unhealthy ones— flow from the role we occupy in our particular family system. Understanding the family system, and the role we play in it, can unlock emotions and behaviors that would otherwise seem impossible to explain.

Tennessee Williams' classic play, *The Glass Menagerie,* offers a typical example of how a family system operates. Laura, the daughter in the play, could easily be considered mentally ill, even schizophrenic. But if we look at the world through her eyes—especially the world of her family—her "crazy" behavior becomes perfectly logical. Indeed, just as in Traci's case, it is vital to the family's survival. Whenever the tension between her mother and brother rises to a dangerous level, Laura steps in with some bizarre type of behavior that takes the focus off their fighting, and shifts it to her and her "strangeness."

Once we understand the concept of the family system, it is not so easy to say simply that Laura or Traci are "sick." Each may well have problems of her own that need to be addressed. However, a good case can be made that there is more to it than that, that each is the way she is because of the family she is part of. Again, it is the family that is sick, not just the individual members.

Many of our behavior patterns—both the healthy ones and the unhealthy ones—flow from the role we occupy in our particular family system.

LINEAR AND INTERACTIVE THINKING

You may remember learning in high school science class the principle that "for every action there is an equal and opposite reaction." This principle is an example of *linear* thinking: If I do "A," then "B" will happen. If it does not, then I know I have not done "A" correctly. This way of thinking is one of the basic foundations of modern science, and it is a tremendous help when you are trying to figure out what is going on in a laboratory.

> Everything occurring in a family, regardless of how carefully it may be hidden, impacts the children. Everything.
> —Robert Hemfelt and Paul Warren, *Kids Who Carry Our Pain*, (Nashville, TN: Thomas Nelson Publishers, 1990) p. 70.

But it is less helpful when you are trying to figure out what is going on in a relationship, let alone in a family. In situations involving human beings, and especially human systems like a family, we have to learn to apply *interactive* thinking. We have to be aware that a given action on our part may or may not cause a given reaction on someone else's part. It may cause a reaction completely different than what we intended or expected. Or it may cause no reaction at all.

The reason is simple: we are dealing with other people, who have their own ideas, feelings, and free wills, all of which enter into the equation. Moreover, we are never dealing with them in a vacuum. An encounter between you and me isn't necessarily "just between you and me." There will frequently be other people, other factors, affecting the situation.

One writer[1] has said that the difference between linear thinking and interactive thinking is like the difference between kicking a tin can and kicking a dog. When you kick a tin can, the results are fairly predictable. You can measure the force being transferred from your foot to the can, factor in the weight of the can and the wind conditions, and calculate pretty accurately where the can will end up.

But kicking a dog is a different matter, simply because the dog has the capacity to act and react on its own steam. When you kick the dog, he may jump. He may politely get up and move over. He may get angry and snarl at you. Or (if he is like my dog), he may simply raise an eyebrow and look up at you as if to say, "Now why did you have to go and do that to poor little me?"

Now imagine that there are two cats napping alongside the dog, a parrot in a cage in the next room, and a group of children playing nearby who see the whole incident take place. When you kick the dog, any or all of these may react in any number of ways, none of which are fully predictable. You may think, when you kick the dog, that you know what will happen next. And you may turn out to be right. But it is at least as likely that the results will be different than you expected, unless you become very adept at understanding the "system" you are part of. The better you understand the system, the better you will be able to make predictions about it, and to adjust your actions in order to produce the results you seek.

All of this is precisely what we try to do when we look at a family as a system. Relationships among family members never proceed according to linear thinking. They are always interactive, and always occur in the context of a system. To use another old saying, "The whole is greater than the sum of the parts." There is more to how a family operates than just the personalities and tendencies of the individual members. Something special is created by the inter-relatedness of family members, something that enters into every facet of family life.

THE HUSBAND WHO SHOVED BACK

Let's give a simple illustration of how this works. Donna had a long-standing frustration with her husband, Fred. She was very social and outgoing. He was a quiet, withdrawn man who had few relational skills and little desire to develop any. They had been married for fifteen years, and Donna had spent most of that time trying to get Fred to be more sociable.

She had tried everything. She got him to attend a Sunday School class at the church that had a lot of social events. She dragged him along month after month for years, until she finally got tired of the hassle and simply quit going to the class herself. She planned events with members of his family, thinking that would draw him out. She put all her plans and desires on hold, trying to figure out how to get Fred to change.

Nothing worked. In fact, it seemed that the harder she tried to get Fred to be more sociable, the more resolute he became about staying in his shell. He did not want to go out. He did not care about seeing his family, or about doing things with other couples. Just let him go fishing once a year, and he was content the rest of the time to simply go back and forth to work and enjoy a quiet life at home.

Donna figured that the way to move Fred in a certain direction was to give him a shove in that direction. What she did not realize was that Fred was shoving back.

Donna was trapped in linear thinking. She figured that the way to move Fred in a certain direction was to give him a shove in that direction. If he did not move, then she simply needed to shove harder. What she did not realize was that *Fred was shoving back*. Every time she pushed him, he resisted. And the harder she pushed, the more stubbornly he resisted.

We pointed out to Donna that her experience reflected a basic reality of linear thinking; that trying harder only gets you more of the same result. We began to look at her relationship with Fred, not just in isolation, but as part of a broader family system. She began to grasp that action "A" does not necessarily produce result "B"—that there might be a host of other factors to take into consideration.

She began to realize that Fred's reclusive behavior pattern had been in place long before she met him. He grew up in a Chaotic family, with an alcoholic father and a nagging mother. The way he had learned to cope with the chaos was to withdraw inside himself and stay out of things as much as possible.

Even now, at his job, the relational dynamics were such that his best course of action often was to "lie low" to keep the boss off his back. In short, almost everything in Fred's life had taught him to deal with people—especially with people who were demanding something from him—by pretending he wasn't there.

By this point Donna could see that her efforts to "help" Fred become more sociable only provoked this well-practiced response, and that "trying harder to help him" was only going to generate more of the same. This realization came as a tremendous relief. If she wasn't the cause of Fred's problem, and if she couldn't "fix" him by working on him, then she felt released to explore some of her own interests.

Interestingly enough, the minute Donna stopped "working on" Fred and began pursuing things she simply liked to do, Fred began to respond. Her nagging kept his reclusiveness in place. Now that she had given up the role of Family Nag, he seemed free to give up the role of Family Hermit. When he saw her doing things she wanted to do, without putting any pressure on him to join in, he started—very tentatively—to come out of hiding.

THE IMPORTANCE OF PUNCTUATION

Anyone who has ever taken a course in grammar knows how important punctuation is. The very same set of words can have entirely different meanings if the punctuation is changed. For example, take the following passage from the Bible: "Let him who steals, steal no more. Let him work" (Ephesians 4:28).

Seems clear enough, doesn't it? But look what happens if we change the punctuation, like this: "Let him who steals, steal. No more let him work."

55

That's a very different message, isn't it? Yet it uses precisely the same words, in precisely the same order. The only difference is the punctuation.

By the same token, our understanding of an event (or series of events) depends on the way we mentally "punctuate" it. Let's go back to Donna and Fred. Donna complained that she was unable to do what she wanted because Fred was so controlling by his passive behavior. Fred simply "moved the periods and commas around" and responded that if Donna would just let up, he would be glad to do more things with her. Donna understood what was happening like this: "He withdraws, I nag. He withdraws, I nag." Fred, however, would have characterized it this way: "She nags, I withdraw. She nags, I withdraw."

Both Fred and Donna are "punctuating" things according to linear thinking, in which there is a single cause and a single result. We might diagram it like this:

Donna nags ————▶ Fred withdraws
Cause   Effect

Or to look at it from the other perspective:

Fred withdraws ————▶ Donna nags
Cause   Effect

Can you see that this way of thinking will lead nowhere? Fred and Donna will go through life sounding like a pair of broken records: "He started it!" "Well, she made me!"

Relationships, as we have seen, are interactive in nature, and require that we think in terms of what are called feedback loops. Once we understand that we are dealing with a feedback loop, however, our diagram looks more like this:

The value of seeing things this way is that it makes clear that *either* party can change the situation by changing his or her own behavior. Before, Donna thought nothing could change in her marriage until Fred decided to be different. But she discovered she could impact their relationship positively by taking certain actions herself. She did not have to "just wait" for Fred. (Of course, the very same principle would apply from Fred's point of view.)

The value of seeing things in terms of feedback loops is that it makes clear that either party can change the situation by changing his or her own behavior.

The case of Donna and Fred is a fairly simplistic one. It involves only two people, and it has a quick, happy ending. Most family systems are far more complex and unpredictable, and the outcomes are not usually so tidy. Still, the story of Donna and Fred really did happen, and the reason it happened the way it did is because Donna learned to see her situation as one component of a system. She learned how to think in interactive terms rather than in straight-line terms.

THE LITTLE BOY WHO WENT TO BED

Let's look at a slightly more complex example. Joey is five years old. He has developed a pattern of throwing temper tantrums at bedtime. Joey's parents represent a fairly typical relational pattern. His father is away from home much of the time but is expected to be "in charge" when he *is* around. His mother is left to cope as best she can with the resulting situation being that she is the one who is "on the scene" most of the time, but without real authority to manage things.

A typical evening finds Dad lost in some television program, while Mom finishes the dinner dishes and begins the nightly process of getting Joey to bed. Joey, being a typically ingenious five-year-old, has developed at least a dozen tactics for delaying bedtime as long as possible, and the resulting ordeal generally leaves Mom utterly frazzled. *Listening* to the bedtime ordeal is also frustrating for Dad, who eventually decides that "enough is enough." He jumps out of his chair, grabs Joey by the arm, and drags him into his bedroom. He then throws Joey's pajamas at him, tells him to get into bed *now*, slams the door, and stomps away.

When he gets back to the family room, his wife is glaring at him. "What's the matter?" he asks. "Why are you so hard on him?" she replies. Dad has been down this path before and knows it leads to a dead end, so he says nothing. He just turns up the volume on the TV and flops back down in his chair.

Mom makes a snack for Joey and takes it to his room. He enjoys a brownie between sniffles as Mom helps him put on his pajamas. She tucks him in and lies down beside him on the bed. In a few minutes they are both asleep.

Dad has no desire to awaken her and run the risk of resuming the argument, so he goes on to bed by himself. For the next couple days, Joey's mom is very cool toward his dad. But Dad acts like he doesn't notice. He goes out of his way to be thoughtful and attentive. Eventually a semblance of peacefulness is restored—at least until the next time the sequence repeats itself.

What is really going on in this situation? Perhaps Mom is angry with Dad because of instead of helping her, he leaves her alone with the dishes and Joey. But instead of confronting him, she tries to stuff her feelings of irritation—which wind up getting vented on Joey instead. Perhaps Dad has had the proverbial "tough day at the office" and feels justified in sitting back and taking a break. Besides, he figures, he deals with problems all day long at the office. Is it really asking too much for his wife to keep things under control at home, so he can catch his breath?

For his part, Joey has simple objectives: he wants to stay up a few minutes later, and he wants a bedtime snack. By now he has learned enough about how the family works to know how to get what he wants. You just resist Mom and make enough ruckus that Dad intervenes, and before long Mom shows up with a peace offering to help you get over Dad's outburst. No one is consciously aware of the strategies they are pursuing, but they play them out time and time again.

Who, then, is "the problem" in this situation? Is it Joey, for being an unruly child? Is it Mom, for being disorganized and inconsistent? Is it Dad, for being quick-tempered and sharp-tongued? In one sense, the answer is, "all of the above." But in a more important sense, the problem here goes beyond the behavior of any of the three individuals *as individuals*. There is a system here, an established pattern of roles and expectations as thoroughly scripted as any stage play. Until that system is addressed, the situation is unlikely ever to change.

RESISTANCE TO CHANGE

What makes families change? Obviously, there are many factors that impact family life in a way that prompts them to become different. Some of these have to do with the normal progression of family life itself. There are a number of natural "turning points" in any family's history: the birth of the first child, and then of each subsequent child; the day the oldest child starts school, and the day the youngest child finishes school; children leaving home; the parents reaching retirement age; and the death of one of the parents. Each of these developments (and many others besides) alters the environment in which the family lives, and prompts the family to adapt—to change—in view of the new situation.

Notice how many of these turning points have to do with the addition or subtraction of family members. Family members can be added in other ways—for example, when an elderly grandparent comes to live with the family. And they can be subtracted in other ways as well, such as through divorce. Whether a given change is seen as positive or negative in itself is not the issue. It is still a stress point, something the family needs to respond to. As we will see in Chapter 3, the ease with which a family adapts to a changing environment is one of the key indicators of its healthiness or dysfunction.

Simply progressing through the life cycle gives families ample opportunities to change. But family systems, like most systems, tend to be resistant to change. There is a kind of inertia to them, which makes them tend to keep going the way they have always gone. They have a remarkable ability to withstand and adjust to outside pressures.

This tendency of systems is called *homeostasis*, which simply means "the same status." Our own bodies demonstrate how homeostasis works. Normal body temperature for most humans is 98.6°. If we suddenly walk into a very warm room, our body immediately adjusts. It activates a variety of "cooling systems" to keep our body temperature stable. Similarly, if we walk into a cold room, our body adjusts in the opposite direction. It is designed to maintain an even 98.6° body temperature, no matter what the external temperature is.

Family systems work much the same way. A pattern of relationships gets established, in which everyone is assigned a role. Powerful forces within the system will work to keep things the same, even as circumstances change.

The shame-bound family system is fixed in its form and highly resistant to change, even though change is a natural fact of life. This system is analogous to peanut brittle, with each person fixed in stereotyped, inflexible roles and relationships to one another.... When change exerts enough force all at one moment upon a rigid system, it may break and splinter. The shame-bound system does not have good capacity to absorb very much stress and still retain its integrity.
—Merle A. Fossum and Marilyn J. Mason, *Facing Shame: Families in Recovery,* (New York, NY: W.W. Norton, 1986) p. 19.

THE DAUGHTER WHO JUST COULDN'T LEAVE HOME

One of the most striking examples I saw of this was Clara's family. When Clara reached college age, life in her family was very tense. For a variety of reasons, Clara had always been the "glue" that held everything together. So the prospect of her departure threatened the family's very existence. Even though she had always wanted to go away to school, Clara persuaded herself that a local community college offered everything she really needed. She lived at home and got a part-time job, which helped alleviate some of the family's financial stress.

No one ever came right out and said, "Clara, you can't go. We need you here. You have to cancel your plans and stay at home." The fact was that no one needed to say anything. The message came through in hundreds of subtle, but powerful, ways. For example, when Clara was twenty-two she applied and was accepted to a university several hundred miles from home. She was even offered a scholarship that would have eliminated any financial obstacle. But that same year her brother graduated from high school, and even with Clara's scholarship there was no way the family could afford to put two children through college. So Clara stayed home. There was never any discussion about it; that was just the way everyone knew it needed to be.

Clara is now thirty-six. She never did go to college, even though she helped pay for both her brother's and her younger sister's education. She still lives at home with her parents, where she continues to serve as a buffer between them. Clara knows she has missed out on a lot, and she confesses to some occasional bitterness and resentment. But she nevertheless insists that she just *couldn't* leave. Her family needed her too much. This is a remarkable example of a family system withstanding enormous outside pressure to change—in this case, the perfectly normal leaving-home stage of an oldest daughter—and managing to stay just as it always was.

What would it take to make Clara's story come out differently? Couldn't Clara simply recognize what was happening to her and decide to take a different course? As a matter of fact, many of Clara's friends expended a great deal of energy trying to get her to do just that. Over and over again they told her she was wasting her life; that she was letting life pass her by; that she would regret it someday when her parents were gone; and so on. It was all to no avail. Not that Clara didn't recognize the truth of what her friends were saying. As they talked, she would nod her head and say, over and over again, "Yes, yes... but..." And nothing ever changed. Clara's friends were applying linear thinking to her situation, when what was needed was interactive thinking—the recognition that it was the system, not just an individual, that needed to be addressed.

Think for a moment about how a thermostat works in your home. Let's say it is set at 70°. If the temperature outside falls and the house starts to get cold, the thermostat sends a signal to the furnace to turn up the heat. If the temperature outside rises and the house starts to get too warm, the thermostat sends a signal to the air conditioner to start sending cool air through the system. Either way, the inside temperature is maintained at 70°.

Now let's say the thermostat is set at 85°—and let's say further that it is kept behind a locked panel so that it cannot be changed. Even in winter, 85° is too warm. Since we cannot adjust the thermostat, we decide to open the window and let in some cold air. What will happen? The more cold air we let in, the more the furnace will blow hot air in its attempt to get the temperature back to 85°.

In Clara's family, it is as though the thermostat is set at 85°. When her friends try to get her to behave differently, it is like trying to cool the house by opening a window. Other parts of the system just work that much harder to keep things the way they were. The only way to make a lasting change in the situation is to adjust the thermostat. And the only way to do *that* is to unlock the panel that stands between the thermostat and us. This means learning enough about Clara's family system to understand the root causes of why it is the way it is. Only then can we "re-set the system." Once again, it is the system, not just the individuals, that we must look at.

FAMILY SECRETS

What are the forces that keep families locked in dysfunctional patterns?

One major factor is simple inertia—the tendency things have to stay the same. Even when a need for change is acknowledged, established roles and patterns can be as hard to break as any stubborn habit. Not only does each individual family member tend to stay the same, but the different members also *reinforce* one another in their customary roles, attitudes, and behaviors. It is hard to become different when everything around you is working to keep you the same.

Not only does each individual family member tend to stay the same, but the different members also reinforce one another in their customary roles, attitudes, and behaviors.

Of course, we do not always recognize the need for change. This inability—or, in some cases, refusal—to acknowledge that a problem exists will keep us from even considering the possibility of change. There are two main things that keep us blind to the existence of problems and the need for change.

One is the family secret. Family secrets are the things that have happened—and may still be happening—that *everyone knows about but that no one ever talks about.*

As you look back at the various families we have met so far, it is easy, in most cases, to see what the family secrets were. Perhaps as you think back through your own life, you are aware of certain incidents, people, or problems, that no one ever discussed, even though it was obvious that everyone was aware of them. Perhaps you can recognize the part you played in maintaining the conspiracy of silence.

That conspiracy was a significant factor in Richard's family. Richard came for therapy with a great amount of reluctance. He was almost overwhelmed by the feeling that he was betraying his family members by talking about their problems to an outsider. "We were taught from an early age that family business stays in the family," he explained.

The main item of "family business," as it turned out, was Richard's father, who suffered periodic mental breakdowns. As Richard poured out his history, he told about the times his father would "flip out." Among the most terrifying memories were the times his father would load the children in the car and drive crazily around town for hours at a time.

Finally, after such an episode, Richard's mother would manage to get her husband into a hospital for treatment. While he was there, she and Richard's brothers would literally pack up and move to another part of town where no one knew them or their awful secret. By the time Richard's father got out of the hospital, the family would be relocated, and his psychotic episode would be buried in the past. Richard said this sequence of events had occurred ten times by the time he turned sixteen.

Finally, Richard's father was committed to the state hospital for good. He remains there to this day. Richard and his brothers visit him regularly. They long ago settled into a rotation, in which a different one goes to visit each week. Interestingly, they manage to do this without ever discussing it. Richard simply takes his turn every six weeks. He has been doing this faithfully for twenty years.

During all those years, whenever Richard's family has gotten together, Dad has emphatically not been a topic of conversation. No one has ever commented on how they thought

> First and foremost, children are taught to disown what their eyes see and what their ears hear. Because of denial in the family, children's perceptions of what is happening become progressively and systematically negated. Overtly or covertly, explicitly or implicitly, they are told not to believe what their own senses tell them. As a result, the children learn to distrust their own experience. At the same time, they are taught not to trust other people.
> —Herbert L. Gravitz and Julie D. Bowden, *Recovery: A Guide for Adult Children of Alcoholics,* (New York, NY: Simon & Schuster, 1985) p. 19.

Dad was doing. No one has ever talked about how it felt to have a father in a psychiatric institution. No one has ever talked about how it felt to have to pull up stakes and move every time Dad had an episode.

Sometimes family secrets are buried even more deeply than this. One day in her therapy group, Marge told how she had just learned two years before that her father was an alcoholic. Someone asked how long he had been drinking. "Oh, all my life," Marge said. "In fact, he was an active alcoholic even before I was born." Marge was forty-one years old when she shared this. That meant she had lived for thirty-nine years with a practicing alcoholic—without even realizing it.

The rest of the group looked at her in disbelief. How could she not have known that her own father was an alcoholic? "It was a secret," Marge shrugged. "Somehow, Mom managed to keep it hidden. And not just from us kids, either. No one in the family knew. No one in town knew. They just thought he was sick a lot." Marge noted that a lot of her father's "illnesses," which had puzzled her at the time, finally began to make sense once she understood her father's real problem. She had wondered about those "illnesses" while she was growing up. But she knew that Dad's health was a closed subject, something you simply did not ask about.

Family secrets are the things that have happened—and may still be happening—that everyone knows about but that no one ever talks about.

Family secrets are like having an elephant in the parlor. You learn at a very young age that the one question you *never* ask is, "Why do we have an elephant in the parlor?" If friends or others outside ask about it, the correct answer is, "What elephant?" As the elephant grows, you put a lamp and a lace doily on it and treat it like part of the furniture. In time you have to avoid the parlor entirely. But you never ask about it or comment on it.

> What is common to all such families is the commitment of all family members to maintain the secrets through rigid rules about what may and may not be talked about. These rules prohibit spontaneity in the family relationships; with spontaneity the real feelings and facts might be revealed.
>
> Family members create powerful myths about their histories, often leaving out the painful historical shapers of the shame. The children in these families are loyal through their lack of questioning about the past, thereby colluding in the family's rules.
>
> —Merle A. Fossum and Marilyn J. Mason, *Facing Shame: Families in Recovery*, (New York, NY: W.W. Norton, 1986) pp. 45-46.

Family secrets are one of the main ways that family systems resist change. Everyone keeps doing what they have always done, as if nothing was wrong. Richard found that in order to break out of his family's dysfunctional system, he had to start talking about his dad. In the same way, Marge knew that she needed to learn more about alcoholism, and about how her dad's drinking had impacted her during her formative years.

You learn at a very young age that the one question you never ask is, "Why do we have an elephant in the parlor?" If friends or others outside ask about it, the correct answer is, "What elephant?"

FAMILY MYTHS

The opposite of family secrets are family myths. Myths are the *things we talk about but never do.* George Bernard Shaw once said that most history was nothing more than "a lie agreed upon." Family myths are like that. They represent a silent conspiracy to pretend that things are different than they are. Ask almost anyone about their family, and the first thing you are likely to hear is one of the family's myths.

The most common of these, perhaps, is the one that says, "Oh, our family was very close." Time and again I have asked people in the clinic to tell me about their families, and the first words out of their mouths are, "Well, you know, we're a very close family." Then they go on to tell me about all the problems, hurts, and disappointments their family has caused them, describing anything but closeness and warmth. But as they finish their account, they invariably conclude by saying, "But our family is really close."

There are other common myths. People will say that their family was very loving or caring. People from strong religious backgrounds will often say that their family was very spiritual, even when there is little evidence of it.

> Our symptoms are born out of emotional denial and they serve to maintain that denial. They are ways that we allow ourselves to live one kind of life while convincing ourselves that we have a very different kind of life. And while they serve to give us the illusion that we are in control, they are in fact clear indicators that what we have really done is to give up healthy control of our lives to something outside of ourselves.
> —John and Linda Friel, *Adult Children: The Secrets of Dysfunctional Families*, (Deerfield Beach, FL: Health Communications, Inc., 1988) p. 23.

Not surprisingly, family myths are frequently connected to family secrets: the one thing the family is most ashamed of will be the thing they try to cover over with a myth. I remember Anne telling me about her family. In between the various problems she described, she mentioned repeatedly that her family was "very supportive." "We're always there for each other," she would say. But about two weeks later, she exploded. "I thought my family was supportive," she said. "But here I've been in the hospital for two weeks, and not a single one of them has come to see me. They haven't even called. It's like they don't want to admit I'm here."

The realization that she was living a myth—painful as it was—turned out to be a key to Anne's recovery. Myths are powerful forces that help dysfunctional families stay locked in their unhealthy patterns. Until we confront them and uncover the reality behind them, everything continues to stay the same.

Where do family myths come from? To some degree, they are simply a social convention, as when someone asks, "How are you doing?" and you answer, "Fine, thanks." But there is more to it than that. We have all been programmed in various ways as to what a "normal" or "happy" family is like. It is like the families we have seen on television programs, or read about in school books growing up. We know what a family is *supposed* to be like, and we have a natural reluctance to acknowledge that our family was not like that. Never mind that the images we have in our minds may be absurdly unrealistic. We want to believe that they are true, and that our life compares well with them. To acknowledge otherwise—to others, and even to ourselves—would be too painful.

This, of course, raises the question yet again: What *is* a "normal" family? And how do we measure deviations from that norm?

In the next chapter, we will hear about Tom and his wife, Margaret. Tom was the undisputed leader in the home and had a rule about everything—including the appropriateness of his wife working outside the home. Was Tom and Margaret's family life normal and healthy, or was it overly rigid?

3

All families are imperfect.
But some families are healthier than others.
How can you measure the ways in which your
own family fell short of the ideal,
so as to better understand
your own need for healing?

CHAPTER 3

My Family
and Me

J UST WHAT *IS* A normal family
anyway?

In Chapter 1 we tried to understand the family in its most
basic form, with an emphasis on *parenting* that expresses itself
in an *unconditional love* that allows for the development of an
autonomous adult. In this chapter, we will spell out in greater
detail what a family therapist means when he or she talks
about a normal family. We will look at some of the more common deviations from this norm, and identify some of the varieties of dysfunctional families that result. Then in later
chapters, we will learn some tools and techniques that will
help us apply this analysis to our own situation.

THE WELL-ADJUSTED FAMILY

Many psychologists and counselors have tried to outline
the characteristics of a healthy family. One writer has developed a description of what he calls the "well-adjusted" family.[1]
He speaks of a balance between "autonomy" and "attachment" in which there is a minimum of *fusion* between people

and, at the same time, a minimum of *distance* between them. He also speaks of a balance between *individual* and *family* needs, and of an adaptability that enables the family to adjust to changing needs and circumstances.

One of the key indicators of a well-adjusted family is that *problems are seen as family problems, not just as individual problems.* In other words, there is a sense that "We're all in this together, and we're *for* each other in whatever problems arise. If *you* have a problem, then *we* have a problem." At the same time, there is a healthy insistence that individuals take responsibility for their own lives, and people deal with one another straightforwardly and directly, rather than through third parties or go-betweens.

The well-adjusted family has found a balance between two seemingly contradictory dynamics: being close and being separate.

In a well-adjusted family there is *a mutual respect that expresses itself in a tolerance for differences.* Indeed, within the context of a common set of basic values, individual differences are not only tolerated, they are encouraged—even celebrated. People who grow up in such a family can interact well with others, and accept a variety of expressions of opinions, attitudes, and emotions.

A well-adjusted family also demonstrates *a respect for members of other generations.* The young do not isolate themselves from the old, nor do the old cut themselves off from the children and young adults. People are connected with their parents; they recognize and appreciate the benefits they derive from one another, as well as the benefits they can provide for one another. Other family members are not seen as emotional

crutches to be used or leaned on, but as resources for learning and growth, for feedback and enjoyment.

In a well-adjusted family, *people are free to "experience their own
emptiness."*[2] All of us experience good times and bad times,
times when we are "up" and times when we are "down." It is
especially in the "down" times that we usually feel most unac-
cepted by others. In the well-adjusted family, people are given
the space to experience and express even the down side of
their emotions without others attempting to judge them or
"fix" them, or encouraging them to repress their feelings.

In short, the well-adjusted family has found a balance between two seemingly contradictory dynamics: being close and

---

Characteristics of a Healthy Family

1. It is balanced; it can adapt to change.
2. Problems are handled on a family basis, not just an individual basis.
3. There are solid cross-generational connections.
4. Clear boundaries are maintained between individuals.
5. People deal with each other directly.
6. Differences are accepted and encouraged.
7. The thoughts and feelings of others are accepted.
8. Individuals know what they can give to, and receive
   from, others.
9. Maintaining a positive emotional climate is a high priority.
10. Each family member values the family as "a good place
    to live."
11. Each learns from the others and encourages feedback.
12. Individuals are allowed to experience their own empti-
    ness.

---

being separate. These dynamics must be balanced within each of us if we are to be healthy as individuals; they must also be balanced in our families. When either of these two dynamics gets seriously out of balance, the result is family dysfunction. In a moment, we will see in greater detail how that happens.

"WHAT ABOUT *MY* FAMILY?"

By now you have no doubt begun to think about your own family, and about how it "stacks up" in terms of the issues and dynamics we have been talking about. As we go along, we will develop a number of tools with which we can assess, or diagnose, various aspects of our family experience. But for now, here is a quick inventory to help you to begin to get a handle on the kind of family you grew up in.

For each statement, write in a number according to the following scheme:

- Write a "1" if the statement was *almost always* true for your family.
- Write a "2" if the statement was *sometimes* true for your family.
- Write a "3" if the statement was *almost never* true for your family.

Respond to each statement based on your own recollection and perception of your family experience. Someone else in your family might have a completely different set of responses. But that doesn't matter. All that matters is how you experienced your family.

Write the appropriate number in the space following each statement.

Put a book marker on this page so you can refer back to it later.

Family Inventory[3]

_____ 1. Family members supported each other when they had problems.

_____ 2. Family members felt free to speak their minds.

_____ 3. It was easy to talk about almost anything with my family.

_____ 4. All family members participated in making family decisions.

_____ 5. Our family did a lot of things together.

_____ 6. In our family, children had a say in how they were disciplined.

_____ 7. Our family loved to be in the same room together.

_____ 8. Our family enjoyed discussing problems and solutions together.

_____ 9. Each of us knew that our friends were also the family's friends.

_____ 10. Everyone shared responsibilities in our family.

_____ 11. Family members shared interests with one another.

_____ 12. Rules changed often in our family.

To complete the inventory, first add up the totals for the *odd-numbered* questions, then add up the totals for the *even-numbered* questions. Write the totals in the spaces below.

_____ Odd-numbered questions.

_____ Even-numbered questions.

THE ADAPTABILITY SCALE

There are two continuums, or scales, that we use to assess family life. One has to do with *adaptability*, and the other with *attachment*. Let's take a close look at each one.

First, the adaptability scale. This measures how readily the family adapts, or adjusts, to change. At one extreme, a family can be rigid; at the other extreme, a family's life can be chaotic. The adaptability continuum looks like this:

Adaptability Scale

RIGID   ADAPTABLE   CHAOTIC

6   7   8   9   10 11 12 13 14 16 18

Your responses to the even-numbered statements in the inventory will locate your family along this continuum. Take the total of your responses to the even-numbered statements and mark it on the diagram. As you read this section about Chaotic and Rigid families, keep in mind where your family was located on the continuum.

Chaotic and Rigid families—families at the extreme ends of the adaptability scale—have several things in common. For one thing, they are both rather poorly equipped for problem-solving. While the Rigid family will make some effort to discuss ways to solve problems, they tend to make decisions quickly and arbitrarily, and then to impose them on family members with little forethought or planning. The Chaotic family, by contrast, will often take a great deal of time talking about a problem, but in a confused, disorganized way that makes arriving at a clear conclusion very difficult. The Chaotic family typically does a poor job of following through with whatever decision it finally does come up with.

78

Both types of families also have a hard time dealing with emotions. The Rigid family tends not to allow the expression of emotions, and those that are expressed tend to be ignored. The result is that a great deal of anger builds up. But it is expressed in indirect and manipulative ways. In the Chaotic family, there is often a lot of expression of emotion, but the structure of family life is such that its meaning and significance get lost in the shuffle. The resulting impulsiveness and volatility also stirs up anger.

Now that we have seen what these two types of families have in common, let's look at them more closely to see what is unique about each one.

THE RIGID FAMILY

The Rigid family is a very authoritarian family. Leadership is clearly defined and recognized: *everyone* knows who the boss is, and everyone knows what the rules are. They tend to be very specific, almost endless in number and scope, and largely non-negotiable. When the rules are broken, punishment is swift and stern.

---

*The Rigid family is a very authoritarian family.
Leadership is clearly defined and recognized:
everyone knows who the boss is,
and everyone knows what the rules are.*

Lydia—the young woman we met in Chapter 1, who had been repeatedly molested by her stepfather—came from this kind of family. Her stepfather was the undisputed leader in the family. His decisions were final, even when they were immoral or destructive; his position in the family was unassailable. Lydia's mother went along with everything because in the context of her family she could do nothing else.

Another man, Tom, also came from a Rigid family, though it was not nearly as dysfunctional as Lydia's. In his own family, Tom was the benevolent dictator. He was utterly rational in the way he led the family. There was a rule or policy to cover every situation that might arise. If one of the children wanted something, they had to be able to present reasons that Tom found persuasive. "Just wanting" something was not enough. The kids found this frustrating, but they knew there was no point in questioning the system.

Tom's wife conformed to Tom's idea of what a wife and mother should be. She would have liked to work outside the home, but that did not suit Tom. He felt that if she started working, she would become unacceptably independent. Controlling the family environment was a major priority for Tom.

As we gradually discovered, Tom's father had run *his* household in precisely the same way. Tom remembers that his father's decisions were always final. Tom's wife, Margaret, had come from a similar background, in which Dad was the unquestioned leader and Mom was the compliant follower. Margaret knew she was following in her mother's footsteps when she married Tom; she can remember how pleased she was to find someone who was so much like her dad.

THE CHAOTIC FAMILY

To speak of the Chaotic family as having a leadership style is almost a contradiction in terms: in the conventional sense, there virtually *is* no leadership in the Chaotic family. Each individual is a law unto himself. No one takes charge in a consistent way. What leadership there is, is exercised sporadically, first by one member of the family, then by another. The rules, such as they are, are largely unwritten and unspoken. They can change without warning at the whim of whoever happens to be "in the saddle" at the moment. Outsiders can seldom discern any pattern or order to relationships; those who marry into Chaotic families find it almost impossible to decipher what is happening at a given time.

Mary, whom we met in Chapter 1, came from this kind of family. The combination of an alcoholic father and unstable mother, plus the fact that both parents were frequently absent, meant that Mary's older brother was often the one in charge. He was a law unto himself. He did what he wanted, and neither Mary nor any of the other siblings could complain to their parents. Even if they did complain, it would not matter. The parents either did not care what the older brother did, or simply were not interested in stopping him.

When Mary got married, it wasn't long until her husband grew intensely frustrated in their relationship. He described his situation as "never being able to do anything right with her." The problem was that Mary couldn't *tell* him what was "right." She had expectations, but she was unable to articulate them to her husband, or even to herself. She just knew that "things weren't the way they were supposed to be." It was only when Mary began to understand her family background that she could begin to identify the unspoken rules she expected herself and others to follow.

Sometimes the chaos is less extreme. Stan described his family as a place where there was discussion that stretched on forever but never reached a conclusion. Everyone seemed to operate according to the principle, "Why decide something today that could be put off until next week, or next year, or forever?" Decisions were not really *made*, they just sort of *happened,* usually when circumstances conspired to force the family's hand.

It wasn't until one of his own daughters threw up her hands one night and exclaimed, "I just want a yes or a no, not an endless discussion," that Stan realized how he had implemented the style he had grown up with in his own family.

The raising and disciplining of children is very erratic in the Chaotic family.

As the experience of Stan's daughter illustrates, the raising and disciplining of children is very erratic in the Chaotic family. Sometimes consequences are applied; sometimes they are not. Sometimes parents mean what they say; other times they seem to forget what they have told the children as soon as the words leave their mouths. The children are often quite vocal about their anger and disrespect, but it has little or no effect. It just becomes part of the chaos.

THE ADAPTABLE FAMILY

The healthy balance between Rigid and Chaotic families is the Adaptable family. It is characterized by an approach that offers clear but flexible leadership and healthy but adjustable discipline. Everyone knows who is in charge; they also know that the leader is someone who can be talked to and reasoned with. They know there are rules, and consequences for breaking those rules; they also know the rules are fair and sensible, and that exceptions can be made when the situation warrants.

Problems are discussed, and the discussion leads to a decision that reflects the input of various members of the family, both children and adults. Roles are clear—parents are parents, children are children—but communication is plentiful. People know what is expected of them, and they know how to negotiate those expectations when legitimate needs to do so arise.

THE ATTACHMENT SCALE

The second major dynamic that helps gauge the health or dysfunction of a family is *attachment.* Attachment refers to the way members of the family bond with one another; to a large degree this flows from the bonding that takes place between young children and their parents, especially the mother.

As with adaptability, attachment can range between two extremes: the *Disengaged* family style and the *Enmeshed* family style. Again, this range can be represented by a continuum scale:

Attachment Scale

Disengaged			Attached				Enmeshed		
6	7	8	9	10	11	12	13	14	16	18

Go back to the inventory you completed on page 77. Take the total of the values you assigned to the odd-numbered questions and mark it on the diagram above. This will give you an initial idea of where your family stands on the attachment scale.

Again, the families located at the extreme ends of the attachment scale—Disengaged and Enmeshed families—will tend to have certain things in common. Both will have difficulty building healthy marital relationships. The partners will struggle to find a balance, but will almost inevitably tend to feel either "too close for comfort" or "too distant" from each other.

This struggle is made worse by the fact that people often seem to marry someone who comes from the opposite end of the scale from themselves. A person from an Enmeshed family, where everyone is constantly dabbling in everyone else's business, will gravitate to a partner whose style is to give others more "space." On the other hand, a person from a Disengaged family will likely gravitate to a situation that seems to provide warmth and closeness. Quite frequently, these two individuals find each other and get married. Before long they discover that they may each have found "too much of a good thing."

Now let's take a closer look at each of the family types along the attachment scale, in order to understand them better.

As adult children of dysfunctional families we operate in a world of extremes—always seeking that healthy balance, the Golden Mean, but always seeming to fall short of the mark. The pendulum swings to one extreme and we feel lonely, isolated, and afraid. We tire of this, and it swings to the other extreme, where we feel enmeshed, smothered, and angry.

—John and Linda Friel, *Adult Children: The Secrets of Dysfunctional Families* (Deerfield Beach, FL: Health Communications, Inc., 1988) pp. 17-18.

THE ENMESHED FAMILY

I don't know about you, but I find that every year at Christmas time the same thing happens to me. I am trying to decorate the family Christmas tree, and when I take out the strings of lights, they are always hopelessly entangled. I cannot tell where one string ends and another begins. It seems to take forever to untangle them before I can put them on the tree.

The members of Enmeshed families are like that. They are so thoroughly entangled in one another that it becomes difficult for anyone to tell where one person ends and the next one begins. Enmeshed families are characterized by an extreme sense of closeness, so much so that almost any expression of independence or separateness is seen as disloyalty to the family. This kind of false loyalty is a very high value in an Enmeshed family.

Take Marti as an example. She expressed a great deal of hostility toward her mother. But then she was overwhelmed with guilt at her "disloyalty." How could she speak of her own mother that way?

Marti had very few friends growing up. Her mother dominated her use of time and energy. Marti felt obligated to check everything she did with her mother, to run all her plans and ideas past her for approval before proceeding. Even after she grew up and got married, Marti felt compelled to seek her mother's approval for decisions she was making about her family. On one hand, Marti greatly resented this state of affairs; she knew it was a way for her mother to keep her under her thumb. But the thought of breaking free from her mother terrified Marti.

The issues along the attachment scale have to do with personal and family boundaries. Where does one person's business, one person's identity, one person's life, end—and another's begin? Within the Enmeshed family, boundaries are virtually nonexistent. Everyone experiences his life as almost totally "overlapping" with everyone else's.

An example of a boundary is our skin. It holds what is inside of us inside, and it keeps what is outside of us outside. Without the boundary of our skin, our organs would simply fall out. Germs and other undesirable things would enter us at will. We would have no protection and no real definition of who we are. A boundary is like a fence around our property—it lets us know where our property ends and someone else's begins.

Where Are My Boundaries?

- Do I regularly find myself saying "yes" to others—especially to other family members—when I really want to say "no"?
- Do I frequently become burdened with other people's problems because they see me as the kind of person they can come to with their troubles? Do I frequently feel resentful about this later?
- In establishing preferences and desires, do I find myself wanting what I want or what "we" want? In formulating opinions, do I ask, "What do we think?" or "What do I think?"
- Do I sometimes find myself feeling what other people feel? Their feelings seem to be mine as well. I am unable to stay objective.

Answering "yes" to these questions may indicate a need to clarify blurred personal boundaries within the family.

Interestingly, however, Enmeshed families tend to have remarkably rigid boundaries vis-à-vis anyone outside the family. Marti said her mother never tired of warning everyone

86

that "family business was family business," never to be discussed with "outsiders."

Enmeshed families can look attractive and inviting from the outside. Take George's family, for example. George had built a successful bakery business in his town. His three grown sons were all very active in the business. Together, George and his sons had established a virtual monopoly on the baking business in their area. They had also established a virtual monopoly on one another's lives.

Consider Tim, the oldest son, who wanted to get married. He was almost thirty years old, and had cancelled three previous engagements because his family did not think the girl would "fit in." Finally he found a girl that everyone approved of. She was quiet and docile, and came from a family in which people were aloof and uncaring. "I finally found a real family," she would say, and Tim's parents and brother would smile contentedly.

In time, Tim's two brothers also married. As with Tim, their wives came from highly detached, uninvolved families. Each was quickly absorbed into their new clan and into the bakery business. This is a classic example of a moderately Enmeshed family—not quite suffocating enough to cause the kinds of discomfort that Marti experienced, but enough to blur the individual members into what one family researcher calls an "undifferentiated ego mass."[4]

THE DISENGAGED FAMILY

As the name suggests, the Disengaged family is marked by its extreme lack of emotional bonding. Neither "closeness" nor "loyalty" are particularly prized by the Disengaged family, as they are by the Enmeshed family. Disengaged families value independence, and relationships outside the family. They experience very little of what we commonly call "togetherness." Family members often know less about one another's plans and activities than they know about most of their friends' and neighbors'. In the Disengaged family, boundaries *within* the family are very strictly enforced, while boundaries outside the family are quite flexible, sometimes almost nonexistent.

> *Disengaged families value independence, and relationships outside the family. They experience very little of what we commonly call "togetherness."*

Larry, whom we met in Chapter 1, came from this kind of a family. Being left on an aunt's doorstep at age five, and never hearing another word from your parents, is about as disengaged as you can get.

A phenomenon that occurs more often in the Disengaged family than in other types of families is the existence of a *family scapegoat*, someone who takes the blame for the "badness" in the family. From a very early age, Larry was the scapegoat for his family. He was the reason why "nothing ever worked out right." He was the "bad boy."

Larry spent much of his childhood living up to this expectation. Being abandoned by his family, and then blamed for its problems, left him seething with resentment and rage. He vented his anger in frequent fights at school and in the neighborhood. As soon as he was old enough to leave home, he did. He joined the army. After being discharged, he drifted for several years, working an array of odd jobs, never staying in any one place for long.

Larry was a classic loner. No one—not even his wife and children—knew what he was like on the inside. Not surprisingly, he grew both lonely and depressed, to the point that he began talking about suicide. It was then that his wife forced him to seek help. In counseling, Larry was able to trace his depression and his "loner" identity to the role he had been forced to play in his family.

Susan's family illustrates a less severe form of disengagement. Her parents had always given her a lot of latitude growing up, which she had valued and enjoyed. But when she became a mother herself, she found it hard to respond to her own children's desire for greater freedom and autonomy. She experienced the natural motherly concern for their safety and welfare; she did not want to risk the consequences of "too much independence too soon." Ironically, it was this experience that prompted her to look back at her own family. Why had her parents given *her* so much freedom? Why didn't they care enough about her to show more concern for her safety and welfare? Learning about the Disengaged family style helped her sort out her own background and the feelings she now had as a mother.

THE ATTACHED FAMILY

While the Enmeshed family feels suffocating, and the Disengaged family leaves the individual feeling isolated, the Attached family strikes a healthy balance. There is a sense of individuality without a loss of connectedness. People in an Attached family enjoy being together and doing things together, but are able to relate to people and be active outside the family as well. When they are away from the family, they do not feel guilty or disloyal. They are able to share outside experiences with the family, knowing other family members will understand and accept their choices.

In the Attached family there is mutual respect that allows freedom of activity, without any hidden agendas that trigger guilt. There is support for individual uniqueness, coupled with shared appreciation for one another's accomplishments. Like all delicate balances, it is difficult to find and maintain, but it is well worth the effort.

While the Enmeshed family feels suffocating, and the Disengaged family leaves the individual feeling isolated, the Attached family strikes a healthy balance.

Earlier we said that each of us faces two primary tasks in our early developmental years: finding our place in a loving environment, and growing as a distinct individual within that environment. These two individual dynamics are mirrored in the family dynamics of adaptability and attachment.

Attachment has a direct bearing on the ability to find autonomy as an individual. People who grow up in Enmeshed or Disengaged families struggle with this. Autonomy has to do with boundaries, both inside and outside the family. Enmeshed families try to prevent us from attaining autonomy; Disengaged families force a degree of isolation on us that makes it impossible for us to get our bearings.

Adaptability likewise impacts ability to relate to other people as a healthy adult. Primarily it does this by establishing how well we can adjust to others. People from Rigid families will have little tolerance for those who are different from themselves. People from Chaotic families lack a firm base on which to develop a sense of self, and frequently end up "hiding" from others out of a resulting sense of insecurity.

COMMON TYPES OF DYSFUNCTIONAL FAMILIES

You can probably see that ultimately there are as many types of family dysfunction as there are families. But it may not surprise you to learn that there are some common varieties of dysfunctional families. Though every situation is unique, most dysfunctional families will fall into one of several recognized categories. Let's look briefly at some of these common types.[5]

Isolated Islands. In some ways, this kind of family bears scarcely any resemblance to a "family" at all, because the individual members are so isolated from one another. They are like some of the island groups in the South Pacific. If you were to view them from a great distance—if you were to photograph them from a satellite in outer space, for example—you would be able to recognize that they do in fact "go together" in some way. But if you were actually standing on one of them, you would think you were all alone on the middle of the ocean. The other islands in the group would be so distant you would not be able to see them over the horizon.

Some families are like that. Because the members share the same last name and address, it is possible to see that they go together. But in terms of the internal dynamics of family life, they are almost totally detached from one another.

This is probably the most severely disturbed pattern of family dysfunction, and the one that has the most negative impact on its members. People from this kind of family are like isolated islands, with few (if any) personal relationships that involve any degree of attachment. Whatever relationships they *do* have are typically devoid of emotional content, existing for utilitarian purposes only.

Let's go back again to Larry, who had been emotionally deserted by his parents long before they literally abandoned him at age five, leaving him in the care of his aunt and uncle. His new family was not much different from his old one. Larry would be quick to point out that his aunt and uncle "took good care of him," that they gave him a warm bed to sleep in and three square meals a day. But emotionally, Larry was raised in a vacuum.

Deep inside, Larry longed for emotional closeness—to connect with someone. But those longings stayed deep inside. Bringing them to the surface—let alone acting on them—was far too frightening a prospect, even with his own wife and children. It was not until his depression deepened to the point of threatening his life that Larry could bring himself to take the terrifying step of reaching out to others—to start building bridges from his isolated island to the world around him.

Generational Splits. The distinguishing characteristic of this kind of family is a lack of significant interaction between parents and children—not just the two generations currently living in the same household, but also between the parents and *their* parents. Significant interaction takes place only within generations.

Interestingly, a frequent pattern in this type of family is for emotional and relational connections to *skip*, or leapfrog, generations. For example, the children in a particular family may be isolated from their parents but experience a high degree of emotional warmth and nurturing from one or both sets of grandparents. When these children themselves grow up and raise a family, their own parents—who largely neglected them—will take a strong interest in the grandchildren. And so it goes, generation after generation.

Rick and Beth provide an example. They had three daughters. But they had remarkably little involvement with them. They were very much involved with one another, however.

They worked together in real estate and took vacations to-gether—without the kids. As a result, their daughters became very close. Outsiders looked at them with admiration; they were so tight-knit, so supportive, so loving. What those out-side observers did not realize was that the girls would have loved for their lives to be different, but they had no choice; there was no one else for them to turn to but each other. While the girls were little, Beth's parents stayed with them a lot. After they died, various of Rick's and Beth's friends filled in until the girls were old enough to care for themselves with-out a sitter.

Now, years later, all three of the girls are married. Rick and Beth have four grandchildren and more on the way. Rick and Beth are virtually obsessed with their grandchildren. They have dozens of pictures of them on the walls of their home and offices. Beth doesn't work much anymore—she spends a lot of time watching the babies. When she and Rick go on vacations now, they often take the older grandchildren along with them. As for the three daughters—they are too busy with their husbands and careers to spend much time with their kids. The pattern goes on.

Gender Splits. This is similar to the generational split except that the split happens along gender lines within families. The men and boys stick together, as do the women and girls. The whole family spends time together and does things together, of course, but very little emotionally-significant interaction takes place across gender lines.

A lot of times this pattern is found in families with a very strong notion of sex-based roles for men and women. Not just that there is "men's work" and "women's work," but that there is a "man's world" and a "woman's world." Women have "their place"—usually the kitchen—and the girls are expected to be there with them. The men have more choices where they go together. (They usually stay away from the kitchen, though, since that is where the women are.)

My own family was a lot like this growing up. Even when we sat down to eat at the kitchen table, my dad and I sat on one side of the table, and my mother and sister sat on the other side. When we went somewhere in the car, the men sat in the front seat and the women sat in the back.

There is a great deal of evidence that children benefit from a strong identification with the same-sex parent. It is especially important for developing a clear gender identity and sexual orientation. But children also need appropriate exposure to their opposite-sex parent and siblings. If they do not get it, they can grow up fearful or disdainful of one another.

There is a great deal of evidence that children benefit from a strong identification with the same-sex parent. But children also need appropriate exposure to their opposite-sex parent and siblings.

The Fused Pair. In this type of family, two members of the family are cut off—or rather, they cut themselves off—from the others. This fused pair becomes the nucleus around which the rest of the family revolves.

Marti, the woman we met earlier in this chapter, came from a family like this. In her case, it was Marti and her mother who became fused together while Marti was growing up. Early on, her mother had dismissed her father as a significant factor in the family because of a "moral lapse" on his part. From then on, her mother invested everything in Marti, in an apparent effort to draw from her relationship with her daughter what was not available to her anywhere else. She paid as little attention as possible to Marti's father and her other two sisters. Being fused with her mother in this way produced Marti's mixed feelings toward her: of bitterness mixed with reluctance to be "disloyal."

In this kind of system, the other members experience the family as extremely disengaged and detached, much like those who grow up in a family of "isolated islands." But the two people who are fused experience the family as being strongly enmeshed. This type of family manages the extraordinary task of occupying both ends of the attachment scale at the very same time.

Queen of the Hill. This is a family completely dominated by one person. It could be anyone, but in the vast majority of cases it is the mother. There is no mistaking where the power lies and who is in charge. Everything must go through Mother. If anyone needs anything, they get it from her; if they want to do anything, they must clear it with her. If they have a problem, they take it to Mother—and nowhere else.

In some extended families, Grandmother is the reigning matriarch. In these cases, Mom is just as subservient as everyone else. But she knows the day will come when she ascends to the throne. She is simply waiting her turn.

Mary—the girl (in Chapter 1) who was raped by her older brother when she was young—came from this kind of family. Even though Mary's mother was gone from the home a great deal, there was no questioning the fact that she was in charge. Mary's father was just as powerless as the children. When Mary tried to tell what her brother had done, and her mother refused to believe her, that was the end of the discussion. No one questioned Mom's decisions.

The Quiet Dictator. This type of family is similar in some respects to the one dominated by a "Queen of the Hill"; however, in this case the dominant member's control over the family is far more subtle and manipulative in nature. A "Queen of the Hill" type tends to be very "up-front" and imperious in her domination of the family, while a "Quiet Dictator" works behind the scenes, pulling the strings quietly and unobtrusively, skillfully manipulating others' emotions.

To the skilled eye, the Quiet Dictator is not hard to identify. Usually this is the one person who refuses to participate in counseling—or if they do show up, either tries to sidetrack the conversation or simply refuses to talk altogether. When a sensitive topic is raised, the eyes of the other members inadvertently turn to this individual for cues as to what to do next.

This family would score very high on both the adaptability and the attachment scales: an extremely rigid family, and one that is highly enmeshed. There are clear, ironclad rules and expectations, enforced by a firm set of roles that the members are to fulfill without wavering.

Families often make one member serve as a scapegoat—
someone who bears the blame for the family's problems.
As you can imagine, being a scapegoat
is not a happy experience.

The Family Scapegoat. We have already mentioned the tendency for families to make one member serve as a scapegoat—someone who bears the blame for the family's problems. The scapegoat image is drawn from the Bible. In the Old Testament, when the Jewish people wanted to be reconciled to God, they would symbolically place their sin on a goat that had been specially chosen for the occasion. The goat would then either be sacrificed or sent away, never to return.

As you can imagine, being a scapegoat is not a happy experience. I remember when Eddie came into our clinic. When we talked to him about inviting his family for Family Day, he hesitated, and asked if he really had to. We asked what his concerns were. "They're all against me," he said. "They treat me like an outsider."

Nevertheless, when Family Day rolled around two weeks later, Eddie had his whole family there. Everything seemed perfectly normal—for a while. Then one of our counselors began leading a discussion group designed to draw out what various family members were thinking and feeling below the surface. It was Eddie's sister who finally blurted out that Eddie "just never fit in." The rest of the family "does just great together," she said. "But whenever Eddie's around, there's tension." She sat back with a relieved look on her face, as though relieved that a dark secret was finally out in the open.

The issue of blame is one that is a theme in a chemically dependent family. It also reflects the extreme thinking and low self-worth of the family system. Adult Children of Alcoholics (ACoAs) continue to seek a scapegoat to explain their own discomfort. Frequently, as in life with active addiction, the family appears to take sides, the same sides, on every issue. There are bad guys and good guys, and everyone knows who they are. Once labeled, it may be very difficult to break out of an expected behavior pattern.

—Ann W. Smith, *Grandchildren of Alcoholics*, (Deerfield Beach, FL: Health Communications, Inc., 1988) p. 19.

The more our counselor probed with the family, it became increasingly clear that Eddie had been treated as a classic family scapegoat. When you talked with Eddie by himself, he was a pleasant, normal person. When you talked with his family, they too seemed like pleasant, normal people. But when you put them together, it did not take long to see that what looked good on the surface was, in reality, anything but that. There were serious tensions—and Eddie, in the mind of everyone else, was to blame for all of them. Inevitably, he himself had begun to accept this assessment of the situation, and played his assigned role perfectly.

So far our discussion about normal and dysfunctional families has been rather clinical, at the level of "concepts" and "dynamics" and "general theories." But what about *your* family? How did *it* operate? What were its unique strengths and weaknesses? How did these qualities affect *you*? In the next chapters, we will learn how to use some tools that can help us begin to better understand our own family system.

4

*There is nothing new under the sun.
The problems your family experiences
frequently have their roots in
patterns of dysfunction that are handed down
from generation to generation.
A simple tool called a genogram
can help you better understand
a heritage of dysfunction.*

CHAPTER 4

The Sins
of the Fathers

O NE OF THE MOST help-
ful tools we can use to
understand the dynamics of our family system is called the
genogram. The genogram is a sort of expanded family tree that
charts the relational and emotional aspects of a family across
several generations. It includes the kind of information that a
typical family tree would contain—names, birthdays, wed-
dings, divorces, deaths, and the like. But it also includes brief
descriptions of family members, their particular strengths and
weaknesses, and aspects of their lives that can have a continuing effect down through the years. It is put together in a way
that makes it possible to identify principles and patterns that
have been at work across the generations.

The genogram is a sort of expanded family tree that
charts the relational and emotional aspects of a family
across several generations.

Those of you who have thumbed ahead through this chapter and have seen what genograms look like may be a bit in-

timidated by them. Let me simply assure you before we go any farther that they are not as complicated as they first appear to be. The various symbols may be new to you, but they are not hard to understand. And when you are working with a genogram of your own family—as you will be, by the time we have finished this chapter—the fact that you are working with familiar names and events will make it easier for you.

> The first step in releasing the past is to become aware of the problems which still exist. Identify what it is from your past that still bothers you, affects you, influences you, or hinders you.
>
> —H. Norman Wright, *Always Daddy's Girl,*
> (Ventura, CA: Regal Books, 1989) p. 208.

Before we get into the "how" of constructing a genogram, let's talk for a moment about the "why." There are three main things we can gain from the use of the genogram.

- The first is *understanding*. As you develop your genogram, you will be able to see and understand your family as more than just a collection of individuals. You will be able to see it as a unified whole, as a system. You will be able to identify patterns and tendencies that may have characterized your family for years, and that impact you to this day. This enhanced understanding will apply not only to your family as a whole, but also to specific generations of the family and even to particular individuals.
- As understanding increases, so does the *potential for change*. It is nearly impossible to change something we do not see or understand. But once we can recognize where problems and weaknesses lie, the potential for changing them becomes available to us.

- This brings us to the third thing genograms help us with, which represents the whole point of this book. Once we start to understand the dynamics at work in our family system, and begin to grasp the potential for change, we are able to consider the crucial step we must take if we are to find freedom from the effects of the past. That step is *forgiveness.*

> If we can move toward gathering a more factual history of our family, and enlarge the context over several generations, we will gain a more objective perspective on family members. We can begin to see our parents, as well as other relatives, as *real people in context* who have both strengths and vulnerabilities—as all human beings do. And if we can learn to be more objective in our own family, other relationships will be a piece of cake.
>
> —Harriet Goldhor Lerner, *The Dance of Intimacy,* (New York, NY: Harper & Row, 1989) p. 199.

DRAWING THE BOUNDARIES

Now let's look at some of the family dynamics that can be clarified through the use of the genogram. The first is the dynamic of *boundaries.* One of the best descriptions we have read of how boundaries work within a family system comes from the book, *Adult Children:*[1]

We are talking about psychological and social boundaries here, although in principle they are the same as physical boundaries around one's property, city, state, or country. For our purposes we will look at three types of boundaries:

1. Individual boundaries: Our personal boundaries which define who we are in relationship to others.

2. Intergenerational boundaries: Boundaries which help us define who the parents and children are, for example. When these boundaries are blurred, the children often become the parent to the parent.

3. Family boundaries: Boundaries which define our family and make it distinctive from other families.

Within each type, we can have three boundary states:

1. Rigid boundaries, which are too strong, can be likened to walls without doors. They are often impenetrable. We cannot move back and forth across the boundary.

2. Diffuse boundaries, which are too weak, can be likened to defining our property by drawing a line in the dirt with a stick. It does not take much to wipe out the boundary. People with diffuse boundaries may say "no" to something, but they change their minds with a little encouragement.

3. Flexible boundaries, which are healthy, can bend when they need to. If the circumstances warrant it, the "no" can be changed to "yes" but never out of guilt or a sense of being forced into something. Flexible boundaries allow the other person to say "no." The person who asked is then able to accept the "no" and find another way to accomplish the task.

The way boundaries worked in your family has a lot to do with how you relate to your world today. A genogram will help you identify the types of boundaries that existed (and still exist) in your family, and the way they may have affected you for good or for ill.

THE ROLES WE PLAY

A second dynamic that can be identified with a genogram is that of *roles* and how they are played out. A "role" is simply any fixed pattern of relating that forces us into set actions, behaviors, and responses, out of "habit" rather than as a freely chosen response to changing circumstances and situations. When roles work like this, they dehumanize us. People do not relate to us as full, free human beings with individual dignity and free will, but only in terms of our role. We are treated, not as "Dave" or "Joan," but as "the Black Sheep," "the Scapegoat," "the Kid Brother," and so on.

Roles can dehumanize us. We are treated, not as "Dave" or "Joan," but as "the Black Sheep," "the Scapegoat," "the Kid Brother," and so on.

We are already familiar with some of the more common family roles—like the Scapegoat—that occur with some frequency in many families. But ultimately, there are as many different "roles" as there are individuals within families. The point is not to draw up a comprehensive list of standard family roles, but to understand the roles that have existed in our own family and how they have affected us:

Families cast their members in roles that they never forget. Although we may be separated, literally or figuratively, from our families of origin, these major roles are indelibly engraved on our memories. We replay these roles over and over again, not just in families we form but often in other groups as well. We are attracted to people who play, and let us play, the roles we know. Sometimes, we do not want the role we played as a child, and choose another role. But that role will also be familiar to us—a role that someone else played in our family of origin.[2]

Thus it is important to know what role (or roles) we played in our family, as well as the roles we play today. It is also important to understand the roles that others played, and how they are all interconnected. Seeing the whole will enable us to better understand the particular parts.

THE RULES WE FOLLOW

Every family system operates according to a set of rules, or what are known in the business world as "standard operating procedures." Rules may be spoken or unspoken. Nevertheless they exist, and they affect our family's activities and behaviors. Even without saying a word, our family lets us know what is and is not acceptable, how various circumstances are to be assessed and responded to, and how different individuals ought to act and react in different situations.

> "Don't rock the boat" is the all-encompassing rule, the master rule and gatekeeper who rides herd over all the other rules in the family. "Don't rock the boat" becomes the rule that rules. This simple but stern injunction, "Don't rock the boat!" locks each individual family member inside a set of unhealthy rules. If left unchallenged, these rules will inevitably suppress change, hinder growth, and obstruct any hope of recovery.
> —Robert Subby, *Lost in the Shuffle*, (Deerfield Beach, FL: Health Communications, Inc., 1987) p. 46.

Unwritten Rules

Children who grow up in dysfunctional families quickly learn the unwritten, unspoken rules of the household. Here are some that are especially common:

1. *We don't feel.* We keep our emotions guarded, especially anger (though often there is one person who is allowed to express feelings openly, especially anger).
2. *We are always in control.* We don't show weakness. We don't ask for help, which is a sign of weakness.
3. *We deny what's going on.* We don't believe our senses or perceptions. We lie to ourselves and to others.
4. *We don't trust.* Not ourselves, not others. No one can be relied upon, no one confided in.
5. *We keep the family's secrets.* Even if we told, no one would believe us—or so we think.
6. *We are ashamed.* We are to blame for everything bad that happens—and we deserve it.

Remember Richard, from Chapter 2, whose father was in a state mental hospital? Richard and his brothers took turns visiting their father every week, but they never talked about it—or about him. "Visit Dad every six weeks" and "Never mention Dad's existence" were both very strong, very clear rules in Richard's family, even though they were never stated out loud.

In any family there are likely to be rules to control such areas as communication ("We don't talk about Mom's drinking"), display of emotion ("Men don't cry; it's a sign of weakness"), how boundaries are to be observed ("We don't hug in this family"), the kinds of people who are acceptable ("We don't marry people like that"), and many more. Often it is hard to recognize these rules when we are living in the midst of them. But when we take a step back and look at our family system as a whole, they emerge more clearly.

Even without saying a word, our family lets us know what is and is not acceptable.

TRIANGLES

We are accustomed to thinking of relationships almost entirely in "one-to-one" terms: my brother and me, my mom and dad, my father and me, and so on. In assessing family systems, we find it is almost always easier to understand how a relationship works by examining it in terms of groups of three, or *triangles*. Instead of speaking about "the relationship I had with my mother," we talk about "the way my mother and I related when we were with my father." This concept is very important and requires more in-depth explanation. We will look at triangles in detail in Chapter 5 to see how they help us fill out the patterns revealed by our genogram.

Toxic shame is multigenerational. It is passed from one generation to the next. Shame-based people find other shame-based people and get married. As a couple each carries the shame from his or her own family system. Their marriage will be grounded in their shame-core. The major outcome of this will be a lack of intimacy.

—John Bradshaw, *Healing The Shame That Binds You*, (Deerfield Beach, FL: Health Communications, Inc., 1988) p. 25.

RECURRING PATTERNS

Another important family dynamic revealed by the geno-gram is the *recurring pattern*. By this we simply mean personal characteristics or relationship dynamics that get repeated generation after generation within a family. Alcoholism and code-pendency are common recurring patterns. In part, this is because alcohol appears to have a biological component that is passed along through our genes. But it also reflects attitudinal and behavioral patterns that increase our vulnerability to becoming alcoholic or to gravitating to alcoholics as friends and even as spouses. Adultery, desertion, abuse, and divorce are all patterns of behavior that sometimes seem to be "handed down" from one generation to the next, and patterns can be spotted using the genogram.

If we do not know about our own family history, we are more likely to repeat past patterns or mindlessly rebel against them, without much clarity about who we really are, how we are similar to and different from other family members, and how we might best proceed in our own life.

—Harriet Goldhor Lerner, *The Dance of Intimacy,* (New York, NY: Harper & Row, 1985) p. 118.

Two of the more general patterns we look for in the geno-gram are the ones we were introduced to in Chapter 3, namely, attachment and adaptability. Do past generations of our family show a tendency to be enmeshed or detached, rigid or chaotic? As we have seen, these are vitally important dynam-ics that show up very clearly in the genogram.

THE HORIZONTAL AXIS

The final family dynamic highlighted by the genogram is what we call the *horizontal axis*. Think of it as a sort of timeline, on which are noted various key life-events that tend to produce stress on the family system. These key events include such things as an untimely death, a divorce, a move or relocation, and other stressful or traumatic occurrences. This dynamic was described as:

> ... the horizontal flow of anxiety [which] emanates from current stresses in the family as it moves forward through time, coping with the inevitable changes, misfortunes, and transitions in the family life cycle. With enough stress on this horizontal axis, any family will experience dysfunction.[3]

The *horizontal axis* differs from the *vertical axis* in that it relates to current issues within the family that are not cross-generational. As we look at a genogram, we cannot explain everything by the generational patterns. Sometimes problems occur simply because life brings problems.

Horizontal stress is not an excuse for dysfunctional behavior. But understanding the nature and extent of these kinds of stresses can help us understand how dysfunctional behavior arises and is sustained.

GATHERING INFORMATION

The first step in building your own genogram is to collect information. You will need as much data as possible about your family going back at least two generations. If you do not have the information to do this, take some time and do the necessary research. Talk to your parents, if they are available and willing to do so. Call your grandparents, your aunts, uncles, and cousins. Frequently there will be one family member (for some reason, it is almost always an aunt) who will have been designated as the "unofficial family historian," and will have already obtained much of the information you will need.

One of our clients, Bill, had a fairly typical experience. When he started asking his parents some fairly basic questions about their families, they became defensive. "Why do you want to know about that?" they asked. "Let the past stay in the past!" Naturally that only served to stir up Bill's curiosity. Over the next several months he managed to chat with a number of his aunts and uncles. Each was able to give him a few snippets of information, but not enough to fill in the picture completely. He was about to give up when one of his aunts suggested that he talk to one of her cousins. It turned out that this cousin had thoroughly researched her own corner of the family and had enough material about Bill's segment to enable him to complete his genogram.

You may not be as fortunate as Bill was. But even if it takes considerable effort to assemble the data you need, stick with it. It will be worth your trouble.

BUILDING YOUR GENOGRAM

Once you have assembled the necessary information, it's time to get started. The easiest way to begin is to get several large sheets of paper—perhaps the big sheets that come with demonstration flip-charts. You can get these at any office supply store. It is important to use large sheets: first, because genograms tend to "take off in all directions" as you draw them up, especially when you are just beginning; second, because when you are done, you can more easily sit back and study the genogram as a whole.

> The chief component in the family as a system is the marriage. If the marriage is healthy and functional, the family will be healthy and functional. If the marriage is dysfunctional, then the family is dysfunctional.
>
> —John Bradshaw, *Healing The Shame That Binds You*, (Deerfield Beach, FL: Health Communications, Inc., 1988) p. 30.

You will need to know some basic symbols in making your genogram. Let's review them quickly. Male family members are represented by squares, females are represented by circles. An "X" drawn through a square or circle indicates that the person is deceased. Close relationships between people are indicated by lines: a solid horizontal line between a man and a woman, for example, signifies a marriage. Two slashes through such a line represents a divorce. Children are listed with the oldest on the left and the youngest on the right.

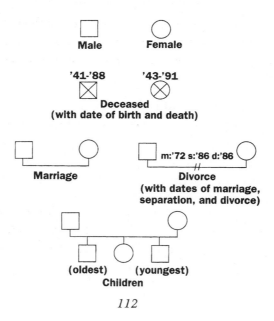

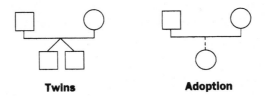

Twins **Adoption**

Now let's start building your genogram.

1. Begin with yourself and your immediate family situation. For example, if you are a married woman with two sons, you would begin like this:

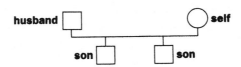

2. Next draw the same kind of diagram for your own family of origin. Let's suppose that you are the oldest of three children. You have two younger brothers, and your father has passed away. Adding them to your genogram makes it look like this:

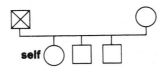

3. Now do the same thing for your husband's family of origin. For the sake of illustration, let's say that he is the younger of two children from his father's second marriage, his father having remarried after the death of his first wife. Let's also say

that he had a daughter from that first marriage. Sounds pretty complicated, doesn't it? But when you see it diagrammed as part of the genogram, it's actually fairly simple to grasp:

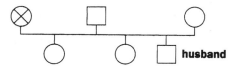

4. The next step is to add the preceding generation for both sides of the family. I will not even try to describe it in words. Here is what it might look like, though, once you have drawn it up:

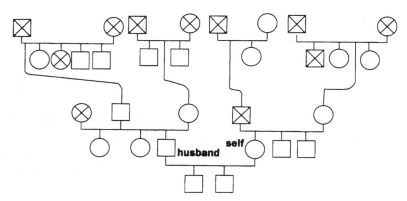

You now have a three-generation family tree in place. This is the core of your genogram. That wasn't so hard, was it?

5. Now go back and add the names of all the individuals, and the key dates that relate to them: birth, death, marriage, divorce, and any other events from the "horizontal axis" that seem significant to you. You can see why it is important to use large sheets of paper! When we do these in our counseling rooms, we usually just tape lengths of butcher paper to the walls and start scribbling. The main thing is to "just get it all up there somewhere." We can always go back and draw up a tidier version.

6. Now go back once more and add brief descriptions of any individuals and relationships that were significant, either in your life or in the life of your family. In the case of individuals, you might jot down key character qualities, personality traits, personal problems, or notable family roles they played, that had a substantial impact on family dynamics. Note especially things like alcoholism or other disorders, those who were the "black sheep" in their families, and so on.

For relationships, note any that were especially close with a heavier straight line, and any that were particularly strained or conflicted with a wavy line. If you become aware of any "fused pairs" (see page 94), indicate them with a double line. Refer back to the chart on page 112 for a simple guide to these symbols. If you know enough about particular family units to score them on the Attachment and Adaptability scales, note that as well. Just write the words "Rigid," "Chaotic," "Enmeshed," or "Detached" next to the appropriate family groups.

A word of caution: thoroughness is important, but so is clarity. Some people really "get into" researching their family tree, and come up with all kinds of intriguing tidbits of family history, amusing anecdotes, and so forth. Trying to cram too much information onto the genogram will make it impossible to read. Remember, the goal is to identify certain kinds of patterns that repeat from one generation to the next. If you fill in too much extra data, you will not be able to see the forest for the trees! Following the steps we have outlined here will help you get the most important data into your genogram. If you have additional information you want to keep, you might want to write it up on separate sheets of paper.

Once you have finished constructing your genogram, your task is to sit back, look at the information it presents, and reflect on any patterns it reveals. Do any key "horizontal axis" events appear over and over? What about significant relationship disruptions, such as divorce? Is there a trail of "Chaotic" or "Enmeshed" families, or of some of the other types of dysfunctional families we mentioned in Chapter 3 (generational or family splits, fused pairs, "Queen of the Hill" families, etc.)? Do certain types of personal problems repeat themselves (alcoholism or other addictions, emotional breakdowns, etc.)? One woman, when she looked back through three generations of her family, counted eleven suicides! She had never thought of suicide as a particular problem in her family until it was revealed by her genogram.

THE COUPLE THAT DRIFTED APART

To get a better idea of how a genogram works in practice, let's look at a couple of real-life examples. The first is actually a composite of several couples who have come to us for counseling over the years.

There was an interesting mixture of love, apathy, and tension in the air when Pete and Amy began to tell their story. They had come to us for marriage counseling. Things had actually been deteriorating in their relationship for some time. They were seeking help now that Amy had recently told Pete she couldn't take it any more and that unless things changed, she was going to file for divorce.

In earlier years, Pete had been a practicing alcoholic. Because of his drinking, he had functioned as an absent member of the family most of the time. When he *was* present, he was hostile and demanding. A few years before, Pete had stopped drinking, through sheer willpower. Much of his overt hostility seemed to have dissipated. But the self-centeredness and demandingness had remained. By now, Pete and Amy's marriage consisted of little more than two people who happened to live at the same address and who, as a result, occasionally did some things together.

Amy had coped with the barrenness of her marriage by pouring herself into her children, which gave her a sense of purpose. She had also expended tremendous amounts of energy trying to please—or at least to appease—her husband. Her overriding goal was to keep things as calm as possible around the house, so as to avoid provoking any unpleasant reactions from Pete.

The current crisis in their marriage was precipitated by two things. First, two of the children had grown up and left home. Amy was faced not only with an empty nest but also with an emptiness in her heart. Second, in an attempt to fill that emptiness, Amy had started to work outside the home. She was doing well at it, too; she had already gained several raises and promotions. She was developing new friendships as well. Her success in the world of work only heightened her awareness of how much of life she had missed down through the years.

Pete barely noticed that the kids were gone, except for the fact that the house was a bit quieter. But Amy's job bothered him. For a while he tried to blame the problems in their marriage on the fact that she was working. When that failed to find a listening ear, he tried another tack: he made some minor gestures toward greater involvement with Amy, and then settled back, thinking that things were improving. But they were not. Pete finally woke up when Amy first used the word "divorce." Before long, they were in our office, looking for help.

PETE'S BACKGROUND

We led them through the same exercise we have just described to you—charting the dynamics of their family system over the past three generations. Their genogram told us a great deal about why they were the way they were. A copy of their genogram is on page 119, so you can refer to it as we go on.

First, look at Pete's side of the family. The dynamics of his parents' relationship were strikingly similar to the dynamics of his own marriage. His father, Ronald, had been an alcoholic who paid little attention to his family most of the time, but he was domineering when he was around. He seemed uncomfortable expressing any kind of emotion. On the other hand, Pete's mother, Sherry, was a nice lady who worked hard to keep the peace in the family—becoming somewhat manipulative, and extremely protective of the children, in the process. Pete was especially close to his mother, but experienced open hostility with his father.

Looking back another generation, we see essentially the same pattern repeated with Pete's grandparents (though apparently without the alcoholism). One trait that shows up clearly and consistently on Pete's side of the family is a strong tendency toward strictness and orderliness, which Pete had continued (and even expanded upon) in his own family.

AMY'S BACKGROUND

Now let's look at Amy's side of the genogram. She came from a family in which there was a lot of open hostility between the parents. Her father, Bob, was very domineering, a gambler who was gone a lot but whose presence instilled fear when he was home. On the other hand, he could at times function as a "family man" who, despite his other behaviors, managed to convey that his family was important to him. They often did things together as a family, even though Amy's mother, Pat, was not a healthy person physically. As a result, most of the work for these family events fell on Amy. Amy's mother could display a nasty side but never toward Amy, for whom she seemed to feel a special closeness.

Amy was unable to learn a great deal about her grandparents. But the little she *did* find out seemed to indicate, in both cases, a combination of meanness and sweetness, with the men living on the fringes of the family and women serving as the mainstays of family life.

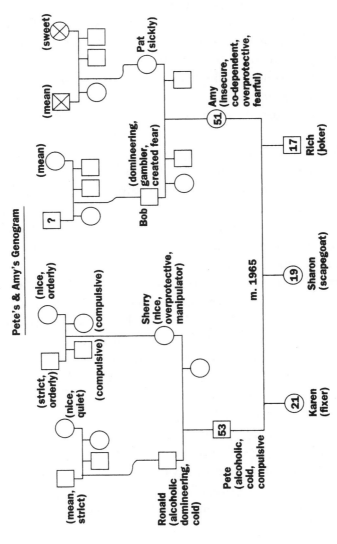

RECURRING PATTERNS

The longer we looked at the genogram, the clearer the patterns seemed to emerge. The main thing we saw was a problem with intergenerational boundaries in both families of origin. In each case, the children had become entangled in the parents' problems: both Pete and Amy found themselves fused with their mothers in an attempt to survive the negative aspects of life with their fathers. As a result, each of them found themselves locked into the patterns they had learned growing up; it was almost impossible for either of them to break away and develop any other style of marriage or family life.

Pete in particular had found himself caught in two very difficult roles at the same time. He was cast in the role of "scapegoat" by his father, who subtly but unmistakably communicated the notion that "if you wouldn't cause so much trouble, this would be a more pleasant place for all of us." At the same time, he was expected to play the role of emotional spouse to his mother when she was feeling alienated from her husband. The two roles reinforced each other in a perverse way. The more Pete's mother leaned on him, the more resentful his father became. Conversely, the more harshly his father treated him, the more Pete's mother tried to protect her "little man." Pete's way of coping with the resulting tension was to withdraw into himself emotionally—and as he grew older, to drown his sorrows in alcohol.

Amy, on the other hand, was clearly taught to assume the role of the "enabler," the one whose steadiness and responsibility makes it possible for others to get away with being erratic and irresponsible. She was the one who was expected to stay calm amid the tensions of her parents' marriage. She was the one who would try to comfort both her mother and her father after they had fought. She was the one who would try to get the family to act like a family when it seemed that everything was flying apart. It was a tough job for a little girl to fill. But the fear of losing her family and being all alone pushed Amy to almost superhuman effort, balancing off all the conflicting emotions in her family. It turned out to be great training for what she experienced with Pete.

Pete and Amy learned some common lessons from their families of origin. Both of them learned, for example, that Mother is the source of nurture and that Father, as the material provider, is allowed to be emotionally distant most of the time and openly domineering when on the scene. Both also learned very clearly the rule, "We don't talk about our problems."

They also learned some lessons that turned out to be contradictory. For example, Pete learned from his upbringing that a marriage and a family could function with very little shared time. Amy, on the other hand, learned from her family that no matter how bad the problems got, you still got together, did things as a family, and acted as if everything was just fine.

> About 85 percent of us end up marrying someone very similar in personality dynamics to our parent of the opposite sex.... We continue what we got used to in childhood.
> —Paul Meier and Frank Minirth, *Free to Forgive: Daily Devotions for Adult Children of Abuse,* (Nashville, TN: Thomas Nelson, Inc., 1991) June 21.

The more clearly we were able to see the dynamics of the families that Pete and Amy grew up in, the more readily we could understand why they had the kind of marriage they had. Pete simply repeated the pattern he had seen modeled by his father, showing little interest in his wife and children. As he drank more and more, the burden on Amy to hold the family together grew heavier.

Pete's retreat from the family triggered in Amy the same fear of abandonment she had experienced growing up. She very naturally slid back into the familiar role of the enabler, taking upon herself full responsibility for holding things together, serving as the children's sole source of nurture. Since neither Pete nor Amy knew how to communicate about what they were feeling and experiencing, the patterns they had learned in childhood were repeated in adulthood. The unresolved hurts of the past were never resolved—just reproduced and intensified.

As we worked with Pete and Amy, helping them understand the dynamics of their respective family systems, two things began to happen. First, the light bulbs began to come on regarding their families of origin. They had already sensed some parallels between themselves and their own parents. But they had not appreciated how their parents' lives had been shaped by their grandparents. Seeing how dysfunctional patterns could carry over from one generation to the next gave them a better idea of what they were really dealing with.

It is not unusual for dissatisfaction to set in with the wife long before it is sensed by the husband.

Second, it became startlingly clear to both Pete and Amy that they were still operating under the same rules and out of the same roles they had known in their families of origin. They were astonished by how precisely they had managed to reproduce the dynamics they had known in childhood in their own marriage and family.

It is not unusual for dissatisfaction to set in with the wife long before it is sensed by the husband, as was the case with Pete and Amy. Men are usually not paying that much attention to relational issues. Much of what we did with them in counseling focused on clarifying, openly and together, the kinds of family rules they *wanted* to establish for their family. They also needed to discuss what roles needed to be abandoned, and how they could be replaced by more suitable and flexible ones, both as regards their relationship with each other and their relationship with their children.

THE DESCENDANTS OF ABRAHAM

Now let's consider a second example. This one is drawn from the Bible. It concerns Abraham and the generations that followed him.

A few comments as we begin. First, it is obvious that we do not know as much about Abraham and his descendants as we would ordinarily know about people who were still living and coming to us for counseling. We cannot ask Abraham and his family members the many questions that we might like to ask, in order to fill out our understanding of their family system. Thus we must be careful of the dangers that always exist when we try to analyze people who are no longer alive.

At the same time, though, Abraham and his descendants do offer us a helpful example of how the genogram works. The Bible actually gives us a great deal of information about them (if you want to read more, see the Book of Genesis, Chapters 12 through 50). And as we will see, the genogram helps illustrate some of the family dynamics that played an important role in biblical history.

To begin with, we have Abraham and his wife Sarah, who have been unsuccessfully trying to have children for many years. In desperation, Sarah finally suggests (according to the custom of the times) that Abraham take her maidservant, Hagar, and have a child by her. A son is born, Ishmael. In those days, everything that belonged to a maidservant was considered the property of her mistress. Thus Ishmael was considered *Sarah's* son.

Some years later, however, Sarah herself gives birth to a son, who is named Isaac. Abraham and Sarah are now, in effect, the parents of two children. Tension soon develops in the family as Sarah begins to reject Ishmael. She says to herself, "Isaac is *mine*—I gave birth to him. But Ishmael isn't *really* mine. He belongs to Hagar." Finally Sarah's jealousy and resentment build to the point that she prevails upon Abraham to send Hagar and Ishmael away for good.

Here we see the first instance of a pattern that will repeat itself in ensuing generations. The parents play favorites. In this case, they agree together on who the favorite is: Isaac. Ishmael is rejected, first emotionally by Sarah, then literally by both Sarah and Abraham.

Let's look at how the genogram would represent this first generation of Abraham's family:

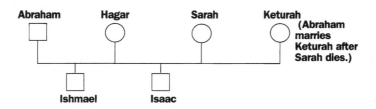

ISAAC AND REBEKAH

Now let's look at the next generation. Isaac meets Rebekah and falls in love. They marry, and Rebekah gives birth to twin boys, Esau and Jacob. Here is how their genogram would look:

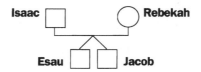

Since Isaac was raised in a family where "playing favorites" led to such tragic consequences—the banishment of his own half-brother—you would think he would be on guard against this destructive dynamic. In fact, though it takes a somewhat different form in his case, in the end he falls victim to the same problem.

The two sons develop into very different types of men. Esau is a ruddy outdoorsman, Jacob more quiet and home-centered. Isaac begins to favor Esau. Rebekah favors Jacob. Did Isaac recognize the unhealthy dynamic that was developing in his family? Did he see it as a repetition of the dynamic he himself had experienced growing up? Did he and Rebekah ever talk about it? We do not know, of course, although there is no evidence to suggest that he did, and much that suggests "We don't talk about our problems" was a strong unspoken rule in Isaac's family. In any case, the favoritism splits the family right down the middle.

JACOB AND RACHEL

Now let's build the genogram for Jacob's family. Jacob's marital history is a bit complicated. He sets out to marry his beloved Rachel, but is duped by his uncle into marrying Leah instead. He angrily confronts his uncle, who tells him to wait a week and allows him to marry Rachel as well. He now has two wives, each of whom has a maidservant, and Jacob has children by all four of them. Here is how the genogram represents Jacob, his wives, and his thirteen children:

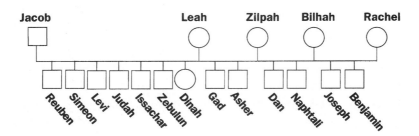

Again, the pattern of favoritism continues in Jacob's family. He has two wives competing for his attention, each of whom has some children of their own and some through their maidservants. In this case, since Rachel is the favorite wife, Jacob picks her firstborn son, Joseph, as his favorite son.

The complete genogram for Abraham's family is on page 127. Can you see the patterns that have reproduced themselves from one generation to the next? For example, in each generation, one of the sons has had to leave the family. Abraham's son, Ishmael, was forced out by Sarah's jealousy. Isaac's son, Jacob, had to leave out of fear for his life: his brother Esau swore to kill him after Jacob finagled Esau out his birthright. Jacob's son, Joseph, was forced to leave because of the jealousy of his brothers, who sold him into slavery.

Each generation also displays a split of some sort between marriage partners that creates an alignment across the generations. Abraham aligns with Isaac against Ishmael. Isaac sides with Esau, against Rebekah and Jacob. Jacob aligns himself with Joseph, against all his other sons. Can you see how each generation has experienced problems that had their roots in the family dynamics of prior generations? That is a very common occurrence, and one that the genogram helps us see very clearly.

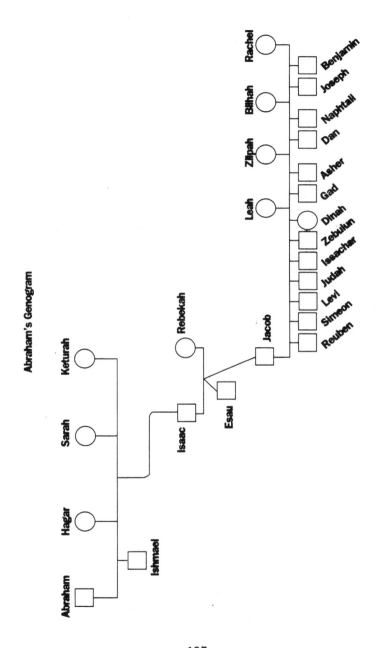

Abraham's Genogram

127

5

We usually think of relationships in terms of one-to-one interactions. To a family therapist, however, relationships happen in threes— in what are called triangles. Charting the triangles in your family can help you understand the dynamics that made you who you are.

CHAPTER 5

Three-Way
Relationships

A S WE MENTIONED IN Chapter 4, family systems researchers have found that the best way to study what goes on in people's relationships is to look at what are called groups of three people, or *triangles*.

This is not what most of us would think. If we wanted to understand, for example, the way a mother and daughter got along, we would probably assume that the logical thing to do is to focus on just the two of them. What do they do when they are together? How do they relate together? How do they communicate?

For many years researchers operated in just this way, and indeed they did learn a number of helpful things about relationships. But they soon began to find that the inner workings of a relationship were really unlocked when a third person was added to the picture.

THE THIRD PERSON

Let's suppose two people have fallen in love—so deeply that they "only have eyes for each other." For months they block out everyone else from their lives. We can study certain aspects of the relationship while they are in this mode. But to a large degree, they are in "a world of their own"; there is much about their relationship that we will not be able to get a handle on until they are forced to interact with "the outside world."

For example, let's say our two lovebirds have a mutual

The inner workings of a relationship were really unlocked when a third person was added to the picture.

---

friend who is dead set against their relationship. When all three of them are together, we are likely to see a very different set of dynamics emerge. We will see how each of them relates to the friend, how they relate to each other in the presence of the friend, and—most importantly—how they deal with the challenges their friend is, implicitly or explicitly, raising in their relationship. All these are very important dynamics, ones we would never have had a chance to observe had we only looked at the original two people.

> Two-person systems are inherently unstable. Anxiety and conflict will not stay contained between two parties for more than a short time. A third party will quickly be triangled in (or will triangle him- or herself in). This process operates automatically, like a law of physics, without conscious awareness or intent.
> —Harriet Goldhor Lerner, *The Dance of Intimacy,* (New York, NY: Harper & Row, 1989) p. 151.

Looking at these "triangles," thus gives us a new and helpful perspective on relationships. For one thing, the third person provides an outside reference point against which the relationship can be compared. In the case of our two starry-eyed lovers, bringing the skeptical friend into the picture takes them out of the "world of their own" and helps us measure them against the real world.

The third person in a triangle can also serve to uncover hidden dynamics in a relationship. Many husbands and wives, for example, grow accustomed to relating to each other according to established patterns, often with a number of secrets, myths, and unspoken rules in operation. When a third person comes along who either does not know the secrets, myths, and rules (or who knows of them and simply refuses to go along with them) the couple is suddenly forced to deal with realities that they are otherwise adept at ignoring or sidestepping. Triangles help "blow the cover" of our denial systems.

Triangles help "blow the cover" of our denial systems.

CHARTING THE TRIANGLES

For these reasons, we have found that examining the "triangle" relationships in a family is one of the best ways to understand the dynamics of that family system. After completing the family's genogram, the next thing we do is to "chart the triangles." This chapter will help you understand how three-way relationships work, and how to chart the triangles in your own family system.

This may sound and look very complex and involved. But as you will see, the concepts are not all that difficult to grasp, and the rewards of coming to grips with them are worth it.

Our triangles will be drawn using two basic symbols: a straight line drawn between two people, and a wavy line drawn between two people:

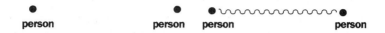

person   person   person   person

A straight line indicates a relationship of *connection or attraction*. A wavy line indicates a relationship of *aversion or absence of connection*. Two people who are comfortable together and feel drawn to one another would be linked by a straight line. Two people who do not get along together or who are simply unable to "connect" with each other would be linked by a wavy line.

Another way to think of the lines is to see them as representing either the presence or absence of a rope tying the two people together. The difference between a straight and wavy line is similar to the difference between two people who "can't stay apart" and two people who "can't stay together."

Often, a straight-line relationship will be marked by harmony and attraction, while a wavy-line relationship will be one marked by discord, even by conflict. Naturally we tend to think of a straight-line relationship as one in which the two people "get along," and a wavy-line relationship as one in which they "don't get along."

But it doesn't always work that way! There are people who remain very strongly attached to each other in a relationship even when that relationship is characterized by a great deal of conflict. Probably all of us know of couples who "only seem happy when they are fighting." That may actually be closer to the truth than we think.

THE MAN WHOSE PARENTS COULDN'T PART

The most extreme example of this kind of relationship that I ever came across had to do with the parents of a man named Brock. His parents had been divorced for more than twenty years when I met him, and both had quickly remarried. But according to Brock, over those twenty years, not a day had passed in which they did not get into a fight with each other over the telephone.

"They still talk to each other?" I asked in disbelief. "Every day?"

"Every single day, without exception," Brock said. "And that's not all. They actually follow each other around the country."

"What do you mean, they follow each other around?" I asked.

Brock explained that shortly after their divorce and remarriage, Brock's father and his new wife moved to a different town. Less than a week later, Brock's mother and her new husband moved to the same town. Brock had no idea how or why it happened the way it did. But he said that over the last twenty years, one or another of his parents had moved more than half a dozen times. Each time it was only a matter of weeks until the other one moved to the same area. The longest they were ever in separate towns was about a month.

All of us know of couples who
"only seem happy when they are fighting."
That may actually be closer to the truth than we think.

As I said, this is an extreme case, but it illustrates the point dramatically. We would have to diagram the relationship between Brock's parents with a straight line. They are clearly connected to each other, and seemingly incapable of disconnecting. Yet their relationship has consisted of nothing but conflict for more than twenty years.

By the same token, it is possible for a wavy-line relationship to be relatively peaceful in nature. A wavy line can represent a relationship marked not by conflict but by distance (emotional or geographic), aloofness, coldness, separation, absence (as with a father who is gone ten months out of the year traveling on business), or simply "not being on the same wavelength." A wavy line often indicates the absence of a solid emotional connection, not just the presence of conflict. I have often used a wavy line to describe the relationship between, for example, a parent and child who never fought or argued at all, simply because they had never managed to forge any kind of meaningful bond.

Sometimes the "third person" in a relationship
can be figurative, as when we say,
"You're just like your mother."
The spectre of an absent third party
can be a very real presence in a relationship.

A note in passing. Usually when we speak of a triangle, we are dealing with a relationship among three flesh-and-blood people who actually interact together on a regular basis. Sometimes, though, the "third person" in a relationship can be more figurative, as when we say things like, "You're just like your mother," or "You remind me so much of your father when you do that." The spectre of an absent third party can be a very real presence in a relationship.

FOUR TYPES OF TRIANGLES

Putting together the various combinations of straight-line and wavy-line relationships produces four types of triangles:

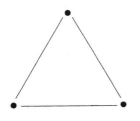

The first triangle is made up of all straight lines. It is one in which all three people are solidly connected with one another and in most cases, get along with one another comfortably. This is the most pleasant type of triangle relationship for all involved.

The second triangle is made up of all wavy lines. It represents three people who either do not get along at all or who are utterly unable to connect with one another. Obviously, being part of such a triangle would be most unpleasant for everyone.

The third triangle has one straight line and two wavy lines. It reflects what happens when two people align with one another and against the third. Examples of this might be when two brothers "pick on" a little sister, or when a mother and daughter align against the father.

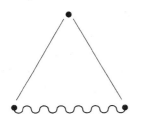

The fourth triangle consists of two straight lines and one wavy line. This occurs when one person is trying to hold together the others who are at odds—for example, a mother trying to keep the peace between a father and son.

THE PRINCIPLE OF BALANCE

Any of these triangles may exist among any group of three people at any given time. But only two of these types are stable and enduring. As relationships grow in intimacy and intensity, and as they continue over long periods of time, three-way relationships will inevitably gravitate to one or the other of these two types. We call these "balanced" triangles.

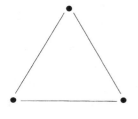

The first *balanced* triangle is the one composed of three straight lines. It is easy to see why this triangle is able to hold together over time. Everyone involved in it is comfortable with all the others; there is no *reason* for it to change.

The triangle composed of all wavy lines is *unbalanced* almost by definition. How could it be otherwise? A relationship of three people who do not get along is hardly a relationship at all; it is bound to either drift apart or—more likely—self-destruct.

The third triangle, in which two are aligned against one, is also *balanced*. While it may not represent a very happy arrangement—at least not for the odd man out—it is capable of enduring for a long time. In fact, sometimes the relationship between the two "aligned" parties draws much of its strength from their mutual distaste for the third person.

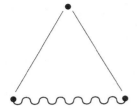

The fourth type of triangle, in which one person has a good relationship with two other people who dislike each other, is by nature *unbalanced.*

It may not be immediately obvious why this last triangle is unbalanced. In fact, most of us probably find ourselves in this sort of situation with some regularity. We may, for example, have two co-workers, both of whom we consider our friends, who cannot stand each other. Can't such a situation remain unchanged indefinitely?

It can, but only as long as the three of you have fairly structured, impersonal relationships—such as being co-workers in a large office. If the three of you were to move into a small apartment together, things would soon change.

In more intense, long-term settings (and within the family most of all) all triangular relationships will, sooner or later, move to a position of balance.

Here's why. Let's say you are the one cast in the role of peacemaker. Sooner or later, one of two things is going to happen. Either you will grow weary from the effort of holding the others together and throw in your lot with one of them against the other, or one of the others will become irritated by your peacemaking efforts and throw in his lot against you! Either way, the relationship becomes two-against-one, which makes for a balanced triangle. (There is, of course, a third possibility: all three of you may get fed up with one another, in which case the relationship breaks down entirely.)

Unbalanced triangles can last in short-term or impersonal

situations. But in more intense, long-term settings (and within the family most of all) all triangular relationships will, sooner or later, move to a position of balance.

THE LITTLE GIRL WITH TWO "BEST FRIENDS"

We actually see this sort of dynamic occur around us all the time. Let's take a simple example. Imagine that you are the parent of a six-year-old girl. One Saturday you invite your daughter's best friend from school to come over to your house for the afternoon. You also invite your child's best friend from church. These two children have never met each other before.

Things go well for a while. But soon the friend from school corners your child and says, "I thought I was your best-best-best friend. Am I?" Your child reassures her that, *of course,* she is her best friend. Immediately this little girl runs to the other guest and says, "I'm her best-best-best friend, and you're not!"

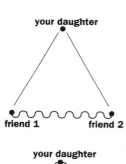

This immediately sends the friend from church running to your child to demand, "Aren't I your best-best-best friend?" And again your child says, "Sure you are." We now have the kind of situation represented by the unbalanced triangle to the left.

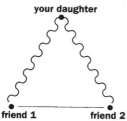

As any parent knows, before very long one of two things is almost certainly going to happen. Either one of the two friends will feel hurt and will start whining that she wants to go home, or *both* of the invited guests will become "best friends" with *each*

other and ignore your child. We now have the situation represented by this balanced triangle.

Children seldom have the maturity and the relational skills to resolve this kind of situation such that *everyone* winds up being friends—even with parents' help. When that does happen, we are usually so amazed by it that we comment about it to others! Nine times out of ten, what happens is that two pair off against one. That is the nature of this kind of triangle, and the reason why we consider it an "unbalanced" triangle.

THE PREDICTIVE POWER OF TRIANGLES

This principle of balance holds true with a remarkable degree of consistency and tenacity. Our experience (and that of other family systems theorists) shows that over time, in a close, intimate setting like the family, *all* three-way relationships will inevitably resolve themselves into one of the "balanced" triangle patterns:

Not only that, but the characteristic of any given two-way relationship (whether it is a straight-line or a wavy-line relationship) will remain the same no matter what third party is added.

Sometimes people will say, "My brother and I always got along great." But then an interesting thing happens. When we draw a triangle to include their mother, there is a straight line between them and their brother. The same thing happens when we draw a triangle to include their sister. But when we try to add in their father, they say, "Well, the three of us never could hit it off together. In that case, you'd have to put a wavy line between my brother and me."

Our response would be, "Something's not right here. Experience shows that the quality of your relationship with your brother should remain the same no matter what third party we include." We will then probe more deeply, to see if the individual is not either idealizing his relationship with his brother in the first two settings, or wrongly estimating the negative impact of his father in the third setting.

> Kids aside, we are always in triangles of one sort or another because we always have "stuff" from our first family (as well as elsewhere) that we are not paying attention to and that may overload other relationships.... Working on triangles means more than identifying issues with our first family that fuel anxiety elsewhere. It also means observing and modifying our current role in key family triangles.
>
> —Harriet Goldhor Lerner, *The Dance of Intimacy*, (New York, NY: Harper & Row, 1989) p. 160.

HIDDEN DYNAMICS

The consistency of the principle of balance is so reliable that we can often apply it in just this way, to "smoke out" hidden dynamics in relationships. For example, we once dealt with a woman named Betty, whose mother had divorced and remarried when she was young. Betty knew she did not get along well with her mother, who had always been aloof and

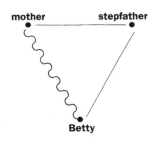

hyper-critical of her. But she believed that her mother and stepfather had a solid relationship. She also insisted that she herself had always felt close to her stepfather as well. When she drew a triangle to represent this relationship, it came out like this.

When we pointed out that the triangle was not balanced, and suggested that Betty take a harder look at the relationships involved, she immediately became defensive—especially about her relationship with her stepfather. "But that's the way it's been!" she insisted. Other members of Betty's group began to ask some probing questions. How had she felt when her mom divorced? How did she really feel when her stepfather first appeared on the scene?

Betty's increasingly agitated responses seemed to indicate that there was more going on than met the eye. A picture of Betty's stepfather began to emerge; that of a genial but distant man who provided materially for his family but who seemed to hold his stepdaughter at arm's length emotionally. We began to ask Betty whether she might not be idealizing her relationship with her stepfather. It would have been quite understandable, we assured her: given her estrangement from her mother, and the trauma of separation from her father after the divorce, clinging to an idealized relationship with her stepfather could have been a way to guard against feeling like an emotional orphan.

As we continued to talk, Betty suddenly began to weep. "But he was a good man," she sobbed. "A *good* man. Just because he used to…"

"Used to *what*, Betty?" we asked gently.

It was then that the painful memories began to rise to the

surface. Betty's stepfather had taken advantage of her sexually. Not in extreme ways, and only for a very brief period, but the molestation was nevertheless quite real. The memories were so painful she had kept them carefully buried for years, all the while telling herself vehemently that her stepfather was "a good man" who loved her. Of course in many ways he was a good man, and he *did* love her. But he had also abused her in a way that had caused her great damage. To face that truth, at a young age, was simply too threatening.

The memories were so painful she had kept them carefully buried for years, all the while telling herself vehemently that her stepfather was "a good man" who loved her.

Betty came to see, however, that it was not disloyal to acknowledge the truth about her past, nor would facing up to it destroy her. In fact, bringing it into the open enabled her to deal forthrightly with what had happened, and it proved to be the key to overcoming the depression that had afflicted her for years.

PETE AND AMY

Let's take a look at how "charting the triangles" works in practice. In Chapter 4, we developed a genogram for a couple we called Pete and Amy. As we examine the dynamics of their family, and of their respective families of origin, three sets of relationships stand out clearly.

In Pete's family, we saw that his father was an alcoholic,

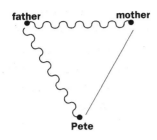

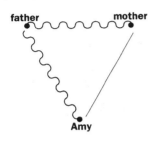

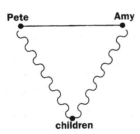

emotionally distant both from his wife and from his son. At the same time, Pete enjoyed a close relationship with his mother. This three-way relationship, when diagrammed, reflects a classic balanced triangle.

Amy's family of origin displayed a similar pattern. Her father, as we saw, was a domineering man who alienated both his wife and his children. Amy's mother, while not an especially warm person herself, nevertheless seemed to hold Amy in special regard. Again, the relationship among these three forms a balanced triangle.

In both cases, we see exactly the same configuration: a coalition between child and mother, with the father left out. With both Pete and Amy having experienced this pattern growing up, is it any wonder they saw the same pattern develop in their own family? They did not *consciously* set out to duplicate the pattern they had experienced as children, but all of their life experience tended to be in that direction. Without consciously *resisting* this dynamic (which they could scarcely be expected to do until they were at least able to recognize its existence), it was simply the most "natural" pattern for them to fall into. That is precisely what happened.

We could, of course, go much further in our analysis of the triangles in Pete's and Amy's family. They have three children; we could draw a separate triangle representing each of the different three-way relationships represented among the five of them. (For those whose math is a bit rusty, there would be ten triangles in all.) We would expect to find that each triangle balanced, and that each meshed with the others in terms of whether the various relationships were "straight line" or "wavy line." But this quick glance is enough to demonstrate how useful triangles can be in illustrating family dynamics.

ABRAHAM, ISAAC, AND JACOB

We can also use triangles to better understand some of the dynamics in the families descended from Abraham. Again, we constructed a genogram for Abraham and his descendants in Chapter 4. Charting the triangles helps us get a better handle on what happened among some of the key characters.

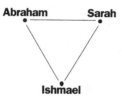

At the start, when Ishmael was born, all seemed well in Abraham's family. We would represent it with a balanced triangle of all straight lines.

But things got more complicated when Isaac was born. Sarah, as we have seen, rejected Ishmael and made Isaac her favorite. This put Abraham in a bind. For him to remain loyal to Ishmael would have driven Sarah—and, presumably, Isaac—away. Here is how we would represent the resulting situation.

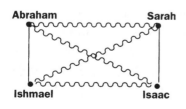

Notice that we overlap two triangles to show the interrelationships among the four people. Notice also that the triangles are in balance.

On the other hand, Abraham had another choice. He

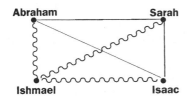

could align himself with Sarah in rejecting Ishmael. This, in fact, is what he did. It too resulted in a set of balanced triangles.

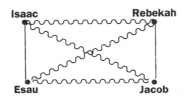

Now let's look at Isaac's family. In the beginning, Isaac and Rebekah had a beautiful romantic relationship. Then the children came along and things got complicated. Isaac, as we have seen, was drawn to his rugged firstborn son, Esau.

Rebekah, on the other hand, favored Jacob. The principle of balance would suggest that we now need to put a wavy line between Isaac and Rebekah. Indeed, when we later read about their interaction after Jacob tricks Esau out of his birthright, we can see the distance and estrangement between them.

Now let's follow the family tree through Jacob's family. Remember that Jacob had planned to marry Rachel, but as a result of his uncle's chicanery he also wound up married to Leah. We can only presume that his relationship with Leah was somewhat strained, and that the relationship between Leah and Rachel was also troubled.

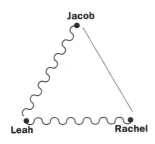

If Jacob plays favorites with his wives, he is also likely to play favorites with his wives' children. He will favor Rachel's son, Joseph, and turn away at least somewhat from the sons borne by Leah and her maidservant and the two sons borne by Rachel's maidservant.

Again, this is in fact what happens. Here is how we would represent this complex situation using triangles:

147

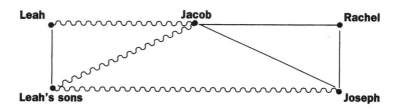

In this case we have three connecting triangles, reflecting the five parties we are considering. Notice that all three triangles are in balance, and the particular one-to-one relationships remain consistent from one triangle to the next.

Again, we are not trying to read more into the stories of Abraham and his sons than is actually in the Bible. But we are told a great deal about this sprawling clan. Charting the triangles helps us to see and understand some of the dynamics at work. In this case, we see a pattern of parental favoritism repeating itself in one generation after the other. The different ways each generation resolves the tensions that it creates have repercussions down through the years.

CHARTING *YOUR* TRIANGLES

No doubt you can see that charting the triangles for a family can become a fairly complicated process. To some degree, this is simply a matter of numbers. The more people involved, the more triangles there will be. We once worked with a family that had fifteen children. If we had worked out every conceivable three-way combination, we would have had to draw 455 triangles! You can see why the arrival of each additional child makes family life so much more complex!

Charting the triangles is also tricky because, as we have seen, the dynamics of relationships are not always clear and simple, and not always what they seem to be at first glance. It can be difficult to completely work out the triangles for your family without hands-on assistance of an experienced counselor.

Even so, you can learn a lot about your family by charting the triangles to the extent that you *are* able to do so. Go back to the genogram you built in Chapter 4. Starting with a fresh sheet of paper, first draw triangles to represent any three-way relationships that you feel confident you understand. Do this both for your own family and for previous generations as you are able. Then see if you can draw other triangles based on the information from those you have just drawn.

What do the triangles tell you? Do they help you understand where potential conflict points in your family may have been? Are you able to detect patterns from one generation to the next, like the ones we saw in our examples? Most important of all, for our purposes, do they help you see more clearly how the dynamics of your family life affected *you*? Do they point out particular relationships that did not work well, particular individuals whose impact on you was harmful in some way?

If so, your tendency may be to get angry or bitter at such individuals. That would be an understandable reaction. But our goal has not been simply to nail down "who did what to whom" so that our blame and bitterness can be more accurately targeted. Rather, our goal has been to get a clearer picture of where the damage lies *so that we can respond to it constructively.*

NOW WHAT?

Up to now, we have focused our energies on understanding how families work—in particular, how they sometimes "go wrong." We have seen how important our family system is in making us who we are. We have seen what a "normal," or "healthy," family looks like, and have reviewed some of the most common ways in which families fall short of this and become "dysfunctional." We have also looked at some of the roles, rules, myths, and secrets that may have been present in your own family.

If you drew up a genogram of your family, and worked out the triangles for as many of the relationships as you could, you should now have a clearer idea of what went right and what went wrong in your particular family. You may well have spotted various dynamics that have affected you negatively, and whose impact is still with you to this day.

In most cases, examining our families in this way points us to certain people in our past who seem like "villains." Their weaknesses, their limitations, their failure to do things they should have done, their having done things they should *not* have done—all may have contributed to difficulties that are still with us in our lives today. The "villain" may be a parent or other adult figure. It may be a brother or sister. Some people even wind up angry at God, for *allowing* bad things to happen to them.

*Whatever others may have done in the past,
what matters is what we do today.*

But the important thing is not just discovering where the problems and who the "villains" are. The important thing is what we *do* with this information now that we have it. Whatever may have been done to us while we were children, we are now grown-ups who must *take responsibility* for our attitudes and actions. Whatever others may have done in the past, what matters is what *we* do *today*.

It is not enough for us to label others as "villains" and blame them for all our troubles. We need to understand what has been done to us *so that* we can take responsibility for our lives as adults and find freedom from our past hurts. We cannot change what has happened to us. But we *can* learn to *respond* to what has happened to us in a way that helps us rise above the negative influences of the past.

How can we learn to respond in such a way that we can begin to experience the freedom of forgiveness? What about those who have hurt us? Can they be released from their pain as well? In Part Two we discover that there can be release for ourselves and others if we and they learn the lesson of forgiveness.

The Freedom of Forgiveness

6

*Once you realize how deeply you may have
been hurt by those in your family,
forgiving them may seem like
the last thing you want to do.
But in fact, forgiveness is crucial
to your spiritual and emotional health.
It is the key to freedom
from the pain of the past.*

CHAPTER 6

Releasing Others, Releasing Ourselves

W HEN MARTI, whom we met in Chapter 3, first came for help, she had no intention of dragging her mother into the picture. She was struggling with insecurity and fearfulness in her own life, which she did not relate to problems within her family. But as we talked (and especially as we constructed her genogram and mapped out the triangles representing her family relationships) the connection became increasingly clear, especially with regard to her mother. Marti was in her forties, but she was still a little girl in terms of her relationship to her mother.

The more we probed this area, the more Marti became aware of how her mother had damaged her, and the more the anger she had bottled up inside came to the surface. One day she turned to me and demanded, "Where is all this going to take me, this therapy? Where is it going to lead?"

I studied her calmly for a moment before replying. "Do you really want to know?" I asked finally.

"Yes!" she snapped. "Yes, I really want to know!"

"Well, Marti," I said, "ultimately, if all goes well, you'll come to the point where you can forgive your mother for the harm she has done you."

"Forgive her?" Marti cried. *"Forgive* her? I will *never* forgive her! Never!"

One of the roots of compulsive behavior is pain that is buried. Pretending that it isn't there or that it doesn't bother you anymore won't solve your problems. Stoicism isn't the answer. Facing your past and forgiving those who wounded you is the only lasting solution....

When buried memories surface, they need to be dealt with. It is important to forgive the parent who hurt you *and* the one who didn't protect you from the hurt.
> —Nancy Curtis, *Beyond Survival,* (Lake
> Mary, FL: Strang Communications,
> 1990) pp. 59-60.

JUST LIKE THAT?

Marti's reaction wasn't all that unusual. People often recoil at the notion of forgiveness. It is not hard to see why. The early phase of counseling often proceeds along the lines of Part One of this book, with an in-depth exploration of the ways our family dynamics have worked against us. Once people have a clear picture of the harm that others have caused them, it's easy to see why forgiving those people might not be the first thing that comes to their mind. "What do you mean?" they cry. "After all that person did to me? After all the pain and confusion they caused me? You expect me to *forgive* them, just like that?"

Our answer is always, "We understand why you are reacting the way you are. We know that in your hurt and anger, forgiving the ones who have damaged you may be the last thing you feel like doing. In fact, we *don't* expect you to forgive them 'just like that.' Forgiving others is not an easy thing. It takes time and effort. But we think you will come to see that ultimately you *must* forgive if you are to be truly free."

Like Marti, you may have been hurt deeply by some important people in your life. As a result of working through the exercises found in Part One, you may be more aware than ever of just how much you have been hurt. And your feelings toward them may be anything but merciful and forgiving. Nevertheless, we are going to urge you on to the high and hard duty of forgiveness, because long experience has shown us that it is the only way to attain genuine freedom from the bad effects of the past.

Forgiveness breaks the cycle. It does not settle all questions of blame and justice and fairness; to the contrary, often it evades those questions. But it does allow relationships to start over. In that way, said Solzhenitsyn, we differ from all animals. It is not our capacity to think that makes us different, but our capacity to repent, and to forgive. Only humans can perform that most unnatural act, and by doing so only they can develop relationships that transcend the relentless law of nature.

—Philip Yancey, "An Unnatural Act,"
Christianity Today, (April 8, 1991) p. 37.

WHY FORGIVE?

We *must* learn to forgive those who have hurt us: that is the message of this book. Forgiveness is important for at least two reasons. We will discuss them in more detail as we go along. For now, let's just note what they are:

- *First, and very important for our present discussion, forgiveness is important for our sake.* We sometimes shock our patients by telling them that they need to learn to be "selfish" about their forgiveness. Often they stare back at us in disbelief. "What do you mean?" they ask. "You want me to be *selfish?* But selfishness is wrong, isn't it?"

  Indeed it is. And we do not mean to be taken absolutely literally, as if we should live our lives in an utterly "me-first" mode. But there is an appropriate way of *caring* for ourselves that can factor into forgiveness.

If we are going to take a loving concern for others, we must also take a loving concern for ourselves. Selfishness says, "Me first; who cares about you?" Appropriate self-care says, "I am going to take care of me so that I can take care of you."

It is similar to what happens when you get on an airliner and the flight attendant explains how to use the oxygen mask that drops into your lap if the plane loses cabin pressure. She tells you that if you are traveling with a child or someone else who requires assistance, you should put your own mask in place first, *then* help the other person. In the same way, if we are going to take a loving concern for others—and we certainly should—we

160

must also take a loving concern for ourselves. Selfishness says, "Me first; who cares about you?" Appropriate self-care says, "I'm going to take care of me *so that* I can take care of you."

- *Second, forgiveness is important for God's sake.* Every wrong is an offense first and foremost against a wise and loving God who does not wish to see any of his creatures harmed and who "takes it personally" when they are wronged. As we will see, an important part of our being able to work out our own forgiveness is drawn from the forgiveness that God himself has shown us.

But think about who your anger is hurting most: It's *you*, as you wallow in your inner turmoil and bitterness. Forgiveness enables you to become fully freed from your anger so that you can develop as good a relationship as possible with your parents. Then, you will also be free to move forward positively in other relationships.

—Anne Grizzle, *Mothers Who Love Too
Much*, (New York, NY: Ivy Books,
1988) pp. 207-208.

CANCELING THE DEBT

Just exactly what does it mean to forgive someone? Does it mean to ignore what they have done? To pretend that it never happened—to "forget" it? To cover things up on the outside while the anger and hurt continue to boil on the inside?

No. Forgiveness is both more simple and more complex than that. The best way I know to understand forgiveness actually comes from the world of banking. Let's say you go to the bank and take out a loan. You now owe money to the bank, which you have every intention of repaying. But let's also say that something unforeseen comes up: a financial calamity, or a major health problem, something that makes it impossible for you to keep up with your loan payments.

When someone does us wrong,
we feel as though they have taken away something
that belonged to us—our peace, our joy,
our happiness—and that they now owe it to us.
When we forgive them, we simply release them
from their debt.

What does the banker do? He could simply insist that you pay back the loan anyway. "I don't care about your problems," he might say. "Just pay me what you owe me." He could keep that debt hanging over your head for the rest of your life.

Or he could, if he wanted to be merciful, decide to simply release you from your obligation. "I'm canceling the debt," he might say. "You don't owe me anything. From here on, I consider us 'even.'" In banking terminology, that is called *forgiving* the loan. It is exactly what we are called to do in our dealings with those who harm us.

When someone does us wrong, when they cause us pain, we often feel as though they have taken away something that belonged to us—our peace, our joy, our happiness, our dignity—and that they now *owe* it to us. We are like a miserly banker, holding an IOU against someone who can never hope to repay us. "I don't care about your problems," we say. "You've hurt me, and you're going to pay." When we forgive them, we simply release them from their debt. We do not have to pretend the debt never existed. We just forgive it; "You no longer owe me anything."

Again, forgiveness has three aspects. First, it has to do with the other person. That is obvious. But second, it also has to do with God, who is—to stretch our analogy a bit—the ultimate creditor, the one to whom all our "debts" are ultimately due. And finally, it has to do with *us*. When we release others from their debts, we also release ourselves from the painful effects of what they did to us. It is a paradox, but it is absolutely true; when we harbor bitterness against others, that bitterness eats away at *us*. The only way to get the poison out of our system is by forgiving.

We said a moment ago that forgiveness has to do with God. Actually, forgiveness is intimately bound up with the very essence of God. He himself is forgiving by nature, and wants us to be forgiving, too.

There are places in the Bible in which we are urged to show forgiveness to others. "Forgive us our debts, as we also have forgiven our debtors" (Matthew 6:12). "Be kind and compassionate to one another, forgiving each other, just as in Christ God forgave you" (Ephesians 4:32). "Bear with each other and forgive whatever grievances you may have against one another. Forgive as the Lord forgave you" (Colossians 3:13).

What stands out in these passsages is that forgiveness begins with God. He does not say, "Forgive or else." He says, "Forgive others *as I have forgiven you*." The reason we can show mercy to others is because he has shown mercy to us. In fact, you could almost say that the mercy we show to others *is* the mercy he shows to us. We simply receive it and pass it on. In other words, our *forgiveness* flows from our *forgiven-ness*.

In answer to a question from one of his disciples, Jesus told this story. Peter had asked, "How many times must I forgive those who hurt me?" In other words, "Just how far does this forgiveness business go? Surely there's a limit to it, right? I mean, if someone just keeps on hurting me, I don't have to keep on forgiving him, do I? Surely there comes a point when I say, 'That's enough!'"

The number of times someone has hurt us is not the issue. Whether the other person deserves forgiveness is not the issue. How we respond to God's grace is the issue.

Jesus' answer makes it clear, however, that there *is* no limit to forgiveness. The number of times someone has hurt us is not the issue. Whether the other person deserves forgiveness is not the issue. *How we respond to God's grace* is the issue. We show mercy to others because he has shown mercy to us.

Someone has said that forgiveness is a "unilateral process." This means it is something we do on our own, regardless of whether the other person responds. So many times we say, "I'll forgive him *if he...*" or, "I'll never forgive her *until she...*"

Forgiveness involves letting go. Remember playing tug-of-war as a child? As long as the parties on each end of the rope are tugging, you have a "war." But when someone lets go, the war is over. When you forgive your father, you are letting go of your end of the rope. No matter how hard he may tug on the other end, if you have released your end, the war is over for you.

—H. Norman Wright, *Always Daddy's Girl,* (Ventura, CA: Regal Books, 1989) pp. 235-236.

But there are no "ifs" or "untils" in forgiveness. It is something we do all by ourselves, whether or not the one we are forgiving even knows or cares we are doing it.

This is important to understand because it sets us free to forgive. We can obtain the wonderful release that comes with forgiving others even without their cooperation!

RECOGNIZING OUR NEED

Jesus makes another point about forgiveness while he is having dinner at the home of a prominent religious leader, a Pharisee, named Simon. They are sitting and talking together when a woman from the town makes an unscheduled appearance. Read what happens next. "When a woman who had lived a sinful life in that town learned that Jesus was eating at the Pharisee's house, she brought an alabaster jar of perfume, and as she stood behind him at his feet weeping, she began to wet his feet with her tears. Then she wiped them with her hair, kissed them and poured perfume on them" (Luke 7:37-38).

Needless to say, Simon is shocked. Jesus becomes aware of Simon's indignation and tells the story of two men who were in debt to a moneylender. (It is worth noting, by the way, that in those days a moneylender was *not* the equivalent of our modern savings and loan officers. He was more like what we would call a loan shark. Falling behind in your payments could be a risky business.) One of the men owed fifty silver coins; the other owed five hundred. Astonishingly, the moneylender decided to forgive both debts. "Now," Jesus asks Simon, "which of these two men will love the moneylender more?" Simon says, "Why, the one who owed the larger amount, of course."

Jesus congratulates Simon for giving the correct answer.

Then he points out that Simon had failed to perform some of the customs that were considered to be part of a good host's duty in those days. "I came into your house. You did not give me any water for my feet, but she wet my feet with her tears and wiped them with her hair. You did not give me a kiss, but this woman, from the time I entered, has not stopped kissing my feet. You did not put oil on my head, but she has poured perfume on my feet. Therefore, I tell you, her many sins have been forgiven—for she loved much. But he who has been forgiven little loves little" (Luke 7:44-47).

Do you sense the sting in these words? Jesus is saying to Simon, "I know this woman has done unspeakable things. But she knows it too, and she recognizes the marvel of God's mercy toward her. That's why she is showing such love and devotion. On the other hand, Simon, you barely showed me the most basic hospitality when I came to your home as a guest. Perhaps that is because you haven't yet realized how merciful God has been to you? Or do you suppose that you have no need of God's mercy? That you are not, in your own way, as needy as this poor woman?"

The point is that we are *all* people in need of God's mercy—indeed, we are all people who have *received* God's mercy. The key is for us to recognize it, and to let it shape the way we treat others. We must let our *forgiven-ness* express itself in *forgiveness*.

THE PROCESS OF FORGIVENESS

The process of forgiveness always begins with a decision. It is an act of the will, something we choose to do because we know it is healthy and right, even though we may not "feel like it" at the moment. I *choose* to take the path that leads to forgiveness. I *decide* to work towards releasing you from the "debt" you "owe" me.

Forgiveness then becomes a process that involves freeing *ourselves* from the emotional effects of what was done to us. When someone has hurt us deeply, it is one thing to say "I forgive you." We can say it with great earnestness, and even *mean* it sincerely. But the pain, the resentment, the confusion caused by the person's wrong action is still there. Sometimes we have to work through our feelings before we can even take the initial step of deciding to cancel the debt. Often we find that even *after* we have made the decision to forgive, our emotions rise up again and make us want to re-impose the debt.

The process of forgiveness always begins with a decision. It is an act of the will, something we choose to do because we know it is healthy and right, even though we may not "feel like it" at the moment.

For example, let us say that you have done something that hurts me. To take a simple example, let's say that while visiting my house, you break a vase that has been in my family for years. You apologize and ask forgiveness. Now what do I do? First, even though I am still feeling sad about the loss of my vase—and still feeling angry at you for breaking it—I know that the right thing to do is to forgive you. And so I do.

Now at this point, in one sense, the debt has been canceled. I have forgiven you, and that is that. But in another sense, I may still have some work to do. I may look at the spot on the shelf where the vase used to be and feel upset that my family heirloom has been destroyed. I may find that I am still irritated at you for destroying it. In time, I realize I am once again "holding against you" the "debt" you incurred when you broke my vase, even though I forgave you.

Now what do I do? I go back to my decision—I have released you from the debt you owe me—I have forgiven you. But now I have to work through all of my feelings about what has happened. I give validity to my loss. I accept the reality of my feelings—I am hurt by your carelessness. I am angry at the loss of something that was important to me. I am saddened over the fact that the vase is gone. I need to "work through" these feelings a number of times before I can really let go of my anger and feel like I have completely forgiven you.

> Remember that no matter how you verbalize your anger, *you must forgive!* Forgiving starts with an *act of the will.* Forgiving is a choice. It may take some time to work through the emotional feelings that are involved. We cannot immediately dismiss the feelings. Again, it takes time to reprogram our computer. It takes time to reprogram the feelings. However, we can forgive others immediately by an act of the will.
> —Frank B. Minirth, M.D. and Paul D. Meier, M.D., *Happiness Is a Choice*, (Grand Rapids, MI: Baker Book House, 1978) p. 156.

This is what we call the *process* of forgiveness, the process by which I not only release *you*, but by which I also find release for *myself.* In time it can happen that virtually *all* the bitterness and hurt is released. I still have a mental recollection of what happened (I am aware that you carelessly broke my vase), and I am still aware of negative consequences that resulted from what you did (my vase can never be replaced). But what happened between us is no longer a "live issue" in the way I think of you and relate to you, or in the way I live my life. I have completed the process of forgiveness. (We will have more to say later about the matter of "forgiving and forgetting.")

---

*The process of forgiveness is complete when
what happened between us is no longer
a "live issue" in the way I think of you
and relate to you, or in the way I live my life.*

THE SIX STEPS OF FORGIVENESS

Let's look at how the process of forgiveness works, in practical terms. There are six main steps. We will briefly review them here. In later chapters we will look more closely at some of the questions and issues that arise as we actually set about the process of working through them.

1. Recognize the injury. "All right," Gail sighed. "I'm ready. I can finally admit my anger over what my parents did to me. I'm tired of getting my head messed up going back and forth between making excuses for them and denying that anything ever happened in the first place. My dad molested me and I feel incredible rage toward him. I feel just as much rage toward my mother because she let it continue all those years. There. That's what happened, and that's how I feel about it."

After more than a year of therapy, being part of a support group for adults who had been molested as children, Gail was engaged in the process of releasing her parents, and herself, from the grip of what had happened in the past.

The process of forgiveness begins when we feel some kind of pain, hurt, or injury. We need to answer some questions.

What happened? Who did it? What effect did it have on me? Adult children of dysfunctional families need to work hard at coming to grips with what happened. Often we are aware of pain and hurt, but we have buried the *cause* of those feelings deeply. We have a hard time remembering what actually happened because part of us does not really *want* to remember what happened. But the remembering is important.

Back in Chapter 1 we met Larry, whose parents had literally abandoned him when he was five years old. Even though it quickly became clear that both his parents had been severe alcoholics and had mistreated him in many ways, Larry had somehow managed to place the blame on himself for everything that had happened. He was at the end of his rope, emotionally and in every other way.

We have a hard time remembering what actually happened because part of us doesn't really want to remember. But remembering is important.

Then one day in the clinic, he and his therapy group were hearing a presentation on the difference between "wrongs done *by* us" and "wrongs done *to* us." Larry suddenly jumped up in his chair. For the first time, he realized that he had been injured, that he had been sinned *against.* That realization triggered a host of memories. For the first time, he was able to remember things that had happened to him in childhood, and understand them properly. He finally recognized the injuries that had been done to him as a child.

Larry said later, "I suddenly realized that I had spent a lifetime turning all my hurt, angry feelings into confessions of things I had done wrong. I even confessed to things I *knew* I hadn't done, 'just in case.'" Remembering the past was the crucial first step in Larry's coming to grips with his past.

This, then, is where the process begins. You might want to get a sheet of paper and make a list of the "wrongs done to me." Be accurate and objective. The goal is not to wallow in self-pity but to lay a foundation of understanding for the steps that are to follow. Take the time necessary to make the list as complete as possible. Reviewing your genogram will help you identify likely patterns of "wrongs done to me" that are characteristic of your particular family.

2. Identify the emotions involved. As you become aware of the injuries you have experienced in your life, you must also try to identify the feelings associated with those injuries. For most of us, three types of emotions will predominate.

Fear. The emotions we associate with past injuries will generally be a composite of what we felt when the injury first occurred and what we are feeling now. The feelings from childhood—when many of the injuries will have taken place—will usually be dominated by fear. It is not hard to see why. Usually, the ones who hurt us as children were grown-ups, people we often looked up to and respected. It was natural for us to be afraid of them then, and that fear will often carry over into our present-day experience.

Guilt and Shame. Adult children of dysfunctional families sometimes seem to have a corner on the guilt market. Most of it is false guilt. We find ways to blame ourselves for our problems, even for things we did not do, just as Larry did. Clarifying exactly what happened helps clear away this kind of false guilt.

It also helps in dealing with shame. Guilt and shame are not the same thing. To put it simply, guilt has to do with *what we have done*, and shame has to do with *who we are*. When we do something wrong and feel badly about it, that is guilt. When

171

we conclude that we are a terrible person because of what we have done, that is shame.

We need to be careful not to let sinful actions lead to shameful self-definitions. If I lose my temper, it is not helpful for me to say, "I'm just an angry person who can never keep his big mouth shut."

---

*Guilt has to do with what we have done,
and shame has to do with who we are.
When we do something wrong and feel badly about it,
that is guilt. When we conclude that we are
a terrible person because of what we have done,
that is shame.*

Shame makes us want to hide from others, lest they find out "what we're really like." We become convinced that there is something inherently wrong with us.

Especially for adult children from dysfunctional families, shame almost always accompanies guilt. It is important to recognize both feelings, and to deal with each one appropriately.

Anger. When we begin to come to grips with the harmful things that have been done to us, and with the feelings of fear, guilt, and shame that those injuries have produced, it usually isn't too long until anger surges to the surface. Many people are astonished at the amount of anger—*rage* is not too strong a word—they have been carrying around with them, stuffed deep inside, for years and years.

Anger is not necessarily a bad thing. There *is* such a thing as righteous anger. It is often an entirely appropriate reaction to having been damaged. In counseling, we find that it is important for people to be able to identify their anger. It clears their vision and helps them see the truth. It also makes it easier for them to continue with the process of forgiveness.

3. Express your hurt and anger. We treat this as a separate step because it is so important. It is not enough to simply identify what we are feeling. We also need some way to *express* our feelings, especially our anger.

If you discovered that there was poison in your belly, it would not be enough just to know it was there, or even to know exactly what kind of poison it was. You would want to get rid of it! That is what the word "express" actually means. It means to "press something out," like squeezing the juice from a lemon. "Expressing" our destructive emotions is important because it gets them "out of our system" so that they cannot poison us any longer.

There are several concrete things we can do to express our feelings. One is simply to "talk them out" with a trusted friend. Make sure to find someone who is willing to listen without trying to problem-solve.

If you discovered that there was poison in your belly, it wouldn't be enough just to know it was there, or even to know exactly what kind of poison it was. You would want to get rid of it! We need some way to express our feelings, especially our anger.

Another way to express feelings is to write them out. Take a sheet and begin writing: "Today I feel..." and then complete the sentence in as much detail as you can. Don't stop to rework or rewrite as you go. The goal is not to produce a piece of enduring literature but to get your feelings out. Once you have finished writing, you may want to share what you have written with a friend. Some people find it easier to interact with others about sensitive topics if they can "work from a script" in this way.

A variation on this technique is to write a letter to the person who hurt you, stating what happened and how it made you feel. One man I know wrote a letter to his long-deceased father, pouring out the disappointment and hurt he felt when his father died. As he wrote, he became aware that he was actually feeling anger at his father for abandoning him just when he needed him most. Writing the letter helped him organize his thoughts and clarify his emotions.

Some people write a series of such letters, one for each person who harmed them in the past. It is extremely important that you *never* send these letters to the people to whom they are addressed. That is not the intention of writing these letters. We gain nothing by "getting even." Our purpose in writing these letters is to help clarify our feelings and emotions. Sometimes we may feel the need to send something to the person involved. If we do, it should be a revised version that has lain on our desk unmailed as we work through our expectations in sending the letter.

When we hear something often enough,
over a long enough period of time, we believe it.
This can work against us, as when we constantly tell
ourselves, "What a jerk I am." But it can also work for us.
Healthy self-talk can help us change and grow.

If you don't like to write, you can talk to an empty chair, in which you imagine the other person is sitting. Tell them what you remember and what you are feeling. Some people find it helpful to switch sides—to figuratively (or even literally) sit in the other chair and try to comprehend the other person's likely reactions and responses.

Talking to an empty chair may feel a bit ridiculous, rather like "talking to yourself." But actually, talking to ourselves is a very important aspect of expressing our feelings. The fact is that we all "talk to ourselves" constantly—we maintain a constant running monologue inside our heads. Making our self-talk explicit helps us understand what is going on inside.

When we hear something often enough, over a long enough period of time, we tend to believe it. This kind of repetition can work against us, as when we constantly tell ourselves, "What a jerk I am." But it can also work *for* us. Healthy self-talk can help us change and grow. The rule for healthy self-talk is simple; make positive statements, in the present tense, that reinforce the values, attitudes, and self-concepts you are trying to develop. Don't say what you will do in the future, just reaffirm what is already true. "I am a worthwhile person because God loves and accepts me. I am working on forgiving my parents and getting free of the hurts of my past."

4. Set boundaries to protect yourself. Boundaries are limits. They are like a fence that we put around our house to define where our property begins and ends, and to keep it separate from other people's property. As children in our dysfunctional families, our personal boundaries were often violated. Physical or sexual abuse are obvious violations. Other ways parents ignore our personal boundaries include: opening the door and coming into the bathroom when we are in there, a father walking in on a teenage daughter while she is dressing, a parent going through a child's drawers or papers without the child's permission, or even reading a child's locked diary.

Some parents see this as their "right." But each is a violation of an important boundary, which will make it difficult for us as adults to set appropriate boundaries in our relationships. We may even have to be convinced that we have the "right" to set boundaries for ourselves.

In our earlier discussion on types of dysfunctional families, we learned about the Attachment Scale. We saw that some families are "Disengaged," meaning that the members live as isolated islands with almost no involvement in one another's lives. Others are "Enmeshed," meaning they are so tangled up in one another that it becomes impossible to tell where each member's identity ends and begins. In working through the process of forgiveness, it often becomes necessary for us to establish some new boundaries, to give ourselves "space" to work in.

Often these boundaries have to do with the way we relate to others, or the way we let them relate to us. For example, we might decide, "From now on, I will decline to accept my mother's suggestions on what I should wear, or how I will do my hair, or how I will clean my house." Or, "I will listen to the advice my dad gives me about how I'm raising my kids, but I won't let myself feel that I have to do anything he says."

---

*In working through the process of forgiveness,
it often becomes necessary for us to establish
some new boundaries,
to give ourselves "space" to work in.*

In many cases, setting boundaries means that we need to physically stay away from other family members, either for a time or for good. I remember Penny, age twenty-two, who had been in and out of several mental health facilities by the time she came to us for help. Each time she went into the hospital, she would make remarkable progress. But within a few months of her release, she would need to go back.

When we constructed her genogram and charted the triangle relationships in her family system, it became obvious that Penny occupied the role of scapegoat in her family. When she was away from them, she did well. But as soon as she returned to her family, she relapsed into her old problems.

Penny decided she needed to live apart from her family for a time. She rented an apartment of her own. When she was released from the hospital she went there instead of going home. She explained to her family what she was doing, and promised to write them a postcard each week to let them know how she was doing. Her family did not like the arrangement and tried to sabotage it, but Penny stuck to her guns.

It was three months before Penny felt that she was able to begin relating to her family again. She began making periodic phone calls, being careful to limit their frequency and duration, and reviewing the kinds of topics she would and would not talk about with her parents. Once when Penny tried to enforce a boundary she had set, by telling her father she did not want to talk about a certain topic with him, he got angry and hung up on her.

Penny was in anguish. Had she done the right thing? She wrestled with the temptation to call her father back and apologize. But then, she thought everything through carefully and decided that she had been right to do what she did. The next day, her father called *her* back. She was elated. "For the first time," she said, "he treated me like I was a real person. It's as though he's started to accept the fact that I'm an adult, and that I have boundaries."

Most people find that some boundaries are only temporary. They give us a little extra space while we work through particular difficulties. Others, however, become permanent. They help make a lasting change for the better in the dynamics of our family system.

5. Cancel the debt. Now it is time to forgive—to "cancel the debt." As we have worked through our injuries and emotions, we may have felt a sense of someone owing us something. That is a useful experience, because it helps us identify where we are holding emotional IOUs and where we need to forgive.

Often it helps to make the act of forgiveness take some concrete, tangible form. For example, some people take the letters they have written to various family members and write "canceled" across them. I know others who have burned or even buried their lists of injuries, to show that all those wrongs are now dead and buried.

Again, it may seem awkward to engage in these kinds of exercises. But our experience is that it can be helpful. Such actions leave us with the memory of a definite time when we tangibly and concretely canceled our debts. We need never be troubled by the nagging thought that "perhaps we really didn't forgive them," or "maybe it wasn't really complete." We know it happened, and we *know* it was real. It can also help to talk about your act of forgiveness with someone who will understand.

---

*It helps to make the act of forgiveness take
some concrete, tangible form. Such actions
leave us with the memory of a definite time
when we tangibly and concretely canceled our debts. We
know it happened, and we know it was real.*

---

6. Consider the possibility of reconciliation. Earlier we said that forgiveness is unilateral; it is something we can do all by ourselves, without the other person cooperating with it or even being aware of it. Reconciliation is different. If two people who have been estranged from one another are going to be reconciled, both must be involved. I can desire to be reconciled with you. But if you refuse to be reconciled with me, there is nothing I can do but wait, and hope that your heart will change.

We will look at reconciliation in more detail later. For now, let's simply note that reconciliation is the ideal outcome of the process of forgiveness—when it is possible. But it is not always possible.

Remember, six steps will help you through the process of forgiveness:

The Six Steps of Forgiveness

1. Recognize the injury
2. Identify the emotions involved
3. Express your hurt and anger
4. Set boundaries to protect yourself
5. Cancel the debt
6. Consider the possibility of reconciliation

There is a worksheet in the Appendix on page 317 to help you work through this process of forgiveness.

Forgiveness is a process that leads us to forgive all those who have hurt us (including, as we will see, ourselves!). It also leads us to seek and accept forgiveness from those *we* have harmed. If our forgiveness is genuine, we will be willing to see it move in both directions: from others toward us, from us toward others. Forgiveness is the key to freedom from the effects of our past.

7

*We all know the old adage,
"Forgive and forget."
But forgetting the harmful things
that have happened to you
is precisely the wrong thing to do.
You must work hard at remembering—and
accepting—what has happened,
in order that you may truly forgive.*

Forgiving, Forgetting, Denying, Accepting

MYRA BURST INTO TEARS. I have seldom heard any-one sob so deeply. I was at a loss to understand this sudden outburst; I had no idea what had caused it. So I sat quietly and waited.

"I can't, that's all," she said. "I just can't."

"You can't what?" I asked gently.

Silence. By now in our discussions, I had learned that Myra's father had physically and sexually abused her from the time she was eleven years old until she ran away from home at seventeen. Later, Myra had married a fine man named Greg, a widower with one son; they now had a daughter of their own. Their marriage was good. They appeared to be a happy family.

Myra had come to me for counseling because she wanted to get free of the bitterness and resentment she felt toward her father. We had met together a few times, and she seemed to be coming to grips with her misery-filled childhood. But today, before we had even gotten started, the tears had begun to flow.

"Myra, *what* can't you do?" I asked again.

She slowly lifted her head and looked at me through tear-filled eyes. "I can't forget what he did to me," she sobbed. "I've tried. I've really *tried*. But I just can't!" She buried her head in her hands and wept quietly.

---

*I waited a moment, then said simply,
"But Myra, you don't have to forget."*

I waited a moment, then said simply, "But Myra, you don't have to forget."

She looked up at me again, a bewildered look on her face. "Say that again," she said.

"You don't have to forget what your father did to you," I repeated.

"But... then how can I... I mean..." Myra stammered.

"Myra," I asked, "who told you that you had to forget what happened?"

She pulled back in her chair, really confused now. "Why—why, the Bible says so. Doesn't it?"

"I've never read that in the Bible anyplace," I said.

"But... it must. I mean... the people at church... everyone says..."

"I know," I said. "Everyone says, 'Forgive and forget.' I don't know where that old saying comes from, Myra. But it definitely doesn't come from the Bible. And to tell you the truth, it's not very good advice. I don't *want* you to forget what happened, Myra. If anything, I want you to *remember.*"

Myra just sat there. She obviously did not know what to make of what I was telling her.

"Listen," I said. "Have you ever burned your fingers?" She nodded silently. "And it hurt, didn't it?" She nodded again.

"Well, Myra, what would happen if you ever forgot how it hurt, or how you did it?"

"I guess I'd be liable to burn my fingers again," she said. I could see the light of understanding beginning to dawn in her eyes.

"That's exactly right!" I said. "That's one of the things our memory does for us. It helps us learn from the past so that we don't have to repeat painful mistakes.

"Now, Myra," I said, "we've talked a lot about forgiving your father. I've told you how important forgiveness is. But listen to me; I do want you to *forgive* your father, but I do not want you to *forget* what he did. Forgiveness has nothing to do with forgetting. Do you understand? *Forgiveness has nothing to do with forgetting.*"

It is easy to become confused. The Bible says repeatedly that God is able to forgive and forget. For example, God says, "For I will forgive their wickedness and will remember their sins no more" (Jeremiah 31:34). But it never says that we are to do the same. We cannot. Only he can. One reason why God can forget is that there is nothing he needs to learn by remembering. There is often a lot of important information that we can learn by remembering, even though we may not want to remember.

I understood how Myra felt. I've felt the same way myself many times. Haven't we all? We want to get rid of the pain of harmful things that have happened to us, and we think that the way to do that is by getting rid of the *memory* of those harmful things. If we can work ourselves around to believing that the hurtful incident never happened, then it can't hurt us any more.

Or can it? The fact is that very often the harmful effects of past injuries stay with us *whether or not we consciously remember the injuries themselves.* This is why we say that remembering, not forgetting, is the key to forgiveness. Only when we are clear on what has, in fact, happened to us can we deal with it effectively.

We may make connections between current difficulties and painful experiences from our past. The way a friend treats us today may trigger memories of the way our parents or siblings treated us years ago. These memories, in turn, may uncover connections to other past hurts. Many of the problems people bring into counseling stem from things in their past that they needed to remember clearly before they could deal with them.

THE WOMAN WHO COULDN'T REMEMBER

Take Carol, for example. For as long as she can remember, Carol has felt abandoned and betrayed. She is a very disciplined person, especially in relationships. She avoids "giving too much of herself" to others. Whenever anyone promises her anything, she immediately begins waiting for them to fail her.

When she got married, it was only six months before she began to be plagued by fears that her husband was going to leave her. She began to suspect him of seeing other women, and accused him of it regularly. If he was even a little bit late getting home, she demanded an accounting of his time. Not surprisingly, her husband did start seeing other women, and did eventually leave her.

Five years later, Carol met Randy. They fell in love. Randy noticed that she seemed a bit possessive, but he didn't let it bother him—at first. As time went on, though, Carol's mistrustful, clinging behavior asserted itself more and more. Finally Randy had had enough. "I need a little space!" he yelled at her during an argument. "I need to be able to live life without having to give you a minute-by-minute account."

Carol realized she was again on the verge of destroying a relationship that meant a great deal to her, because of attitudes and actions she could neither understand nor control. That was when she came for help.

As we talked about Carol's family background, she was finally able to recall some of the pain from her childhood. Carol grew up in a family with two working parents. The oldest of three children, she wound up shouldering much of the responsibility for her two brothers. She saw little of her parents except on weekends. Then her parents divorced, and her father moved out of state.

"You know, I've always tried not to think about all that," she said. "Put it all behind me, you know? I guess I just didn't like to think about the miserable childhood I had. But now I see the connection between what happened then and what happens to me now. I've never gotten over being abandoned by my parents, have I?"

Carol will always remember how her parents failed her
and damaged her when she was younger.
But those injuries won't disable her any more.
Because she was willing to remember them,
she was able to overcome them.

That recollection was the beginning of the healing process for Carol. By remembering her past hurts, she began to be able to identify and release negative feelings. Carol will always remember how her parents failed her and damaged her when she was younger. But those injuries won't disable her any more. Because she was willing to remember them, she was able to overcome them.

> You will know that forgiveness has begun *when you recall those who hurt you and feel the power to wish them well.*
> —Lewis B. Smedes, *Forgive and Forget: Healing the Hurts We Don't Deserve,*
> (New York, NY: Harper & Row, 1984)

That is how forgiveness works. The past is still with us, but now it is truly in the past. It no longer has control over what happens in the present. Its power to dominate our lives is cut off. Forgiving does not mean forgetting. It is draining the past of its power to hurt us.

A psychologist friend of mine once said, "Those who try to cut themselves off from the past have no future." What he meant was this: when we ignore the past, or try to forget it, its hold on us actually grows stronger. Something from "back then" remains unresolved, and interferes with our ability to function in the present.

TRYING TO FORGET

Well-meaning friends often urge us to "try to forget" bad things that have happened. "Just let it roll off, like water off a duck's back," they say. "The person who hurt you isn't worth wasting your time and energy on, anyway." When people say this, they are in effect saying that our inner pain is trivial. Now, our pain might indeed appear to be of little significance to someone else. But in reality, it might run quite deep. If so, we need to learn how to remember it in a healing way, not try to forget it.

"Trying to forget" what has happened to us is virtually impossible anyway. It is like trying not to think about something.

Try this: for the next thirty seconds, do not think about pink elephants. Think about anything else you like, but no pink elephants.

Could you do it? If you are like many people, you spent the entire thirty seconds saying to yourself, "I will not think about pink elephants. I will not think about pink elephants. I will not think about pink elephants." The result, of course, was that your very effort not to think about pink elephants made it impossible to think about anything else!

The more you say to yourself, "I will not remember what my father did to me when I was younger," the more firmly the memory will be planted in your mind.

"Trying to forget" works exactly the same way. The more you say to yourself, "I will not remember what my father did to me when I was younger," the more firmly the memory will be planted in your mind.

There is a word for what happens when we try to forget painful memories instead of dealing with them straightforwardly. The word is "denial." When we deny what has happened to us, we do not really forget it, in the sense of getting it out of our system entirely. We just pack it up and store it in our emotional deep-freeze. It is like lying to ourselves: by telling ourselves that something bad did not happen—when of course we know that it did—we are only deceiving ourselves.

That self-deception never lasts, and it does not free us from the harmful consequences of the past. Though the painful memories are buried, they are still there, still having their effects on us—as Carol discovered.

"Don't you see?" Judy said. "If I don't remember, then it's as if nothing ever happened. That was how I kept my life together for a long time. I just didn't remember..."

"... Or *want* to remember," Alice added. "Sometimes it just hurts too much to remember."

"If I persuade myself that it never happened, then I never have to deal with it, do I?" asked Carrie. "That was my method for many years."

There is a word for what happens when we try to forget painful memories instead of dealing with them straightforwardly. The word is "denial."

These three women were members of a group who met weekly for therapy. All eight women came from abusive backgrounds. Four had been sexually abused. All had known the trauma of growing up in seriously dysfunctional families. When the group started, six of the eight women had no

---

As children we are developmentally and constitutionally incapable of understanding that our parents may be sick. We don't see that their sickness is the reason they do the things they do. We experience the neglect, the abandonment, the verbal, sexual, and physical abuse, but we don't understand it—we don't see the sick codependent logic that fuels the abusiveness of our parents.
—Robert Subby, *Lost in the Shuffle,*
(Deerfield Beach, FL: Health
Communications, Inc., 1987) p. 93.

memories of their lives before the age of ten. As they eventually came to recognize, they had employed an unconscious strategy to cope with the pain of the past.

Loss of childhood memories is fairly common among adult children of dysfunctional families. It is, of course, a form of denial. But denial *may* be a helpful process at the time of injury or abuse. Especially when we are young, it may be our only means of coping with a situation we cannot comprehend. "And it worked," as Carrie once said. "We survived, didn't we?"

But while denial can be a helpful device during childhood trauma, it becomes a harmful trap later on. As adults, we no longer need to block our memories. Quite the opposite, we often need help in uncovering the truth, in getting in touch with what happened, and in forgiving those who caused us pain.

In dysfunctional systems the catastrophe that hits us is a continuous one and denial becomes a way of life, rather than a protective measure to be used only in extreme circumstances. The pain of living in a dysfunctional system is akin to slow torture as opposed to dying an instantaneous death. Day-by-day, year-by-year, decade-by-decade, we crawl deeper and deeper into a shell of denial, defensiveness, isolation and emptiness that is fueled by our shame and embarrassment at the thought of anyone ever finding out what is really going on inside of us. That is the nature of dysfunctional systems—they are closed and implosive, ever more self-destructive. In that sense, they are just like malignant tumors in the body.

—John and Linda Friel, *Adult Children: The Secrets of Dysfunctional Families*, (Deerfield Beach, FL: Health Communications, Inc., 1988) p. 102.

THE PROCESS OF INTEGRATION

Children come into the world with no fears of life and no prejudice against others. Their initial task, as we saw earlier, is to form an attachment with a figure who will make the world a safe and reliable place—usually, the mother. In their undeveloped thinking process, they absolutize things: everything is either all good or all bad, all right or all wrong. They have no concept of anything but the extremes. Mom, of course, is all good in their view. She is loving and caring, the unfailing source of everything they need and want.

But by the time they reach the crawling stage, they begin to make some very startling discoveries about Mom. They begin to realize that the wonderful supplier of all their needs is the same person who did not come to feed them when they were hungry, or did not change their diaper when it was uncomfortable.

Prior to this discovery, the person who did not do these things was "simply out there." There was no identity to them. Now they begin to make the connection that this unidentified person is the same Mom who is so good at taking care of them. They begin to see some badness in Mom.

Infants are thus faced with a terrifying dilemma. They desperately need Mother to be good, in order to keep their scary world safe. How can Mom, who is—who must be—all-good, be bad? Infants resolve this dilemma by putting the blame—the badness—on themselves.

If the child's emotional development progresses properly, he or she will resolve this dilemma by a process known as *integration*. During this process, the child begins to integrate—to put together—things that used to seem incompatible. Mom is not just the "perfect parent personified"; she is good *and* bad, right *and* wrong.

This integration process will continue as long as no trauma or interferences come about. Children will gradually come to understand that parents are human. They are capable of making mistakes, of getting angry, of doing wrong—while remaining capable of loving and caring for us.

Often, children from dysfunctional families don't develop the ability to see that their parents have both good and bad qualities.

What often happens with children from dysfunctional families is that the integration process gets short-circuited. They do not develop the ability to see that their parents have both good and bad qualities. They continue to operate from an unconscious belief that things must be either all good or all bad. As we will see in a moment, this results either in outright rejection of the parents, or—what is far more likely—unhealthy idealization of the parents.

THREE TYPES OF MOTHERS

Typically, when the process of integration has been blocked in a child's development, we find that the mother in the family was one of three types. (This isn't meant as an attack on motherhood, by the way—heaven forbid!) But our experience shows it to be true more often than not.

1. The Intrusive Mother. She has to be in control at all times, because she is the only one who really knows what is best for everyone.

Evelyn was one of four children. She, her two sisters, and her brother all lived in the same city even after they grew up and got married. Their mother was in her seventies, and she expected each of her children to either call or visit her every day.

One day Evelyn's mother mentioned to her that she hadn't heard from Evelyn's brother in several days. Evelyn got angry. She started to dial her brother's telephone number, already rehearsing in her mind how she was going to read him the riot act. But suddenly she stopped and asked herself, "Why? Why does he need to call her every single day?" In that moment Evelyn understood something about her mother's intrusiveness and about her own reaction to it. Her mother manipulated her with guilt. If Evelyn didn't call her mother every day, she felt as though she had done something awful. Evelyn was forty-one years old when this happened.

When the Christmas holidays came that year, Evelyn and her family went away on a two-week trip. Late on Christmas Day, she called her mother. "There, you see, I *knew* you'd finally call," her mother said. "Both your sisters invited me over for Christmas dinner. But I didn't go. 'Evelyn hasn't called yet,' I told them. I'll just sit here and wait for her. You can send over something to eat. I'll be fine."

Evelyn felt awful. There was her poor mother, sitting there all alone on Christmas day, waiting for her to call. Evelyn apologized profusely. She even made up a phony excuse to explain why she hadn't called sooner. Only later did it dawn on her that she'd been "had" again. "Mom knows where we are," she realized. "She has the number here. She doesn't have to sit around all day, making herself miserable, waiting for the phone to ring. She could call me anytime she wants." Life with an intrusive mother is often like that—a long series of guilt trips.

2. The Abandoning Mother. This kind of mother doesn't always literally run away from her children—though some do. More common is *emotional* abandonment, simply neglecting the kids because Mom is too busy with other things, such as her job or friends.

Frank grew up in an ethnic community in the midwest. "My parents believed that children would control the whole family if they were catered to, so they made sure they never 'catered' to us. If we cried, they checked to see if we had wet diapers or were sick. If not, they just left us alone." Frank grew up with many unmet emotional needs. Although he eventually married a wonderful woman, he engaged in a series of affairs. "I felt compelled to develop these relationships," he said. "I needed to be loved so badly, that no one woman could possibly meet all my needs."

Some people speak of growing up too quickly because, as children, they had to attend to their parents' needs. This is especially common with children of alcoholic parents. Their own needs go unmet, and this seriously hinders their development.

3. The Unpredictable Mother. Sometimes she is warm and nurturing, holding her children and whispering words of love in their ears. At other times—and with no warning—she is cold, indifferent, and critical. Her children grow up in the land of inconsistency. They survive by expecting the unexpected, never sure of what life is going to bring their way next, distrustful of others, and robbed of basic security.

Some adults speak of growing up in a family system made from "interchangeable parts"—mom's (or dad's) sequential live-in lovers, along with their respective offspring, members of the extended family coming and going, or an ever-changing array of outside relationships produced by frequent geo-

195

graphic moves. I remember two little twins, Reggie and Regina, who became close to our own children. They came around the house all the time over a two-month period. Then suddenly they disappeared.

About a year later they turned up again. My wife, told them how much she had missed them. "Oh, we just moved again," Regina explained.

"I hope you'll stay this time," my wife said.

Reggie shook his head. "No. We'll be moving on."

"Yeah," Regina said matter-of-factly. "Soon as Daddy stops paying the rent and the landlord says we can't stay, we'll be leaving again."

Reggie sighed. "I did ask Daddy if this time, maybe we could just move somewhere else in this same part of town." A few weeks later they were gone. We never heard from them again.

BLACK AND WHITE?

Children raised by one of these kinds of mothers became stuck in their emotional development. The intrusive mother makes all our decisions for us, so we never develop the ability to judge things for ourselves. The abandoning mother and the unpredictable mother make life feel unsafe. But in all these cases, children aren't able to recognize the harmful effect stemming from the mother's dysfunctional behavior. They attribute the "badness" they experience in their mother to themselves.

This helps illustrate something called "splitting," which is one of the earliest defense mechanisms that develops in children. It is more or less the opposite of integration: the inability to see that good and bad qualities can co-exist in the same person.

"It took me a long time to realize that life wasn't just black or white," one man said. "I finally discovered that there are also gray areas. In fact, I learned that life also has all kinds of reds and greens and yellows, too."

"Splitting" is one of the earliest defense mechanisms that develops in children. It is more or less the opposite of integration; the inability to see that good and bad qualities can co-exist in the same person.

As we have seen, one of the first things we do in life is to divide reality into all-good and all-bad. If we are able to mature emotionally, we will come to see that life is not so easily categorized. We are able to integrate seemingly contradictory experiences. When we are prevented from maturing emotionally, we continue to force everything into one of two categories: all-good and all-bad. When our parents are in question, the pressure is almost overwhelming to consider them "all-good" despite their problems.

It's not hard to see why, when we look at parents through the eyes of a small child:

- Adults are bigger.
- Adults are smarter.
- Parents have power.
- Parents can hurt children.

If we accept these notions about our parents—and as children, we really have little choice—then we have to conclude that they know what is best for us, and that they are always right. This tendency to always view our parents as all-good is called *idealization.*

Idealization often occurs in families that are very religious, especially in those kinds of religious homes that draw very

197

strict boundaries to define acceptable and unacceptable attitudes and behaviors. The high value that is placed on family, and on respect for parents, makes it almost impossible for children to integrate their parents' failings and weaknesses.

The tendency to always view our parents as all-good
is called idealization.

THE "SAINTLY" MOTHER

This was made clear to me by the experience of a pastor friend of mine in Atlanta. He was twenty-three and had just been installed in his first parish. Desiring to get acquainted with his new parishioners, he made appointments to visit all of them in their homes.

One day he visited three sisters, all single, all in their late fifties. They lived together in a large home built by their father. He had died when they were young, and they were raised by their mother. Their mother had been dead at least fifteen years by the time my pastor friend arrived on the scene. But as he was to discover, she was still a powerful presence in their lives.

The sisters led the pastor into the living room, which was dominated by a large painting of a middle-aged woman. "That is our mother," one of the sisters said in a hushed voice.

"An absolute saint," said the second sister.

"The perfect mother," added the third.

For a full forty minutes, the conversation centered around the angelic mother. The young pastor had never encountered anything like it, and was overwhelmed by their adoration. Yet he couldn't believe that anyone could be quite *that* wonderful.

Later he mentioned his experience to one of the older

members of the congregation, who had become a friend and confidant. The man laughed. "Why, their mother was about as mean as a woman could be," he said. "Ran their lives like a dictator. I don't think she ever let them go out on a date or develop any real friendships."

Adult children who have practiced this degree of splitting and idealization tend to be driven by fear. First, there is fear of being abandoned. "I was always afraid my mother was going to leave us," one woman remembered. "When we did something bad, she threatened to walk out and never come back. I remember many afternoons when I ran home from school, afraid that the house would be empty when I got there. She never actually left, but I always feared she would."

None of us can control life completely, and the more we try, the more out-of-control we feel.

Such children also fear loss of control or loss of autonomy. For children growing up in a dysfunctional family, control is all-important. It is the only answer to the chaos that surrounds them. The problem, of course, is that none of us can control life completely, and the more we try, the more out-of-control we feel. But the fear of losing control drives us to try all the harder, despite the suffering and frustration it causes.

BLAMING OURSELVES

Children need the protection of the adults in their lives, who can love them and help orient them to the world around them. When children grow up in dysfunctional homes, when these basic needs are not met, when they are abused, neglected, exploited, or deceived—they are damaged and their development is short-circuited.

The blame for all this has to land somewhere. If children idealize their parents, they become the only available targets. Children grow up thinking *they* are the bad ones. Even if others try to tell them they are good, inwardly they don't believe it. How could it be true? Other people just don't realize how awful they really are. "I have trouble whenever anyone says, 'I love you,'" one woman explained. "In our family, whenever I heard those words, it meant I was about to be taken advantage of."

The normal reaction to these kinds of injury should be anger. But since children in hurtful environments are often forbidden to express anger—or are too young even to realize what is happening to them—they repress their feelings and

---

Blame has to land somewhere. If children idealize their parents, they become the only available targets. Children, then, grow up thinking they are the bad ones.

---

they deny their memories of what has happened.

But even when denial shuts out the source of pain, the feelings of anger, helplessness, despair, suspicion, fear of rejection, abandonment, anxiety, and pain are still present. They may find expression in psychological disorders or in such self-destructive behaviors as substance abuse or suicide. When these adult children become parents, they may take revenge on their own children for the mistreatment they received in childhood. Or their unresolved negative emotions may find expression in destructive acts against others, even leading to criminal behavior.

When denial is allowed to continue into adulthood, it opens the door to many problems. The answer to those prolems is never to "forget." It is remembering that makes healing

> Not everything that is faced can be changed, but nothing can be changed until it is faced.
> —James Baldwin

and freedom possible.

ACCEPTANCE

The key to remembering is *acceptance*. We need to accept the reality of what happened to us, so that we can deal with it.

One man said that his dad beat him at least twice a week while he was growing up. Later, as an adult out living on his own, he would visit his father and try not to remember the terrible things that had happened in years past. But he couldn't do it. He thought of the places where the beatings had taken place, the belt his dad had used, even the lamp that had fallen and broken during one incident. "Trying not to remember didn't help," he said. "He beat me. It happened."

Accepting the reality of what happened in the past is especially difficult—and especially important—for victims of sexual abuse. One man said, "I kept thinking, 'I must be making this up. My older sister would never have done such things to me.'" He tried for years to persuade himself that the assaults never happened. But it did not work. In the end he had to say, "She did it. It happened. I can accept that now."

These men accepted the reality of their pain. They learned that there could be no freedom without this acceptance. Forgiveness can occur only after we have acknowledged and accepted that there is something to be forgiven.

We must accept the fact that we hurt. We have suffered because of someone else's actions. What makes it worse is that "someone else" is usually very close to us, someone with whom we have a strong, lasting bond: our parents, our siblings, our spouses, our children, our friends. Occasionally we experience injury from more distant figures, or from some impersonal entity like an organization. The choice is always the same: to accept the reality or to deny it. Denying it—repressing it, pushing it down inside us—only intensifies resentment and stops the healing process.

What has happened to us has happened. Our parents hurt us. Our friends let us down. Our neighbors treated us badly. Our co-workers deceived us. We cannot change those facts. They remain so for all eternity. But with the help of God, we *can* change the *meaning* of those facts. It happens through the process of forgiveness.

Many Jewish people celebrate *Krystalnacht* each November, on the anniversary of the night in 1938 when the Nazis smashed the glass in synagogues all over Germany. A few years ago I attended a *Krystalnacht* service. Among those who spoke were two survivors of the Nazi concentration camps.

The first speaker, a bent-over woman with a deeply lined face, recounted in a calm, controlled voice the terrible inhumanities she had suffered. She cried only when she told how her husband and son had been sent to the gas chambers while she stood by, watching helplessly. As she concluded, she straightened up, looked out at us, and said, "We forgive the Germans. But we can never forget."

I thought to myself, "She understands what forgiveness is all about." It has nothing to do with forgetting. The power lies in the fact that we forgive *even as we remember.* If we really forgot, we could not forgive. How could we forgive an offense we are not even aware of? The power of forgiveness is that, even in the face of inescapable reality, it liberates us from the inner anger, the resentment, the quest for vengeance that eats away at us and, in the end, destroys us.

The power lies in the fact that we forgive even as we remember.

BEYOND DENIAL

Forgiveness begins with remembering and accepting what has happened in the past. Acceptance is an act of integration. It is a movement toward wholeness. It is how we incorporate the past into the present, and build for the future.

A word of warning. Once we accept that "it happened," we begin a process that will not be without its share of pain. It hurts to get in touch with how deeply we were hurt as children, to realize how those who should have loved us and protected us actually caused us harm. But as an old saying puts it, "You have to feel in order to heal."

This goes against the grain for us. We grew up becoming experts at controlling, avoiding, and numbing our pain. Doing an about-face and choosing to *feel* our pain will hurt. We are reopening an old and deep wound. It is similar to what happens when people stop using tranquilizers, or alcohol, or other drugs to cope with life and begin feeling their emotions for the first time.

Many of us will find ourselves mourning over lost childhoods, realizing that we were cheated out of some of the normal stages of growth and development. I think of one man whose father committed suicide when he was little. He now says, "I was never really a child. I was just a short adult."

When we open ourselves to feel the pain in statements like that, it can be overwhelming. As Marti, whom we met in Chapters 3 and 6, started to work through the issues with her mother, she became aware of a child-like part of herself that had been neglected or locked away for years. As she worked through the pain of those lost years, she experienced intense rage, overwhelming depression and hopelessness, and at one point, thoughts of suicide that led to her needing to come into the hospital.

Some of her pain was so deep it didn't have words. It took someone else to put words to what she was feeling. At times she would say, "If I had known how much this was going to hurt, I don't think I would have started this journey." But then she would add, "But then I started the journey because of a different kind of pain. I don't know which is worse at this point." I would point out to her when she said that, "At least this pain is the pain of recovery—the other was a dead-end."

Adult children of dysfunctional families often pass through the classic stages of grief: anger, denial, despair, and so on. We mourn over who we might have been, over what we didn't get out of childhood, what we didn't get from our parents. We may feel cheated, and stripped of self-worth. But it is important that we let ourselves feel these emotions, work our way through them, and then move on past them. Mourning is therapeutic. It is healing. It is letting go of our bitterness, canceling the emotional IOUs we are holding, so that those who hurt us no longer dominate our lives as they once did.

We can never change what has happened to us in the past. But we *can* change the way we *respond* to it in the here and now. That is the point of remembering: we remember so that we can accept and forgive. "Forgetting" is not the answer. It's just another dead-end street. We feel regret over what happened, and we wish it hadn't happened. But it did. Now we can accept it, and let go.

8

Forgiveness—true forgiveness—takes time.
It is a process you must not short-circuit.
When you forgive too quickly,
without adequately working through
what has happened and how you feel about it,
your forgiveness is incomplete.

CHAPTER 8

Superficial Forgiveness

OVER LUNCH IN THE company cafeteria, John listened as Brian told him about a situation that happened in his office that morning. Brian's boss had walked in, slammed the door behind him, and started barking out questions and accusations.

"Sounds like a bad scene," John said, shaking his head. "What did you say?"

"Say? I didn't say anything," Brian shrugged. "I couldn't get a word in edgewise. I was trying to explain to him what happened, but it was obvious he didn't really want to listen. He just wanted to unload."

"So you never got it cleared up?" John asked.

"Well, he eventually settled down and I was able to explain a little bit," Brian said. "He only had about half the story, and even most of that was inaccurate. But it didn't really matter. Like I said, he just wanted to unload on someone. I just happened to be the closest person. Tough luck for me."

"So how do you feel now?" John asked.

"Well... okay, I guess," Brian sighed. "I was pretty ticked off this morning. But it's over and done with now, I guess. I've forgiven him."

Brian started to talk about something else, but John put his hand up. "Hold on a second," he said. "What do you mean, you've forgiven him? You don't *sound* like you've forgiven him. In fact, you still sound pretty angry to me."

Brian looked at him with a puzzled expression. "I do? I mean, I was angry at first, but..."

"Just listen to you," John said. "Your voice, the expression on your face, even the way you're sitting—you seem uptight."

"I guess you're right," Brian admitted. "A lot of what he said really got to me. I mean, I *knew* he had the facts wrong, and there was nothing I could do about it.... But like I say, it's over now. I've forgiven him."

John smiled. "But that's just my point, Brian. I don't think you really *have* forgiven him. Not completely, not all the way down inside."

Most of us are uncomfortable with conflict.
Rather than take the time and effort
to really resolve conflict, we try to brush it off,
pretend it wasn't important—even
pretend it never happened.

Most of us are uncomfortable with conflict. Rather than take the time and effort to really *resolve* conflict, we try to brush it off, pretend it wasn't important—even pretend it never happened.

Often I have seen people who have done wrong, *know* they have done wrong, and try to pass it off as "no big deal." At the same time, I have seen people who have been wronged, who *know* they have been wronged, who know they are still feeling the sting, and try to ignore the pain and forget what has happened. One person mumbles a perfunctory apology and the other mumbles a perfunctory acceptance; they both go their way as if everything is resolved. But is it really?

Isn't getting quickly past our pain a sign of our strength and maturity? Yes and no.

Most of the time, the answer is no. Genuine repentance and genuine forgiveness both take time and effort. It takes time and effort to acknowledge and accept what has happened and to sort out the feelings and emotions involved. We need to come to grips with genuinely releasing the other person from the "debt" we hold against him. If we skip all this and rush to an "Oh-I'm-Sorry-That's-Okay" conclusion, we haven't really gone through the process of forgiveness.

But haven't we been taught to "bury the hatchet" quickly? Aren't we supposed to keep a stiff upper lip? Isn't getting quickly past our pain a sign of our strength and maturity?

Many Adult Children of Alcoholics and Grandchildren of Alcoholics have tried to forgive others without stopping first to forgive themselves. Sometimes it is easier to see and accept a reasonable explanation for the crazy behavior of others but not our own. Forgiveness is a gradual change in attitude and feelings, not a moment of truth or a sudden realization. It is truly a spiritual process of getting centered with oneself. It involves standing back with some objectivity and looking at the choices you have made, realizing that you did the best you could do at the time with the tools available to you.

—Ann W. Smith, *Grandchildren of Alcoholics,* (Deerfield Beach, FL: Health Communications, Inc., 1988) p. 141.

Yes and no. There *is* a way of dealing swiftly and straightforwardly with conflict that *is* a sign of strength and maturity. But
there is also a need to work through the full process of forgiveness if we are to remain emotionally healthy.

"My mother always said, 'As soon as someone offends you,
just cut it out of your heart.' But sometimes I'd wonder:
if I keep doing this, will there be anything left of me
or my heart?"

A woman named Glenda once told me, "My mother always
said, 'As soon as someone offends you, just cut it out of your
heart.'" Glenda said for years she had a mental image of a pair
of scissors literally snipping off a piece of her heart every time
someone hurt her. "By rushing to forgive, I used to feel I was
cutting away a piece of myself just so we could have peace,"
she said. "But sometimes I'd wonder: if I keep doing this, will
there be anything left of me or my heart?" Good question!

Don't we all tend to think, like Brian, that forgiveness should
be quick and bloodless? Don't we think, like Glenda, that if
we're hurting we just need to "cut the pain out of our heart?" It
sounds so noble, so virtuous, so spiritual. But in reality, it tends
to leave us with a lot of unfinished business, with unresolved
anger and bitterness that can come back to haunt us later.

Earlier in Chapters 3 and 6, we met Marti, the woman who
was shocked when I told her that the goal of therapy was to
enable her to forgive her mother. Her first response was to
cry, "Never! I'll never forgive her for what she's done to me!"
But only a few minutes later she said, "You know, now that I
think about it, I have forgiven her—hundreds of times. Every
time she did something that hurt me, I'd forgive her. I guess it
didn't work so well, did it?"

No, it didn't. And that is precisely the point: that what passes for "forgiveness" among us much of the time really isn't forgiveness at all. At best it is a social convention used to smooth ruffled feathers. At worst it is something that buries the hurt even deeper inside us. An important point about forgiveness that excludes the processing of our emotions is that it ends up being *excusing.*

Now, we need to distinguish forgiveness as a *decision* from forgiveness as a *process.* Forgiveness as a decision means choosing not to hold onto an emotional "debt" against another person. Forgiveness as a process means working through our own inner reactions until what was done to us no longer dominates us.

THE MINISTER WHO WOULDN'T FORGIVE

I went on to tell Marti about an experience that a pastor friend of mine had several years ago. He was invited to join a dozen other ministers for a day-long retreat. At one point during their discussions, my friend—without any conscious thought of offending anyone—said something that deeply hurt one of the other ministers named Dan. It was immediately obvious what had happened; Dan's face flushed and his body stiffened.

A few minutes later, during a coffee break, my friend went up to Dan and said, "Look, I'm really sorry if what I said offended you..."

"*If* you offended me?" Dan interrupted. "You *know* you did!"

"Yes, yes, you're right," my friend said, "And I'm sorry. I really am. Please forgive me."

"Look, I know you didn't mean anything by it," Dan said. "And I know you're sincere in your apology. So I forgive you. But it doesn't really end there. I'm going to need some time to work this through." And with that he turned and walked away.

About a week later my friend's phone rang. When he picked it up, it was Dan on the line. "I just wanted to get back to you about what happened at the retreat day," he said. "I do forgive you. I really do. I mean, I forgave you that day, and I meant it, but…"

"I understand," my friend said. "I know just what you were struggling with. I'm glad you didn't put on a plastic smile and tell me, 'Oh, it was nothing.' I knew you forgave me that day, but I'm glad you went ahead and really worked things through."

In the case of Dan and my friend, the injury was a current one. Even though it hurt Dan deeply, it was nothing like the wound that Marti had carried for more than thirty years. If Dan took a week to process his feelings and come to a place of complete forgiveness over something that was current, then how much time might Marti need to resolve the hurts she carried inside?

"Now, I'm not saying you should carry this around and nurse a grudge forever," I told Marti. "But you've already seen how inadequate your past attempts at superficial forgiveness were. Why not give yourself time and space to do it *right* this time?"

SUPERFICIAL REPENTANCE

Earlier we commented that in conflict-resolution situations, there can be a tendency for both the repentance and forgiveness to be shallow. In a close or ongoing relationship, it can sometimes be appropriate to press someone who has wronged us and only expressed superficial repentance.

Let's say, for example, that I have a habit of making snide but very funny jokes about Jim. These always get plenty of laughs, but always at his expense. I know this bothers Jim, but I keep cracking the jokes and apologize later. Jim may well be justified in wondering whether I am really sincere when I tell him how sorry I am.

One day it happens yet again. I say, "Jim, I'm really sorry. Please forgive me."

"Look, Dave," he says, shaking his head, "this is at least the twentieth time you've done this, and…"

"I know, Jim," I interject. "I know. And I'm really sorry about it."

"But Dave, you were really sorry the last time, too, and the time before that, and the time before that…"

Now let's suppose I decide to play my trump card. "But Jim," I say, "You've got to forgive me. It's the right thing to do."

"Well… okay, I guess," Jim says grudgingly. "I forgive you."

What has really happened here? Have I really repented? Not really. Has Jim really forgiven me? Probably not. We have both said the appropriate words. But Jim knows that offense number twenty-one is on the way; it is only a matter of time until I hurt him again.

Jim may well wonder if I am really being sincere in my repentance. Maybe I have just learned how to manipulate him into forgiving me without my really having to change. I say the magic words—"Please forgive me"—and he is obligated to do so. Presto! Everything is made right!

Or is it? Clearly, it is not. All that has really happened is that I have maneuvered Jim into excusing my wrong action—into letting me off the hook. It is as if he had simply said, "Oh, that's all right," or, "Don't worry about it, Dave."

But if I am doing something to cause him pain, I *should*

"worry about it," at least in the sense that I should take it seriously and make a good faith effort to change. And Jim
shouldn't have to stuff his hurt feelings and set himself up to
be wounded again. He owes it to himself—to both of us,
really—to press me to make my repentance real and to work
through the full process of forgiveness for himself.

THE WOMAN WHO SAID SHE WAS SORRY— AND MEANT IT

Consider Cheryl. She worked for a major corporation with
several other women. One of the women she worked with,
named Alexa, had recently gotten engaged. Cheryl knew
Alexa's fiancé, Louis, because their work sometimes inter-
sected.

It was at the office Christmas party that Cheryl was chatting
with Alexa's roommate, Nancy. The subject of Alexa's engage-
ment came up. Nancy asked Cheryl what she thought of Louis.

"He's all talk," Cheryl said. "He's always saying he's going to
do this or that, but he never follows through." She then gave a
couple examples of projects Louis had volunteered for but
failed to carry out. "Not a very responsible person, I'd say,"
Cheryl concluded.

Just as Cheryl finished her sentence, she turned around
and realized that Alexa, Louis' fiancée, had been standing
behind her, listening. Cheryl was not sure exactly how much
of her negative assessment Alexa had heard, but the look on
Alexa's face seemed to indicate she had heard plenty. "Sorry
you had to hear that," Cheryl said. "But it's the truth." She
walked away.

*The first step of repentance is acknowledging that we have done
wrong.* In the days that followed, Cheryl fretted over the

exchange she'd had with Alexa. The chilly mood around the office confirmed that Alexa had indeed heard her putdown of Louis and didn't appreciate it.

Cheryl's first reaction was to blame the others for what had happened. Why did Nancy have to ask for her opinion in the first place? Cheryl had always lived by the motto, "If people are going to ask, they had better be able to hear the answer." Nancy must have had some questions of her own about Louis—she *was* Alexa's roommate, after all—or she wouldn't have asked.

And Alexa—why had she snuck up behind Cheryl like that? She had been eavesdropping, plain and simple! She had no business listening in on a conversation without making her presence known. If what she overheard hurt her, it was her own fault. That was the risk she ran for eavesdropping.

But the longer Cheryl struggled with the whole episode, the more she realized that she *had* said some unkind things about Louis. She had not lied or exaggerated—if anything, she had softened her assessment of him. Still, Alexa and Nancy were her friends, and Louis was her co-worker. It wasn't right to talk to them about him like that. Cheryl finally admitted that she had been unkind. "I was wrong. I shouldn't have said what I said."

The second step is to decide to repair our wrongdoing. Even after acknowledging that she had done wrong, Cheryl tried out a few more rationalizations, looking for some kind of "escape clause" that would get her off the hook.

Maybe I should just forget about it, she thought. *I'm sure everyone else has. Besides, why should I apologize for telling the truth? Everyone knows I'm a person who speaks her mind. And maybe I even did Alexa a favor. Maybe I saved her some future disillusionment by letting her know what she's getting herself into.*

But in the end, Cheryl realized none of these arguments

would do. She had been wrong, and that was that. Moreover, she had done this very thing many times before. Just because she was "a frank person" didn't excuse her hurting other people. She couldn't expect others to simply accept her candor. She needed to apologize.

The third step is to admit our wrongdoing and ask forgiveness. That morning at coffee break, Cheryl went to Alexa. "Look," she said, "I'm really sorry about what happened at the party the other night. You know, the things I said about Louis. My big mouth is always getting me into trouble. I shouldn't have said the things I said. I'm sorry. Will you forgive me?"

"Sure," Alexa said. "Don't worry about it." Then she turned and walked away. From then on, she spoke to Cheryl only when it was necessary to discuss business matters. A few weeks later, Alexa transferred to another department. Cheryl heard that the wedding was lovely. She didn't have the opportunity to find out for herself; Alexa didn't invite her.

Steps to Repentance

1. Acknowledge that we have done wrong.
2. Decide to repair the wrongdoing.
3. Admit our wrongdoing and ask forgiveness.

This story illustrates not just the process of repentance, but also what happens when we practice superficial forgiveness. Did Alexa forgive Cheryl for the harsh things she said? Yes and no. After all she did say that she accepted Cheryl's apology. But Cheryl certainly did not feel as though she had genuinely been forgiven. In fact, she felt worse *after* she apologized than she had *before*. It was as though Alexa had slapped her in the face, using the right words but with the wrong attitude. Even if Alexa had said, "Don't worry about it," it wouldn't have meant anything.

Still, Cheryl took personal responsibility to repair the damage her words had done. She could neither control nor predict Alexa's response.

THE GIRL WHO FORGAVE HER MOTHER

Diana's earliest memory is of lying in bed, terrified, pretending to be asleep. Her terror was caused by her father, who was sexually molesting Diana's older sister in the next bed. Diana did not fully realize until later what had been going on. No one ever talked about it, or even acknowledged it. Diana just knew that whatever it was, it was bad—and that it could happen to *her* at any time. She now feels fortunate that her father died when she was only ten years old—before she became of any interest to him sexually.

In later years, Diana found that she harbored a lot of frightened feelings about her dad. But she also found that she carried a lot of anger toward her mother, for not protecting her or her sister.

Just because her mother's failings were understandable did not mean that Diana should ignore her own reactions to them.

It bothered Diana that she felt that way. She searched for reasons to excuse her mother's failures. Surely there were many good reasons why her mother *couldn't* protect her daughters. For one thing, she herself was terrified of her husband. He had beaten her on several occasions when he was drunk. Diana's mother simply tried to stay out of his way as much as possible.

Diana and I talked at great length about her anger toward her mother, and about how uncomfortable that anger made her feel. "I agree with you, Diana, that your mom had her hands full just trying to protect herself from him," I said. "But that doesn't change the fact that you have feelings about the way things were in your family, and the way your mother tolerated such chaos and terror, not just for herself but for you and your sister, too." I wanted Diana to see that her feelings were valid, and she needed to pay attention to them. Just because her mother's failings were understandable did not mean that Diana should ignore her own reactions to them. If she did that, she would just be practicing superficial forgiveness, and she wouldn't get free of the hold her anger had on her.

Diana made the investment of time and energy to work through the process of forgiveness toward her mother. She did a lot of writing in her journal about how she had felt as a child, while all the painful things were happening. She talked to her mother, asking her questions about how her mother experienced her father in those days. Once she asked her mother, "What were *you* afraid of?" Her mom went on for more than an hour, telling through tears how trapped and helpless she had felt, both as a wife and as a mother.

Diana didn't blame any of her own negative experiences on her mother. Her goal was not to add to her mother's pain, only to get a better handle on her own. Then, as she worked through her forgiveness of her mother, she was able to do so thoroughly but without adding hurt upon hurt, which would have made the difficult situation even worse. This was a case where the forgiveness was primarily for Diana's sake: not so much releasing her mother from wrongdoing, but releasing herself from emotional bondage.

"THE SAME OLD THING"

Let's go back to the scenario involving Jim and me. I had just made another bad joke—for about the twentieth time—and Jim is struggling with how to respond to my request for forgiveness. Finally, he lets me manipulate him into saying the magic words, and I go merrily on my way—leaving Jim with the sure knowledge that I'm going to hurt him again, probably soon.

Now let's illustrate a healthier response. Again, let's say I have just come to Jim after my twentieth offense and apologized.

"Jim, I'm really sorry. Will you forgive me?"

This time Jim answers, "You know, Dave, this is about the twentieth time this has happened. You keep apologizing, but you also keep on doing the same old thing over and over. I know you mean it when you say you're sorry, but I can't just say, 'Sure, Dave, I forgive you,' and let it go at that."

I try my trump card again. "But Jim," I interject, "you *have* to forgive me. It's the right..."

---

*As much as we might like forgiveness to be quick
and easy, it is a process.*

"I know that," Jim says firmly, "and I intend to. I'm not trying to hold anything over your head. Like I said, I know you mean it when you say you're sorry. But for my own sake, I need to take things a bit further. I'm tired of getting hurt by what you do. I need to work through how I'm feeling about this, and I need to find a way to protect myself. I don't want to go through episode number twenty-one if I can help it."

This is what I consider an honest way of handling the situation. Jim is signalling that he acknowledges the apparent sincerity of my apology, and that he isn't holding a grudge against me. But he is also telling me that he and I are going to need to work together on our relationship.

Most of all, he's not placing himself in a false position by extending superficial forgiveness before he has had a chance to process his feelings and reactions. There is nothing wrong with needing time to work through the process of forgiveness. I can respect Jim for being firm in granting himself that time. Our relationship will be stronger in the end for his having done so.

In his book, *Caring Enough to Confront,* David Augsburger says, "Forgiveness is a journey of many steps." That little sentence sums up much of what we have been saying. As much as we might like forgiveness to be quick and easy, it is a process. It is a journey, which can take many steps. The first step— choosing to forgive, choosing not to hang on to the emotional IOU—is important and should not be overlooked. But the other steps are important, too, and we should not pass over them.

We can learn a great deal from forgiveness. Being hurt by someone only teaches us to protect ourselves and to mistrust others. Forgiveness, however, presents us with a choice as to how to respond. We can brush off what has happened by extending superficial forgiveness, ending up bitter and resentful. Or we can choose the path of true forgiveness, and learn lessons along the way that will shape our lives for the better.

If we are going to take God's principles seriously, we will see that forgiveness isn't optional. It is essential. What is optional is whether we choose the quick and easy path of superficial forgiveness, or the harder but more rewarding path of genuine forgiveness.

9

Many people are uncomfortable with anger.
They have been taught that getting angry
is always wrong—that "nice people"
don't get angry. In fact, anger is a normal
human reaction to being hurt.
And working through your anger
is an important part of forgiveness.

What's Anger Got to Do with It?

W OULD YOU AGREE or disagree with the following statements?

Without anger, most forgiveness is superficial.
Genuine forgiveness almost always includes anger.

Long experience helping people deal with dysfunctional family issues leads us to *agree* with these statements. However, many people are bothered by them. They tend to have a certain amount of mistrust concerning anger, and are especially uncomfortable connecting it with something like forgiveness. But the fact is that anger and forgiveness tend to be intimately connected. In most cases, we cannot really forgive until we have dealt with our anger. To put it another way, working through anger is often a crucial step in the process of forgiveness.

A lot of confusing ideas circulate about anger. Many of us were brought up to believe that all anger is wrong, even sinful. But anger is a fact of life. It happens to us. We experience it. What do we do then? Many of us play word games with it. We say we are "a little irritated," or "out of sorts," or "a bit upset."

We go to great lengths to avoid coming right out and saying, "I'm just plain *mad*."

In most cases, we cannot really forgive until we have dealt with our anger.

But the fact is, we often *are* just plain mad—and there is not necessarily anything wrong with that. The emotion of anger, in and of itself, is not wrong. Let me say that again, to make sure you get it: the emotion of anger, in and of itself, is not wrong. It just *is*. It is part of the "standard equipment" that comes with being a human being. It is what we *do* with our anger that makes it either right or wrong, good or bad, healthy or unhealthy.

We can *use* our anger wrongly, or *express* it in unhealthy ways. A simple example is when we "fly off the handle" at someone we love without good cause. Unhealthy anger separates us from people we love and want to be with.

But we can also use our anger for healthy purposes. For example, anger can energize us to overcome some challenge or obstacle. Who among us has not had the experience of

---

Healthy anger drives us to do something to change what makes us angry; anger can energize us to make things better. Hate does not want to change things for the better; it wants to make things worse.

—Lewis B. Smedes, *Forgive and Forget: Healing the Hurts We Don't Deserve*, (New York, NY: Harper & Row, 1984) p. 21.

"getting good and mad" at some stubborn problem, and find-ing that the energy produced by that anger gets us over the hump?

Anger can also alert us to the need to set boundaries, or limits, with other people. It is one of the ways we protect our-selves. In Chapter 8, we looked at a hypothetical problem that Jim and I had. After repeated offenses, Jim got angry: not red-in-the-face angry, but definitely motivated to make something change in our relationship. He might not have used the word "anger" to describe how he was feeling. He might have said he was "fed up," or just "frustrated." But it was still anger that pro-pelled him to make a very healthy response to the situation.

---

*The emotion of anger, in and of itself, is not wrong.
It just is. It is what we do with our anger that makes it
either right or wrong, good or bad, healthy or unhealthy.*

We may have trouble accepting the notion that anger is a normal, inevitable part of life. We have been carefully taught that anger is always wrong, that "nice people" don't get angry.

Nonsense. The simple fact of the matter is that "nice peo-ple" get angry all the time. The problem is that these folks often don't *realize* that they are angry, or don't know what to *do* with their anger. We'll talk more about those problems as we go along.

But to repeat what we said before: anger is not wrong, in and of itself. The capacity to feel and express anger is part of what it means to be a healthy human being. When we run across someone who seems to have lost the ability to feel or ex-press anger, or who has become expert at stuffing their anger deep inside, we recognize that as a problem not as a virtue.

ANGER AS A VIRTUE

Good people get angry. Even Jesus did. Listen to this passage from the Gospel of Mark:

> Another time he went into the synagogue, and a man with a shriveled hand was there. Some of them were looking for a reason to accuse Jesus, so they watched him closely to see if he would heal him on the Sabbath. Jesus said to the man with the shriveled hand, "Stand up in front of everyone."
>
> Then Jesus asked them, "Which is lawful on the Sabbath: to do good or to do evil, to save life or to kill?" But they remained silent.
>
> He looked around at them in anger and, deeply distressed at their stubborn hearts, said to the man, "Stretch out your hand." He stretched it out, and his hand was completely restored. **Mark 3:1-5**

Here we find Jesus confronting a crippled man who wants to be healed. A group of religious leaders unbelievably do not want Jesus to heal him because, according to their understanding of God's law, it is the wrong day of the week. We see Jesus responding to the situation with the full range of human emotion. Surely he must have felt compassion toward the man with the withered hand. But what did he feel toward the religious leaders? It says he was "deeply distressed at their stubborn hearts." It also says that he looked at them in *anger.*

Here again, we see healthy anger serving a good purpose. Jesus uses it to communicate his displeasure to the religious leaders. He also seems to use it to energize himself to push past their opposition and heal the man.

Paul also wrote some helpful things about anger. Much of the content of his letters in the New Testament has to do with wisdom for daily living. In a letter to the church at Ephesus, he is making the point that all Christians belong, in some sense, to one people. He then goes on to give practical advice on how to live together as part of a united family, including: "Therefore each of you must put off falsehood and speak truthfully to his neighbor, for we are all members of one body. 'In your anger do not sin': Do not let the sun go down while you are still angry..." (Ephesians 4:25-27).

Notice the line, "In your anger, do not sin." That line can also be translated, "Be angry, but do not sin." Paul seems to be saying—

- that there is a difference between "anger" and "sin";
- that it is possible to be angry *without* sinning;
- that there are times when it is actually *right* for us to be angry, so long as we do not sin in doing so;
- some anger can be sinful.

The line, "In your anger, do not sin," is actually a quotation from the Psalms: "In your anger do not sin; when you are on your beds, search your hearts and be silent" (Psalm 4:4).

The image of lying on our beds at night, quietly searching our hearts, helps to give meaning to Paul's warning: "Do not let the sun go down on your anger." On the one hand, we can take this literally. Paul warns that anger is a destructive force, both in terms of our own spiritual health and in terms of our relationships, and we should make dealing with it a priority. If possible, we should try to clear up whatever is standing between us and the person we are angry with. That is not always possible, of course. Perhaps you have seen the cartoon of the couple dozing off in the marriage counselor's office? The husband lifts up his head and, through bloodshot eyes, says, "Well, you told us not to go to bed angry, so we haven't slept for a week."

If we cannot resolve our anger at the interpersonal level, we should at least deal with it in terms of our own emotions, getting it out into the open so that the poison does not fester within us. We've discussed in earlier chapters about how to "express" feelings in this sense: writing them down, sharing them with a friend, even vocalizing them to ourselves.

Resentment is like a poison we carry around inside us with the hope that when we get the chance we can deposit it where it will harm another who has injured us. The fact is that we carry this poison at extreme risk to ourselves.

—Bert Ghezzi, *The Angry Christian*, (Ann Arbor, MI: Servant Publications, 1980) p. 99.

This helps us grasp another, somewhat more figurative, understanding of Paul's words. We can hear him saying, "Do not let your anger go into the darkness—into that place where you cannot see it, or feel it, or even acknowledge its existence." We have already seen how harmful it can be to repress our feelings; anger can be one of the most harmful feelings to repress. It is like an acid that eats away at us from the inside.

Anger that is left unresolved, or that is buried in the darkness of denial, takes root and produces bitterness and resentment. The longer we postpone dealing with anger, the more bitterness and resentment it engenders, and the harder it becomes for us to get in touch with its existence and purge it from our hearts. Once we are aware that we are angry, we know immediately that we must at least begin the process of forgiveness, and keep our anger in the daylight where we can deal with it.

ANGRY? ME?

One of the main problems posed by anger is that we sometimes do not even realize that we *are* angry. This is especially true with people who believe that anger is always wrong or sinful. They do not even let themselves become aware that they are experiencing anger. Instead they repress it, give it a different name, or pretend it doesn't exist.

Remember the story of John and Brian, from Chapter 8? Brian had had a conflict with his boss that morning, and was still experiencing some ill effects from it. But it took his friend John to point out that he was still *angry*. This is not an uncommon scenario. Sometimes we need to have our anger pointed out to us, whether by a friend or a counselor.

Once between sessions at a conference, I overheard one of the leaders yell at another person in obvious anger. His voice was strident and his words were harsh. It was an unpleasant exchange to listen to—never mind being on the receiving end of it!

Later that day I had a chance to talk to the man who had done the yelling. I mentioned that I had overheard what had happened. "Oh, that," he said. "It was just one of those things that happens sometimes. No big deal."

No big deal? I thought to myself. *It sure sounded like a big deal to me.* "Tell me," I said, "what were you feeling while you were... uh... *talking* to him?"

"Feeling?" he said, looking at me quizzically. "I don't know. I wasn't feeling anything. There were some things I needed to say to him, and..."

"Didn't you feel angry?" I interrupted.

"Oh, no," he said quickly. "No, not at all. I wasn't angry. I was just...," he let the sentence trail off.

As we talked, it became clear to me that he was convinced

that anger was bad. Because of this, he could not admit to me, or even to himself, that he had been angry. I believe he was utterly sincere in what he was saying to me. Yet I had seen a man whose face was flushed, whose voice thundered, whose hands trembled, and whose words could have peeled paint off the walls. He was a classic case of someone *experiencing* anger without being able to *acknowledge* it.

Perhaps the most damaging consequence of being shame-based is that *we don't know how depressed and angry we really are*. We don't actually feel our unresolved grief. Our false self and ego defenses keep us from experiencing it. Paradoxically, the very defenses which allowed us to survive our childhood trauma have now become barriers to our growth.

—John Bradshaw, *Healing The Shame That Binds You*, (Deerfield Beach, FL: Health Communications, Inc., 1988) p. 137.

Vic had come to see me about a long-standing depression he suffered from. He had been to a therapist several times, trying to break the hold it had on him, but without much success.

Somehow, we got to talking about his father, who had died when Vic was only ten years old. Vic could not talk about his father without crying, even though he had died almost thirty years earlier. It seemed clear that his dad's death was somehow connected to his depression.

At one point I asked Vic if he had ever been angry with his father for dying. He looked at me with a shocked expression, as if I had violated something sacred. "Angry?" he said. "How could I be angry with him? He didn't die on purpose."

I agreed, but went on to explain that much of the grieving process has to do with working through anger, including anger at the deceased one for leaving us. Vic listened intently for a while, then dismissed the subject with a wave of the hand, saying he couldn't see any connection between his depression and anger.

Several sessions later I brought up the subject again. This time Vic admitted that what I had said bothered him. If he really thought about it, maybe there *was* a little anger there after all. But not at his dad. At the doctors, maybe, or even at God. But not Dad!

I decided to try another tack. "Let me ask you something, Vic," I said. "What do you think you lost because of your dad dying while you were so young?" He thought for a while. Then he began listing a number of things he had missed out on by not having had a father: someone to watch his little league games, someone to help him with his homework, someone to tell him about girls, someone to guide him through major life decisions, and so on. Vic went on for quite some time.

When he finished, I quietly commented, "You know, I think I'd be angry at someone who took all those things away from me, even if he didn't mean to do it." I could see the realization slowly begin to dawn in Vic's eyes.

Later, after Vic had been able to identify some of the anger he held toward his father, he was able to talk about why it was so hard for him to think of being angry with him. Like many people, Vic simply did not know how to deal with anger, either his own or other people's. It made him uncomfortable. So he just pretended that it didn't exist. As we have already seen, ignoring strong emotions doesn't make them go away, it just drives them deeper inside, where they continue to effect us without our consciously realizing it.

> As adult children become increasingly aware of having been cheated out of their childhood, a wave of anger is likely to ensue. The adult child may want to be forgiving, but will still feel angry. Sometimes the anger is directed not at the alcoholic, but at the sober parent—the parent who seemingly should have known better and should have protected the child.
>
> —Herbert L. Gravitz, Ph.D. and Julie D. Bowden, M.S., *Recovery: A Guide for Adult Children of Alcoholics,* (New York, NY: Simon & Schuster, 1985) p. 31.

It was no surprise, then, that even in his adult life, Vic turned out to have a problem with anger. Whenever things went wrong, it would send him off on a rampage that left him feeling embarrassed and guilty. I explained to him that self-control in the emotional area is one of the things that a father might teach a young boy. "Another thing I missed out on," he said.

Vic had never entertained the notion of needing to forgive his dad for anything. He had idealized him to the point that Dad was a virtual saint in his eyes. To even think of being angry at Dad was preposterous. To think of him needing to be forgiven for anything was inconceivable.

Coming to grips with his anger, not only gave Vic an awareness of some important losses he had sustained in life, it also set the stage for him to work through some important forgiveness regarding his father. Not because his father had, in the strict sense, done anything wrong. Vic was quite right in saying that it wasn't his dad's fault that he died. But even without realizing it, Vic was still holding some IOUs against his father—debts he needed to cancel for the sake of his own health.

ANGER AS REACTION, ANGER AS RESPONSE

Anger is one of those concepts that gets more confusing the longer you study it. One problem is that we use the word in such a variety of contexts. I get angry over the car not starting, angry with my father for dying thirty years ago, angry at racial injustice, and angry because there are homeless people in a land as prosperous as ours.

I like to think of anger in two basic ways: as *reaction* and as *response.*

Reaction anger is what happens in us "automatically"
or "instinctively" in answer to some stimulus.
Response is what we decide to do
in response to some stimulus.

Reaction is what happens in us "automatically" or "instinctively" in answer to some stimulus. This is the way we tend to think of anger as an emotion. Someone says something that hurts us, or does something that harms us, and the emotion of anger wells up inside us. We don't plan it or think about it, and we can't prevent it. It just happens.

Response is what we *decide* to do in response to some stimulus. It is, at least to some degree, conscious and deliberate. Our reactions happen to us, but we choose our responses.

Obviously, the same stimulus can give rise to both a reaction and a response. To take a simple example, let's say you come along and, for no apparent reason, slap me in the face. Immediately I experience a reaction: my face flushes and my muscles tense up. I begin to snap, "Why, you…"

Then I stop and reflect on what happened. I take note of my reaction. I also take note of the context in which you did what you did. Maybe there was some good reason why you did it, or some good reason why I should let it pass. I may decide that the appropriate response is to simply turn and walk away. Or I may decide that the appropriate response is to confront you about your behavior.

If I choose the latter response, we would probably say that I am expressing anger rather than patience. The point is simply to note the difference between reaction—what "just happens"—and response—what I choose to do.

Anger is a normal human reaction to such experiences as pain, fear, and frustration. When someone does something against us—whether intentional or not—anger is likely to be one of our first and strongest reactions.

It often helps to take a closer look at what goes on inside us when we have an anger reaction. (Usually, of course, we have to do this well after the fact, when we've cooled down a bit!) For example, suppose I have been teaching a seminar. During the discussion period someone named Herb mentions that he disagrees with my views on anger. He is utterly convinced that anger is always wrong. In answer, I review for him the points I have been advancing here: that anger is inherently neither good nor bad, merely a fact of life; it is our *response* that makes it either good or bad.

"Well, there you go again, Dave," Herb snaps. "You're the expert. You're always right, and everyone else is always wrong. You think you're so smart. Well, actually you're overbearing, pompous, and obnoxious."

What do you suppose is going on inside me as Herb is speaking? First, of course, I recognize that I am being insulted. This comes as a shock. I see myself as being utterly pristine, acting from the purest of motives, guilty of nothing but being who I am and saying what I honestly believe. Overbearing? Pompous? *Me?*

Along with this comes the realization that Herb doesn't

regard me as being valuable enough to deserve better treatment. If he respected me, he wouldn't talk to me like this in front of other people. The message I get is, "You don't count, Dave."

Can you imagine that by this point I am beginning to experience an anger reaction?

Now, I may be able to fend off that reaction. If my self-esteem is in good shape, and if I have had a good night's sleep, I may be able to simply say to myself, "Well, that's just not true. I'm not any of those bad things Herb says I am. He just has an inaccurate perception of me as a person." If so, I may well short-circuit the anger.

But maybe I'm not so confident, or maybe my defenses are down for some reason: because I'm tired, or hungry, or not feeling well. I might be tempted to believe the things Herb said. "Maybe I only got what I deserve," I might think to myself. But even if I do, my next thought is likely to be, "How dare he say that in front of all these people!" Now my anger is giving birth to resentment.

Or I may simply reject Herb and his message. "That's absurd. He has no right to say those things? Why, I ought to…" Now my anger is in full flight.

Why? Because Herb has touched something significant. He has managed to get down to my inner self, to the core of my being. He has, to use the popular expression, "pushed my button."

"CALL WAITING"

All this helps understand "the anatomy of a reaction." But the only reason to understand our *reactions* is in order to help us select an appropriate *response*. Let's suppose we are in a situation where "our button has been pushed" and our anger reaction is in full swing. What are we to *do* with our anger?

There are four basic responses we can make:

1. We can repress the emotion. Some people can be insulted, cursed, yelled at—all but stomped upon—and they seem to respond to it like a stone. At the conscious level, at least, they simply don't feel anger. They have learned, probably from a young age, that it isn't safe—or simply doesn't pay—to allow themselves to experience the emotion of anger. So when it begins to rise up in them, they push it back down. They *repress* it.

Repressed anger is similar to the "call waiting" feature on the telephone. You can go on with your life as if it weren't there—but it is there. It won't go away. It will find ways to "leak out," in the form of depression, bitterness, mistrust, self-pity, anxiety, criticalness, and so on.

Repressed anger is similar to the "call waiting" feature on the telephone. With call waiting, you can be talking to one person on the phone and the receiver will alert you that another call is trying to get through. You can continue with your current conversation, and try to ignore the second call. But the periodic "beep" reminds you that the call is there, and it gets increasingly difficult to ignore.

Repressed anger is like that. You can go on with your life as if it weren't there, trying to ignore it—but it is there. Until something is done with it, it won't go away. It will find ways to "leak out," in the form of depression, bitterness, mistrust, self-pity, anxiety, criticalness, and so on.

In recent years, doctors have learned that repressed anger

can even contribute to physical disorders. Cancer researchers have profiled what they call the "typical cancer personality," traits that people with cancer seem to exhibit to an unusually consistent degree as compared with other people. There are four main components:[1]

- Poor self-image.
- Inability to form or maintain long-term relationships.
- Tendency to self-pity.
- Tendency to hold resentment and inability to forgive.

The fourth component relates directly to repressed anger. Much of the work done by cancer therapists has to do with helping patients to bring their anger out into the open, where it can be worked on and processed. Many patients who did so experienced remarkable remissions of their disease.

Repressed anger is like steam building up in a pressure cooker. A pressure cooker has a main valve and a safety valve. If we continue to repress our anger while trying to keep all the valves shut, eventually the lid will blow off! The pressure can build for only so long before it has to be released. The steam *will* come out. The only questions are how and when—and who gets hurt when the lid blows.

2. We can vent our anger. Years ago, people recognized the dangers of repressing anger, and in response they have pushed the pendulum all the way to the other side. "Anger," they said, "must be fully and freely expressed the instant it appears. Don't delay. Don't hold back. Be 'authentic' with your feelings."

Perhaps you have had the misfortune of being around someone who has taken this approach to the limit. They are constantly unloading on those around them. If they are sad, they spread gloom everywhere. If they are frightened, they panic everyone else. And if they are angry, look out! A lot of innocent bystanders have been hit by a full dose of someone else's angry authenticity. They can tell you it's no fun.

Perhaps you have had the misfortune of being around someone who has decided to be "authentic" with their feelings.

Authenticity may be well and good in its place. But running around yelling, cursing, and being destructive is no solution to anger. These ways of venting our anger may make us feel better, at least for the moment. But they ruin relationships, and in time they undermine our own emotional health.

I remember one man who came to our clinic. "Whenever I get angry, I just haul off and yell at whoever is handy," he said defiantly. "I always feel so much better afterward—you know, like a load has been taken off me."

His problem? "The reason I need to talk to you," he said, "is that I don't have any friends. Everybody seems to act—I don't know, like they're *afraid* of me. They say they don't like being around me." Small wonder!

3. We can feel our anger but decide not to express it right away. "A fool gives full vent to his anger, but a wise man keeps himself under control" (Proverbs 29:11). This means that we let ourselves experience our anger—we don't repress it—but we also choose to handle it in productive and healthy ways. In other words, we decide to *respond* rather than *react*. It is as if we say to ourselves, "Yes, I'm angry, but I'm not going to do any-thing until I've had a chance to think it over."

When we are angry, we usually do not see things clearly. We do well to ask for grace to help us remain calm until we can be more objective. The old adage of "counting to ten" also fits here (though sometimes we may feel we need to count to a million!).

4. We can learn to confess our anger to someone we trust. First of all, let's get clear about the word "confess." At root, it simply means "to say the same as," or "to give accurate verbal expression to what is real." In this sense, it doesn't carry the connotation of "admitting guilt." It simply means we are being candid and honest about what is going on.

In terms of our emotions, confessing our anger means that we share, openly and honestly about what is going on inside us. "I'm really feeling angry right now about..." Or, "When she said that to me, I got so mad I just wanted to..." The goal is to get the feelings out on the table, where we can understand them more clearly and decide how best to respond to them. "When it first happened, I felt like (slugging him, screaming at him, running away). But now I can see that the best thing to do is..."

SUPPORT SYSTEMS

This points up the importance of having a support system of some kind—people in our lives whom we can trust, with whom we can be open. Anger that is carried alone will often wind up getting repressed, and it will reinforce our sense of isolation. Talking out our feelings with someone else helps us process our feelings in healthy ways.

Response number 4 was the approach that Vic opted for. He handled his anger in the context of a relationship of trust. He was able to let himself feel anger at the loss he had sustained, which opened the door to a more comprehensive grieving process.

Four Basic Responses to an Anger Reaction

1. We can repress the emotion. Watch out! Repressed emotions create pressure that will eventually result in an explosion.
2. We can vent our anger. "Don't delay. Don't hold back. Be 'authentic' with your feelings!" Following such advice can provide momentary relief, but it eventually ruins relationships and undermines our own emotional health.
3. We can feel our anger but decide not to express it right away. Often it pays to "count to ten." This strategy gives us the space to respond rather than react.
4. We can learn to confess our anger to someone we trust. The goal is to understand our feelings so that we can decide how best to respond to them.

In the beginning, Vic made use of the third option—where he felt the anger but chose to remain in control of his response. That in itself was new for him. Usually, whenever Vic felt anger, his normal course of action was to attack, which only compounded his problems. Eventually deciding to talk about his anger with a trusted third party helped him to work through it fruitfully. In his case, that was a crucial first step in embarking on the process of forgiveness.

Remember Herb, the man in the hypothetical example who insulted me in front of a room full of people? In that story, I contemplated a number of responses, both internal and external, that I might make to that situation. Perhaps the healthiest response I could make would be to say, "Okay, Herb's angry right now. I don't know exactly why. But I *do* know I can't help the situation by matching his anger with my own. For now I'll just keep my peace. Later I can ask someone to help me sort out what was going on with Herb and what I needed to do with him.

10

*People who grew up in dysfunctional families
often feel that everything that goes wrong
in the world is their fault.
Understanding how you
have been victimized is important.
So is learning to take responsibility
for your life, and not blaming
all of your problems on others.*

CHAPTER 10

The Blame Game

"IF ONLY SHE COULD GET what she deserves."

I was taken aback by the bitterness in Meg's voice as she virtually spat out these harsh words. The "she" Meg was referring to was her twin sister, Martha. The two sisters had not been on speaking terms for more than thirty years.

It all went back to the time when they were both single. They were young, attractive, and vivacious, with many potential boyfriends. Meg had dated a young man named Jeff. She had gotten quite serious about him. She was shocked then, when Jeff abruptly broke off their relationship and started seeing her sister, Martha. Meg flew into a rage at her sister for luring her man away.

Jeff and Martha eventually got married. Martha would have liked for Meg to serve as her maid of honor, but Meg refused. In fact, Meg wouldn't even come to the wedding. Ever since, she has blamed every misfortune, every disappointment, every setback in life on her sister. "She stole the only man I ever loved," had been Meg's constant refrain for thirty years.

I knew Meg for many years. She was grouchy and cantankerous—not an easy person to like. I tried many times to help her see how fruitless it was to blame all her woes on something that had happened so many years before. But it never made a dent in her conviction that Martha was the cause of all her problems. "When she confesses to what she did and apologizes for ruining my life, then I'll forgive her," Meg said. Somehow she did not see that this demand was inconsistent with her refusal to allow Martha even to speak with her. She seemed incapable of viewing life except through the lens of what she saw as her sister's act of treachery.

"When she confesses to what she did and apologizes for ruining my life, then I'll forgive her."

When I last saw her, Meg was in the hospital dying of pancreatic cancer. She flatly refused to allow her sister to visit her. "I wish Martha could slowly drown for all the suffering she's caused me," Meg said. "If only she could get what she deserves."

Martha never came to the hospital, but she did come to the funeral. "I tried so many times to make things right with Meg," she told me. "You know, I probably *did* steal Jeff away from her. It was a game we played for years, flirting with each other's boyfriends. We both did it. But it stopped being a game when I truly fell in love with Jeff. Meg hated me ever since. I guess she felt I had finally won the game once and for all. She would tell anyone who'd listen to her that I didn't really love Jeff and she did."

How many others are there like Meg, consumed with an impossible demand for vengeance? We all know the saying, "An eye for an eye, a tooth for a tooth." Did you know it comes from the Bible? Originally, it was God's way of *limiting* the vengeance that people took on one another. In Old Testament times it was not uncommon for people to extract a *life* in payment for even a minor injury. But in time God introduced the standard of mercy, not the standard of vengeance, as the guiding principle in our relationships.

Even when the guilty parties have been punished, those who have been wronged still have no peace. The memory of the offense remains the source of anguish and turmoil.

Still, the only way many people deal with an offense is to punish the offender. Interestingly, even when the guilty parties have been punished, those who have been wronged still have no peace. The memory of the offense does not go away. That tortured memory remains the source of anguish and turmoil. Bitterness and resentment linger; anger continues to rage.

Sometimes those who have been hurt will take out their frustration on others without even realizing they are doing it. They become irritable and insulting. Their friends find them increasingly difficult to get along with—while they still have friends. In the end their resentment destroys their own freedom. They become incapable of *not* acting spitefully, so thoroughly has the poison of resentment infiltrated their system. That is the inevitable outcome of the blame game: those who play it *always* end up losers.

Have you ever noticed that it's fun to blame others? That's one of the reasons why we do it. If we're honest with ourselves, most of us will admit that we get a kind of perverse pleasure out of blaming others. We may even share our "somebody-done-me-wrong" tale with others whom we know we can count on to add their understanding and sympathy. In effect, we throw a "pity party," focusing on our pain and our resentment, having a fun time in a twisted sort of way.

Sometimes we blame others as cover-up for fear, fear of punishment, embarrassment, responsibility, and the like. Self-protection is a strong drive in all of us.

At the most basic level, our tendency to blame others probably stems from our fundamental conviction that we ourselves are blameless. Isn't that right? We might never come out and say it, but deep in our heart we know we are just, honorable, and upright. When things go wrong, it *must* be someone else's fault. Surely it couldn't be ours!

"I *HAD* TO BLAME *SOMEONE*"

We regularly see an interesting phenomenon occur among adults who were abused as children. They experience an overwhelming need to cast blame *somewhere*. Because of the dynamics of childhood—where adults are bigger and more powerful, and therefore perceived as "always right"—abuse victims invariably place the blame on themselves.

But they soon start accepting the fact that they were only children, innocent, unable to either choose or prevent the things that were happening to them. "For the first time I realized that I wasn't to blame for all the problems that existed in the world," one woman said. "I felt I *had* to blame *someone*. I couldn't blame the adults, because after all, they were *adults*. So the only one left to blame was me."

Once this realization hits, they often start blaming others with a vengeance. Some are simply programmed to blame others for everything. One man named Jerry, remembers growing up in a family where *everything* was regarded as someone else's fault. He can remember times when they hoped for a sunny day and it rained. His father would say, "Even God is against us today." Jerry grew up very confused about the matter of responsibility. If he himself didn't bring about the wrong, then he had to point an accusing finger at someone else.

A more mature understanding of the world tells us that sometimes things just don't work out the way we hoped. There are disappointments, unexpected developments, changes in plans, that are no one's fault in particular. To paraphrase the popular bumper sticker, "Stuff Just Happens." Being able to accept this reality, without always having to point the finger of blame, is an important component of personal maturity and emotional health.

Some people are simply programmed to blame others for everything. One man remembers growing up in a family where everything was regarded as someone else's fault.

THE PATH OF BITTERNESS

Face it: we want to blame. When we have been hurt—or *think* we have—something in us wants to place the blame somewhere (usually on someone else). But the more we blame, the farther we walk down the dangerous path of bitterness. That path never leads us to health and happiness, only to deeper distress.

Recently I came across a story that shows how tragic it can be to walk down the path of bitterness.

Leonard Goldenson's gentlemanly manner running ABC is well chronicled. Not so well known is his feud with Frank Sinatra. In *Beating the Odds*, Goldenson tells his side.

"Frank's career was in the doldrums. He'd just finished *From Here to Eternity*, but it was months away from release. Nobody yet knew it was going to be the smash hit that would restore Sinatra to superstardom.

"I said, 'Frank, do you have any money?'

"He said 'no.' I said, 'I want you on ABC.' Eventually we agreed to form a production company together. I thought a musical variety show hosted by Sinatra held great promise."

Eternity was a smash, earning Sinatra an Oscar. He lost interest in the TV project, and it faltered. Goldenson flew to Las Vegas to see him about doing specials. For three days Goldenson waited to see him. Then, he had had enough.

"I wrote Sinatra a letter in longhand. 'Never in my life have I experienced such treatment,' I said. 'I have no respect for anyone who lacks the character to appear for an appointment. When you were down on your luck and had no money, we went out of our way to make a capital gain for you.... I want nothing further to do with you.'"

They have not spoken once since the 1954 incident.

Leonard Goldenson, *Beating the Odds*,
USA Today, February 27, 1991.

It would seem from this account that Leonard Goldenson is an intensely bitter man, at least as far as Frank Sinatra is concerned. He obviously blames Sinatra for a missed opportunity. Now, let's suppose that Sinatra were to call Goldenson on the phone one day and say, "You know, Leonard, you're right. It was wrong of me to do what I did." Would Goldenson feel vindicated? Perhaps. Would that brief moment of satisfaction be worth thirty-five years of blaming and bitterness? I doubt it.

This is the who-started-it game—the search for a beginning of a sequence, where the aim is to proclaim which person is to blame for the behavior of both. But we know that this interaction is really a circular dance in which the behavior of one partner maintains and provokes the behavior of the other. The circular dance has no beginning and no end. In the final analysis, it matters little who started it. The question of greater significance is: "How do we break out of it?"

—Harriet Goldhor Lerner, *The Dance of Anger,* (New York, NY: Harper & Row, 1985) p. 56.

THE PATH OF FORGIVENESS

A lot of psychologist jokes focus on shifting the blame for all our problems to someone else—usually to Mom. I sometimes tell people, "If you want to play the blame game, I can move you through it real quick. Do you want to know why you have the problems you have? Because of your mother. And why do you suppose your mother treated you so badly? Because of *her* mother. And what was *her* mother's problem? Why, her mother before her, of course."

Do you see where this leads? Eventually we get all the way back to Eve—who, as we have seen, shirked her own responsibility as well. In other words, the blame game leads nowhere. All it does is prove that we are *all* flawed, imperfect people living in a flawed, imperfect world where "stuff happens." So why bother playing it at all? Why not get off the path of bitterness and get on the path of forgiveness?

Playing the blame game just gets in the way of resolving our problems and moving past them. It keeps us mired in them forever. *Blaming other people for our problems doesn't solve our problems, even if we're right.* Think about it: as long as our energies are absorbed with blaming another person, we are really under that person's control. The image of that person becomes the focal point of our whole life. The hurt doesn't go away just because we figure out who the "villain" is. The hurt goes away only when we work through the process of forgiveness.

Some people are blamers without realizing it. They *think* they are taking appropriate responsibility for their actions, but by attaching "stingers" to their words, "I was wrong" turns into "It's all your fault." For example:

"Honey, I'm sorry I yelled at you last night," a husband said. "I'm also sorry you didn't get supper on the table when I asked you to."

One of the ways to spot an unconscious blamer is when "you" statements creep into "I" statements.

"I feel bad today because you..."

"I wouldn't have said what I said if you hadn't..."

"I wouldn't have wrecked the car if you had been ready on time so I didn't have to speed to get there."

It is easy to blame our parents for our present problems. The fact of the matter is that we have faced a lot of decisions and made many choices in life along the way. If we don't grow out of our problems and make the right choices, it is no one's fault but our own.
—Frank Minirth, Paul Meier, Richard Meier, and Don Hawkins, *The Healthy Christian Life*, (Grand Rapids, MI: Baker Book House, 1988) pp. 201-202.

An interesting twist on this is what happens when we are clearly in the wrong, recognize it, and still blame the other person for our actions. "I guess I shouldn't have done it. But he really had it coming. He thinks he's so superior to everyone else." Or, "I shouldn't have treated him that way. But he's such a jerk! Everyone says so."

This is nothing more than rationalizing our misbehavior by claiming that the other person *deserved* to be treated badly "on general principles." But it is not up to us to decide what others "deserve." Our job is to take responsibility for our own actions.

REMEMBERING OR BLAMING?

Back in Chapter 7, when we talked about forgiving and forgetting, we made the point that getting clear about "who did what to whom" was crucial to the process of forgiveness. Trying to forget the offenses we have suffered, or to pretend they never happened, is a dead end. We need to *remember* and *accept* the painful things that have been done to us.

What is the difference between this and "blaming"?

Sometimes people say angrily, "He doesn't deserve my forgiveness. What he has done just isn't forgivable. In fact, he's just a jerk." It may be true that this person does not "deserve" your forgiveness, but the real question is whether *you* desire mental and physical health. Do you want peace of mind? Or do you want the natural consequences of holding a grudge and perpetuating your bitterness?

—Frank Minirth, Paul Meier, Richard Meier, and Don Hawkins, *The Healthy Christian Life,* (Grand Rapids, MI: Baker Book House, 1988) p. 88.

"Blaming" is shifting onto others the responsibility that should be ours, or using the fact of others' guilt to *excuse* ourselves from having to *respond* in healthy ways to what was done to us.

Actually, what happens early in the process of forgiveness— the "remembering"—feels the same as blaming. The truth is, for a little bit of time, we need to blame someone else. When we are dealing with wounds and injuries that go back to childhood, our tendency is to place the blame for what happened on ourselves. If we are going to work through the process of forgiving properly, we need to balance out that tendency by lifting the false blame from ourselves and placing it where the blame really belongs. We need to clearly see that it was not our fault, that we really were victims of someone else.

Blaming can be seductive. If we are not careful, we can reverse the pendulum and become a "blamer." That is why it is essential that we try not to work through this forgiving process alone—we need the wise counsel of someone we trust. We need to blame at this stage so that we can get an accurate picture of what happened, so that our forgiveness can be solidly grounded in reality. When that happens, we let go of the blame, and take responsibility for our own recovery.

Rhonda described herself as a "flaming codependent." Codependency points to destructive lifestyles and emotional patterns that develop from prolonged exposure to an oppressive way of life—usually from living in a close relationship with someone who is "dependent" on alcohol or drugs, or who is in some other way severely dysfunctional. As the sick person's life becomes unmanageable because of his or her dependency, the codependent person's life also becomes unmanageable as a result of trying to cope with them.[1]

"Blaming" is shifting onto others the responsibility that should be ours, or using the fact of others' guilt to excuse ourselves from having to respond in healthy ways to what was done to us.

When Rhonda's husband began to drink heavily, she moved into a classic codependent stance toward him. She became what is called a *caretaker/enabler*. She cast herself in a role that enabled her husband to avoid facing the consequences of his alcoholism, thus making it easier for him to continue to operate as an alcoholic. If he had a hangover and felt too bad to go to work, she called in and made excuses for him. She figured out ways to hide his drinking from the children. She made life easier for him, thinking she was doing the most loving and helpful thing.

He did not seem to care, or even to notice all the things she did for him. In fact, he became increasingly abusive toward her as time went on—even insisting that his drinking problem was her fault. "If you were a better cook," he'd shout, "I wouldn't drink so much." Or, "You're such a stupid woman, drinking is the only way I can stand to live with you!"

The tragic part is that Rhonda, in spite of herself, believed him. For fourteen years she lived under these conditions, convinced that his drinking really *was* her fault, that she *deserved* the treatment he gave her, and she was not entitled to a better life. Her husband had learned to play the blame game, and she was the perennial loser.

One of the steps Rhonda had to go through in getting free from her codependency was to assert and accept that she was *not* the cause of her husband's problems. She was *not* stupid and her cooking skills (or lack thereof) had nothing whatsoever to do with her husband's drinking. He did not drink because of anything she did or did not do. He drank because he was an alcoholic. The fact was that he was a sick and abusive man who had in fact done her great harm.

Rhonda needed to release herself from false blame and accept the reality of her situation. Not that she turned around and played the blame game herself, laying all her difficulties at her husband's doorstep and absolving herself from all responsibility. Rhonda still had much to learn about responding well to the things that had happened to her, and about living a healthy and fruitful life in her own right. The goal was not to *shift* blame but to *do away with* blame, not to make her husband the villain but to acknowledge and accept what he had done, *so that she could forgive him.*

Rhonda's situation was actually rather mild as codependents go. Perhaps the core problem of codependency is this willingness to take all blame upon ourselves for problems that are simply not of our making. People can be beaten, raped, humiliated, half-starved, verbally abused—victimized in any of a dozen ways—and all the while think, "This is my fault. I did something wrong. I made him lose his temper. If I had just been quieter, or if I had responded quicker when he called me, or if I had only sensed his mood when he came in, this wouldn't have happened."

It is absolutely crucial that such people be able to see that it is *not* their fault, that *someone else* is causing their pain. It is the indispensable first step in coming to forgive that person, which is the only path to freedom, health, and sanity.

THE BOY WHO LOOKED TOO GOOD

Dick was a strikingly handsome young man who, as a child, had been sexually molested by a deacon at his church. The abuse had gone on until Dick was twelve years old. Shortly after that, an older boy in the neighborhood also abused him; and this too, went on for some time.

Dick's problem was that he blamed himself for what had happened. "*Look* at me," he would say. "I *made* those people want me. I must have given off the wrong vibes or something. I mean, if I just weren't so good-looking, they wouldn't have been interested in me!"

"What happened to me, happened. I can't change it. But I can accept it, and decide for myself how I'm going to respond to it."

I had to say to Dick over and over, "Dick, this has nothing to do with your looks. It has nothing to do with 'giving off bad vibes.' You were a victim. They took advantage of you. Those people really did hurt you, and *it wasn't your fault*."

Finally, Dick was able to accept what had happened and to place the responsibility where it belonged. "They made me do something I didn't want to do, didn't they?" he asked. "I mean, even if I was the best-looking kid in the world, it was still my body, wasn't it? They shouldn't have done what they did."

That recognition and acceptance were important starting points. But I had to caution him as well. "Dick," I said, "this doesn't end it for you. You were a victim, yes. But you don't have to *stay* a victim—and you shouldn't. You have to move on until you're free of blame and bitterness."

To assign responsibility for past hurts in an objective, truthful way and then to let them go, takes time and work—not to mention prayer and understanding. It is not easy for any of us to say, "What happened to me, happened. Those who hurt me, hurt me. I can't change it. But I can accept it, and decide for myself how I'm going to respond to it—and how I'm going to go on with my life." But that is precisely what we *must* do if we are to stop playing the blame game once and for all, then get on with the process of forgiveness.

> If you are the adult child of a dysfunctional parent, you will almost certainly find blame surfacing in your thoughts. You tell yourself that whatever happened in the past must have been your fault. It's not a rational blame, but that doesn't make it any less painful.
> —Robert Hemfelt and Paul Warren, *Kids Who Carry Our Pain,* (Nashville, TN: Thomas Nelson Publishers, 1990) p. 162.

"I" AND "YOU" STATEMENTS

Earlier we saw that one of the telltale signs that a session of the blame game was in progress was the presence of "you" statements creeping into our "I" statements. One of the ways to free ourselves of the blaming syndrome is to consciously and deliberately turn this dynamic around. We can learn how to state our feelings without using the word "you."

"I feel out of sorts today."

"I was wrong to say what I said."

"It's my fault the car got wrecked. I was driving too fast."

"I'm feeling very angry right now."

"I'm hurt over what happened."

"I'm feeling unsafe right now."

"I'm angry. I need to get this out of my system."

Now, any of these statements could easily be accompanied by a "you" statement. And in time it may be appropriate to assess the role others may have played in causing the difficulty. But by deliberately avoiding the word "you" at this stage, we avoid getting into blaming. This leaves ourselves better positioned to handle the situation peacefully and fruitfully when the time comes.

SHARING OUR PAIN

What do we do with our painful emotions? The blame game calls for spreading our bitterness to others, throwing ourselves a pity party. But instead of that, one thing we can do is to share our pain with someone who can help us. Sometimes just knowing that another person understands what we are feeling makes it hurt a little less.

I remember Kent. He came in to see me, quite stressed and suffering a lot of emotional pain. He started telling me how bad he was feeling. He talked for almost thirty minutes before he stopped and looked up at me. "You know," he said, "I'm feeling a lot better right now."

Why? I hadn't given him any magic pills. He just talked about his pain, and I just listened. It seems like such a little thing, but it is not. Listening to others—when we are listening with gentleness and empathy and compassion—is tremendously healing. It seems to help get rid of the poison that builds up inside us.

Walking the path of forgiveness often involves sharing our pain with someone we trust. Sometimes we are so weighed down it is hard for us to travel the path. But sharing our pain with others lightens our load.

Don't we all need someone—or a group of someones—who can be there when we need help? Someone with patience and wisdom to walk along beside us when the path gets rough? Shouldn't we make it a point to "be there" for one another in this way?

Walking the path of forgiveness is a journey of many steps. Learning to avoid the blame game will help us stay on that path, and not stray off into bitterness and resentment.

11

Sometimes, going to those who have harmed you and "clearing the air" is helpful. But before you confront, you must carefully discern your motives and assess your expectations. You must also understand that you can, and should, forgive others even if you cannot be reconciled to them.

CHAPTER 11

Confrontation, Retaliation, and Reconciliation

As a child, Mel remembered two things about his father. First, he remembered that his father was distant—almost silent—around him. When he did speak, it was only to complain that Mel had done something wrong. Second, Mel remembered that his father drank heavily. Sometimes when he drank, he would laugh and tell funny stories. Other times he became abusive and hit Mel. Mel never knew which to expect.

Years later, after he had grown up and left home, Mel felt he needed to be free from the harsh memories of life with his father. After an intense struggle, he was able to work his way through the process of forgiveness and release his father from the emotional IOU he had held against him. It was a great day when Mel could finally say, "I've forgiven him."

He then decided to take what seemed like the next logical step—to reconcile with his father. Knowing that he had released himself from the grip of his past was wonderful, but Mel wanted to go further. He wanted to patch things up with his dad and restore their relationship. Although he now lived almost a thousand miles away from his father, he made a special trip just to spend time with him. "Dad," he said, "could we talk?"

Without saying a word, Mel's father sat down in his favorite chair. Mel pulled up another chair and sat down facing his dad. For nearly thirty minutes, Mel told his Dad about the pent-up anger and hurt he had grown up with. He never accused, and carefully avoided saying anything condemnatory about his father's actions. He spoke only of himself, reporting simply and objectively what he had experienced, and how he now wanted to make things right.

At the end he leaned forward and took his father's hand. "Dad," he said, "I've put aside all my anger and hurt. I hope you'll forgive me for the many ways I've failed you. I've always wanted to be a good son, to make you proud of me. That's what I want now—just for us to be a real father and son."

Mel's father had listened the entire time without saying a word or expressing any emotion. Now, as Mel finished, his father pulled himself up from his chair, looked down at Mel, nodded his head slightly, and said, "Well..." Then he turned, walked down the hall to his bedroom, and quietly closed the door. He did not come out that night, or even the next day before Mel left.

Several months later, Mel's father suffered a stroke. He died two hours before Mel reached him.

In reviewing his attempt at reconciliation, Mel spoke of his confusion. When he left his father's house that day, Mel still had no idea how his father felt about what he had said, about what had happened between them, about him—about anything. His dad never gave him the slightest response.

"Why did he act like that?" Mel said. "What did I do wrong?"

"Let's try a different question," I suggested. "What did you *expect* to happen when you talked to him?"

"Expect?" Mel said. He shrugged his shoulders. "I don't know what I expected. Nothing, I guess."

"Really?" I replied. "If you didn't have any expectations, then how could you have been disappointed?"

Mel pondered that for a moment, then began to speak. The words tumbled out. He had hoped for an apology. He had hoped for at least some attempt on his father's part to respond. He had hoped his father would say, "I love you," or at least, "I forgive you." Most of all, perhaps, he had hoped his father would say, "Please forgive me."

"And now he's gone," Mel said with great sadness. He had *forgiven* his father. But he had not been able to *reconcile* with him. It was one of those sad facts of life that so many of us must live with. Mel struggled for a long time over what he considered to be his own failure. Surely he could have made the reconciliation happen if he had just said the right things, or said them the right way, or...

"The only failure," I finally told Mel, "is that you lumped together two things that are really separate. Forgiveness and reconciliation are not the same thing."

Forgiveness is unilateral. It is something we can do all by ourselves. Reconciliation requires the participation of another person. We cannot "make it happen," no matter how hard we try.

TWO DISTINCT PROCESSES

Forgiveness and reconciliation are not the same thing. It is vitally important that we grasp that distinction. Forgiveness is unilateral. It is something we can do all by ourselves, something we can "make happen" by our own decision. Reconciliation, how-

263

ever, requires the participation of another person. We cannot "make it happen," no matter how hard we try.

Forgiveness and reconciliation are two separate and distinct processes. We *can* have one without the other. Working through the process of forgiveness is essential to our personal well-being, and should always be pursued. Reconciliation is immensely valuable to us, and should be pursued whenever possible—but it isn't always possible.

Forgiveness and reconciliation are two separate and distinct processes. We can have one without the other.

Mel was stuck on this point. He did not consider his forgiveness of his father to be complete because he and his father had not reconciled. They had not established a relationship of mutual love, or at least mutual respect. He was confusing the two processes.

I pointed out to Mel that as long as he continued to hold this view, his father could continue to hold him hostage, even in the grave. What Mel needed to see was that forgiveness and reconciliation were separate things—that he *had* forgiven his father, fully and completely, even though they had not reconciled.

Mel's situation is not unusual. I frequently find myself listening to someone describe their inner struggle to forgive someone—especially someone close to them, and then tell of their frustration over the way their relationship is now continuing. "Now what?" they ask. "Now that I've forgiven them, why can't we get along?" In effect, they are assuming that the other person, by refusing to be reconciled, can "undo" their forgiveness. But that is not the way it works.

"How you relate to them is a different matter," I usually say.

"We can address that later if you like. For now, I just want you to see that you really have forgiven them. You have done what you needed to do, what you *could* do. You have canceled the debt and freed yourself from the obstacles that held you back from inner peace. I know you're not reconciled with them. But you *have* forgiven them. Nothing can change that."

"But I still can't even *talk* to them," one woman, named Jill, objected. Her parents and two sisters had turned against her years ago, when she had gotten heavily involved in drugs. Since then, Jill had changed. She stopped taking drugs, and finished school. Now she held a responsible job in an advertising firm and had been married for three years. "I mean, they won't *let* me talk to them," she continued. "When I call, they hang up as soon as they recognize my voice. All my letters come back marked, 'Return to Sender.' I don't know what to do."

"Have you forgiven them?" I asked her.

"Well, yes, but..."

"Then you've done all *you* can do," I said. "Forgiving is *your* job. It's under *your* control. But reconciling—for that you need their cooperation, which doesn't seem likely. There's nothing you can do about that, as far as I can see. But that doesn't mean you haven't forgiven them. You have!"

Jill understood. She continues to hope—as do I—that one day her family will relent, and the door to reconciliation will open up. In the meantime, she can only continue to work through the process of forgiveness whenever bitterness or resentment rise up, and grieve over a family that isn't there—at least not for her.

A TWO-WAY STREET

Reconciliation is a two-way street. It requires two people who are at least somewhat "in sync" with each other. It can occur only when both parties to a relationship want it to happen; when both have accepted their own responsibility for what went wrong, have sorted out their emotions, and worked through the processes of both repentance and forgiveness. You work through your side of it and ask for my forgiveness; I work through my side of it and ask for your forgiveness. Then we can be reconciled.

Reconciliation can occur only when both parties to a relationship want it to happen.

In the well-known story of the Prodigal Son, a young man takes his inheritance, leaves his family, and wastes all his money in a far-away city. Broke and hungry, he makes the difficult decision to come back home and seek reconciliation with his family. In heart-rending terms, he begs his father to take him back: "Father, I have sinned against heaven and against you. I am no longer worthy to be called your son; make me like one of your hired men" (Luke 15:18-19).

Clearly, the young man has had a change of heart. Whatever grievances he once held against his father (those things that prompted him to run away in the first place) have clearly been dealt with. He canceled whatever "debt" he once held against his father, and came to him repentant, seeking to be reconciled.

How does the father respond? He, too, appears to have released his son from whatever IOUs he may have held against him. "But while he was still a long way off, his father saw him and was filled with compassion for him; he ran to his son, threw his arms around him and kissed him" (Luke 15:20). What a classic picture of repentance, forgiveness, and reconciliation!

But then we meet a third character—the older brother:

> Meanwhile, the older son was in the field. When he came near the house, he heard music and dancing. So he called one of the servants and asked him what was going on. "Your brother has come," he replied, "and your father has killed the fattened calf because he has him back safe and sound."
>
> The older brother became angry and refused to go in. So his father went out and pleaded with him. But he answered his father, "Look! All these years I've been slaving for you and never disobeyed your orders. Yet you never gave me even a young goat so I could celebrate with my friends. But when this son of yours who has squandered your property with prostitutes comes home, you kill the fattened calf for him!" **Luke 15:25-30**

The older brother, in contrast to his father, offers us a picture of reconciliation spurned. Clearly he still bears great resentment toward his younger brother for his reckless behavior. He also seems to be bitter toward his father for welcoming the younger brother back. As the story unfolds, we see the father attempting to be reconciled to his eldest son, trying to explain his actions in forgiving the younger brother. As far as we know, the older brother was unwilling to be reconciled to either his brother or his father.

Rifts between me and my relatives or former friends can often be healed by swallowing my pride and making the first overtures toward reconciliation. Even if only a little of the blame was mine, the generous gesture will benefit me.

—*One Day at a Time in Al-Anon*, (New York, NY: Al-Anon Family Group Headquarters, Inc., 1987) p. 175.

Reconciliation is a two-way street; in this case forgiveness flowed in only one direction and reconciliation was not possible. The father and the younger brother were free from the prison of their bitterness and resentment; the older brother was still held bound.

A FORM OF LOVE

Forgiveness is ultimately a form of love, a love that accepts others as they are. It meets them with a compassion that springs from an awareness of our own weaknesses, faults, and destructive tendencies.

We cannot pay for what is freely given to us. The beauty of both forgiveness and reconciliation is that they are free actions that come from the heart.

As we have seen, the one who knows he has offended another must apologize, and must work through the process of repentance. This must never be allowed to become a form of "buying back" the relationship. Such a person may struggle with the desire to make some impossible act of restitution, or to be punished in some unhealthy way—as though by doing so, he or she could *earn* forgiveness. It may be right to make restitution for a wrong done, but restitution can never earn forgiveness. It is freely offered as an act of love, and freely accepted as an act of humility.

We cannot pay for what is freely given to us. The beauty of both forgiveness and reconciliation is that they are free actions that come from the heart. When we have wronged someone, and that person has forgiven us and has opened the door of reconciliation to us, the only thing we can do is accept it. This can be difficult indeed. Accepting unconditional love may make us more keenly aware of our own failures, or the wrongness of our own actions. I suspect it was this prospect that rendered Mel's father incapable of accepting his son's offer of reconciliation. As we saw in that case, this refusal to accept forgiveness and love makes reconciliation impossible. Reconciliation is based on mutual acceptance.

Reconciliation requires not only mutual forgiveness but also mutual acceptance. Acceptance is based on:

- Both parties being able to accept themselves.
- Both being willing to admit their own failures.
- Both desiring healing for the ruptured relationship.
- Both being prepared to surrender their demand for self-justification.
- Both being prepared to set aside their desire to punish the other.
- Both acknowledging that it is not easy for people to receive unconditional forgiving love.

RECONCILIATION WITHOUT FORGIVENESS

We have pointed out that it is possible to forgive without reconciling. We should also note in passing that it is possible to reconcile without truly forgiving. This happens, for example, when we:

- "Overlook" the pain caused by someone's actions.
- Deny we've been hurt.
- Excuse inexcusable behavior.
- Fear we'll lose the relationship if we speak up.

"I could be reconciled to my wife," one man said to me. "It's easy. I've done it dozens of times. All I have to do is admit that

I've been the monster she says I am, and that all the hurtful things she says are true. And just like that, we're reconciled."

"And you end up despising yourself," I offered. With pain too deep for words, he nodded slowly.

Let's take another example. You've wounded me in some way. It cuts deeply. I go to you and tell you how hurt I am. But immediately I add, "I know you didn't mean it the way I took it. If I could only get over my sensitivity about things like that." I end up apologizing to *you* for your hurting me!

How absurd! Yet many of us do it, all the time. We have been taught that we must be willing to do *anything* to bring about peace—even deny the truth and inflict wounds on ourselves. We end up struggling to find some way to persuade the other person (and ourselves) that we caused the rupture in the first place.

Superficial forgiveness leads only to artificial reconciliation.

It's easy to be "reconciled" under that approach! But the fact is what has happened isn't really reconciliation at all. Reconciliation has to proceed from forgiveness. The work of forgiveness has to take place in both parties before we can make any step toward one another. Earlier we spoke of "superficial forgiveness." Now we can see that superficial forgiveness leads only to artificial reconciliation.

THE DAUGHTER WHO AMBUSHED HER PARENTS

Dennis and Bonnie told me of going back east to visit their daughter Jean. While they were there, Jean asked if they'd mind coming to a joint session with her therapist. Dennis and Bonnie weren't too sure what it was all about—they hadn't even been aware that Jean was seeing a therapist—but they agreed to go.

"It was the most awful thing I've ever been subjected to," Bonnie said later. "Now I know what people mean when they talk about 'parent bashing.' We sure got bashed by Jean and that therapist of hers."

Apparently what happened was this. When Jean learned that her parents were coming for a visit, she mentioned it to her therapist, who said it would provide the perfect opportunity for Jean to tell her parents everything she was feeling toward them. Jean worked feverishly for more than a month, trying to record every complaint she could remember concerning her mom and dad. Then she and the therapist pulled the list together. I don't know if they ever stopped to consider what the outcome was likely to be—or even what they *wanted* it to be.

In fact, the outcome was that Dennis and Bonnie were devastated. They were certainly open to acknowledging that they had not been perfect parents, and even that they had done things that had hurt their children. They understood many of the things Jean said to them, and were truly sorry for the way some aspects of their parenting had caused her pain.

But the session with Jean and the therapist seemed to make Jean's anger more intense, rather than less. This left Dennis and Bonnie very uncertain how they could relate to their daughter. They tried to stay at Jean's for the remainder of their visit, but wound up checking into a hotel two days before they were scheduled to leave because of another angry, tearful clash with her. They left for home wondering whether they would ever be able to spend time together as a family again.

As soon as we begin to talk about reconciliation, the subject of *confronting* is sure to come up. Some people see it as vitally important—more so than forgiveness itself. The way we see it, there are some important issues that have to be balanced against one another.

Undeniably, it is important to bring hidden things into the light so that they can be dealt with. Family secrets, family myths, seriously harmful actions that have been buried under mountains of denial—these kinds of issues can often be addressed fruitfully by going directly to those involved and bringing things into the open.

Most people, when they think of confronting others, are thinking mainly of themselves; they want to stand up and "tell off" those who have harmed them.

But we must also stop to reflect on our *motives* in confronting others, and on the *effects* the confrontation is likely to have. As far as motives are concerned, it is important to root out any drive for retaliation, revenge, retribution, and spitefulness. We'll talk more about this in a moment.

As to effects, we must try to envision what outcome the confrontation will have. Will it really make the situation better? Or will it make things worse by rupturing relationships that are already strained, putting undue pressure on people who may not be ready to bear it? In short, will confrontation enhance or inhibit the chances for forgiveness and reconciliation?

Most people, when they think of confronting others, are thinking mainly of themselves. They want to stand up and "tell off" those who have harmed them. They see this as a declaration of independence from the emotional bondage of the past, a way of saying to all the world, "What happened to me was wrong and I'm not going to let it happen again." Their instinct is to rush ahead and "have at it." That is seldom the wisest course of action. In order to be effective, confrontation calls for thoughtful preparation.

Confrontation is simply and essentially a sharing of facts and feeling. It is not a vindictive attack or an argument. It is not intended to alienate or change anyone. You do not confront someone for the purpose of releasing your anger against them. In fact, it is best to release your anger before a confrontation. You do not confront someone to punish him, get even with him, frighten him or make him suffer. Rather, confrontation is a way of bringing closure to a painful relationship from the past that would continue to fester if it was not openly discussed and dealt with.
—H. Norman Wright, *Always Daddy's Girl*, (Ventura, CA: Regal Books, 1989) p. 218.

THE WOMAN WHO CONFRONTED HER PRIEST

A well-prepared confrontation *can* have a strikingly success-ful outcome. I know of one instance where a young woman had been seduced by her parish priest. She was nineteen when it happened. She and her therapist discussed the situa-tion at length. The young woman had solid reasons for believ-ing that others had been similarly violated. It seemed to her, and to the counselor, that the man had broken faith with his church, his vows, and the people he was supposed to care for. He had used his position to take advantage of at least one—and probably several—women.

The therapist contacted the priest's bishop. After lengthy consultation, the bishop in turn spoke with the priest, who admitted what he had done. A few weeks later the young woman, her therapist, the priest, and the bishop met together. The priest offered heartfelt repentance, and the young woman responded with genuine forgiveness. The church offered to obtain help for both the woman and the priest who, for his part, agreed to come under the discipline of his superior and undergo treatment.

Not all confrontations have such happy endings. One major reason why this one worked as well as it did, was because those involved proceeded thoughtfully and prayerfully at every stage, always checking their motives and always weighing the impact of each step along the way.

THE DAUGHTER WHO CLEARED THE AIR

It may seem obvious that confrontation is called for in a case where wrongdoing is so great. But even "minor" injuries can benefit from a well-thought-out confrontation.

Carla had been in our clinic for several weeks. As the time drew near for her to return home, she asked if I would help her confront her parents about some issues. I couldn't recall

---

Substantive change in important relationships rarely comes about through intense confrontation. Rather, it more frequently results from careful thinking and from planning for small, manageable moves based on a solid understanding of the problem, including our own part in it. We are unlikely to be agents of change when we hold our nose, close our eyes, and jump!
　　　　　　—Harriet Goldhor Lerner, *The Dance of Intimacy*, (New York, NY: Harper and Row, 1989) p. 15.

---

her talking about any kind of trauma, such as molestation or physical abuse, so I asked her what she wanted to focus on.

"Oh, there's nothing major, like what some folks here are dealing with," she said. "There are just some things I want to say to them, and I could use some help figuring out how to say things in the most helpful way."

Carla and I spent several sessions talking through what she wanted to say to each of her parents. She also spent a lot of time between sessions reviewing her points, narrowing things down to a few basic issues. Then we spent some time talking about what she expected from her parents as a result of this encounter.

This was particularly important with Carla, because one of her major complaints had been that her folks never seemed willing to take the time to really listen to her, to hear what was in her heart. Her mother minimized everything. Her father would usually just clear his throat and sputter, "You'd better talk to your mother about that." These, in fact, were the responses Carla expected when she confronted her parents now.

"Why, then," I asked her, "do you still feel the need to confront?"

"I'm feeling stronger as a person, and I just want to get this stuff out on the table. What they do with what I tell them is up to them. So I'm not expecting any real response. I don't think I need them to do anything more than just be in the room while I talk." I agreed to set up the appointment.

When I met her parents, they seemed pretty much as she had described them. I chatted with them for a while, explaining the basics of what we were about to do, trying to help them feel comfortable. "Carla has some important matters she'd like to discuss with you," I said. "I'm here as a sort of interpreter, to help everyone hear what the others are saying." Then I turned to Carla and said, "You're on."

I watched her parents' faces as Carla told them how she had

felt when they didn't really listen to her. She told them what had made her hurt and angry, but never let herself become hurt or angry in the process. She simply reported her feelings in a simple, straightforward way—no angry accusations or judgments. At one point she even asked if they understood what she was saying, and they nodded.

Finally, Carla told each of them individually what she wished she could experience in their relationship. Tears started to flow at that point, but she pressed on bravely. When she finished, Carla asked her parents to respond to what she had shared. Both of them expressed surprise that she felt the way she did. But they acknowledged that they had, indeed, often responded to her without considering what she was really feeling, or without listening to what she was really saying. As the session ended, they all hugged and embraced warmly.

The next time Carla and I got together, she seemed to walk a bit taller. "It hasn't all been as smooth as when we were hugging," she laughed, "but it's really gone quite well. Mom was a little hurt, I think, but she worked hard at receiving everything the right way. Dad seemed almost relieved. It's like some invisible barrier was broken, like I gave him permission to relate to me."

Carla's story illustrates an important point: we need to think seriously, before we confront someone, about what we really hope to accomplish. Confrontation has to do with *expectations*. Though it sounds callous to say it, confrontation works best when we expect little or nothing to happen as a result. We must be sure we are willing to face such responses as:

- Denial ("I never did any such thing!")
- Countercharge ("But you begged, seduced, drove me.")
- Minimizing ("You're really making too much of this.")
- Ambiguity ("Are you sure? I don't remember anything quite like that.")

One reason it's important to be clear about expectations is that sometimes the response to a confrontation is exactly what we feared it would be.

Though it sounds callous to say it,
confrontation works best when we expect little
or nothing to happen as a result.

THE MAN WHO WASN'T IMAGINING THINGS

Donald felt like the "lost child" in his family. No one took him seriously, especially his brother and his father. Sometimes his dad would put him down, and other times he wouldn't even pay that much attention to him—he just treated Donald as though he didn't exist. Donald remembers trying to talk to his mother about the situation. "It's your problem," she said simply. "You'll have to work it out with them."

When Donald came to the clinic and learned about Family Day, he was both interested and afraid. Part of him wanted to get his difficulties with his family out in the open, and part of him dreaded what might happen if he did. We urged him to take his time before deciding on a course of action. After observing a few Family Days, he decided to invite his own family to the next session. He and Jim Masteller worked all week preparing what he might say and how to say it.

Family Day arrived, and so did Donald's family. Some other patients shared openly with their families, and the effects were good. Encouraged by this, Donald took a deep breath and shared what was on his heart, that he felt abandoned when his dad and brother "ganged up on him" and his mother left him to deal with the problem alone.

277

The response? Donald's father laughed and dismissed Donald's story as ridiculous. His brother immediately chimed in and agreed with Dad. They both sat back as if nothing had happened.

Even Jim—who is a veteran of many such situations—was stunned by what he saw. After what seemed like a "forever silence," Jim commented to the father and brother that it seemed to him they had just done the very thing Donald had described. The other patients and families in the room nodded; they had just seen what Donald had been talking about.

A rather animated discussion ensued. Both Donald's father and brother stoutly refused to acknowledge any problem with what had just occurred. During the whole time, Donald's mother sat off to one side, in total silence. When Jim asked her a question, trying to help her enter the discussion, she just shrugged her shoulders and then started to cry. Finally Jim went on to another family.

Donald was an emotional wreck after the session. Later that day, in a follow-up group, Donald told everyone he thought he must be crazy. He said that his perceptions were completely off. Nothing of what he was feeling was true.

The group rallied to his support. "No way!" one man said. "You're not crazy. It's real. We all saw it. It happened just the way you said."

"Then why couldn't *they* see it?" Donald asked. He was encouraged by the group's support, but still bewildered by his family's actions. The group talked about the dynamics of denial. They reaffirmed the point that when we confront, we must be prepared for the possibility that nothing will happen in return. Donald nodded his head sadly, though he eventually noted that at least one thing *did* happen as a result of the confrontation: the others in the group helped him recognize that what he felt was real, and not just his imagination.

THE FATHER WHO CANCELED CHRISTMAS

James' father was pastor of a large denominational church. One Christmas he decided that James—then age nine—had too many toys and clothes, especially by contrast with the many poor people in the southern city where they lived. Without so much as a word with his son beforehand, his father announced from the pulpit one Sunday that James was not going to open any presents that Christmas. Any gifts he received would be taken to the homes of poor children. James' father would deliver them personally.

"A lot of people told me what a wonderful Christian I was," James said. "But the fact was, I still wanted the toys. I never had a choice in the matter."

As an adult, James was having to work through that experience, along with other painful memories of his childhood. "I find myself thinking of all kinds of ways to get even with my father for what he did to me," James said. He had joined a support group because he was so troubled by these thoughts of revenge.

Others in the group shared their own thoughts of "getting even." One man told of schemes he used to devise to ruin his parents financially. Another told of childish fantasies like letting the air out of his mother's tires.

In time, James began to see that vengeful feelings were a normal by-product of the healing process—part of what he had to work through on the road to forgiveness.

When I talk with children who have been molested or physically abused by adults, they often talk about "getting even" someday. These desires may be accompanied by rather shocking fantasies of revenge. That such yearnings appear at early ages only shows how natural the desire for retaliation is in all of us—natural, but not healthy.

Similar sentiments often emerge from adults as they begin

to realize how deeply they have been hurt by others. "I *can't* forgive," they say through clenched teeth. "It's the *principle* of the thing." They may use other expressions:

"He needs to learn a lesson, and I'm the one that's going to teach it to him."

"Everyone's been too easy on her. She needs a good dose of hard reality."

"I just can't let her get away with it. I have a *duty* to stop her."

"Just wait 'til he gets what he deserves."

For such people there can be no forgiveness without punishment. Their attitude seems to reflect a desire for justice, but the appearance of justice is just that: appearance. It is a mask covering a face of spitefulness and rage. As we have seen, genuine forgiveness flows not from vengeance but from love and grace.

How often do we find ourselves saying, "I'll forgive him, but he's got to pay the consequences." Real forgiveness does not add "but" or "however" or any other conditions to itself. Forgiveness says, "I'm through carrying this hurt." Period.

Persuasive arguments have been made against forgiving. Some say that forgiveness is unjust because the wrongdoer should not be let off the hook. Others say that forgiveness is a sign of weakness, not strength. Bernard Shaw called it "a beggar's refuge." I disagree. Vengeance never evens the score. It ties both the injured and injurer to an endless escalator of retaliation. Gandhi was right: if we all live by an "eye for an eye" kind of justice, the whole world will be blind.
—Lewis B. Smedes, *Forgive and Forget: Healing the Hurts We Don't Deserve,* (New York, NY: Harper & Row, 1984) pp. 194, 232, 308.

REVENGE IS SOUR

There are times when it is right to bring wrongdoers to justice, both for their sake and for the sake of others. The story we recounted earlier, of the young woman who had been violated by her priest, was an example of such a time. But with most of the hurts we suffer, the question is not one of legal recourse but simply of dealing with our own unresolved conflict. Just because the law might be able to punish someone doesn't mean that pressing for punishment will be the best thing for us to do.

James, the minister's son, started to work through his childhood pain and his desires for revenge against his father. Months later he said to the others in his group, "Living a happy life is the best way of 'getting even,' isn't it? We can be happy because we can forgive."

The old saying says that "revenge is sweet." But the truth is that revenge has a way of turning sour once we've tasted it. People who have been deeply hurt don't need any more pain—especially not the bitterness that always accompanies a desire for vengeance.

LETTING "BYGONES BE BYGONES"

I want to emphasize that I believe in the importance of reconciliation whenever it is possible and mutually beneficial. But reconciliation doesn't happen in every instance, no matter how much one party may want it.

For one thing, as we have seen, reconciliation requires that both parties be willing participants. That may not happen. You may go to the other person having fully forgiven them, and with the genuine desire to be reconciled—only to have them reject your efforts. We have seen several examples of this dynamic already.

Sometimes efforts at reconciliation are not advisable. In cases of physical, sexual, or other kinds of abuse, it may not be safe to reconcile with the people who have wronged us. Such people may still be dangerous to us, and it may be better to avoid them. Or they may be in such a fragile condition that confronting them with the past might devastate them. There *are* times when it is wisest to let "bygones be bygones," at least as far as confrontation and reconciliation are concerned. However, it is *never* necessary or advisable to bypass the process of forgiveness.

There are times when it is wisest to let "bygones be bygones," at least as far as confrontation and reconciliation are concerned. However, it is never necessary or advisable to bypass the process of forgiveness.

WHEN THE OTHER PERSON IS NO LONGER LIVING

Sometimes, of course, confrontation and reconciliation are not possible because the other person is no longer living. The most common example is when we want to be reconciled to a parent who has died. There may, however, be ways to apply the dynamics of confrontation even in such instances.

- Glen went to his father's grave. There he poured out his heart about the things that had happened between them and how Glen wished things could have been. "I don't know if he could hear me," Glen said. "I guess it doesn't really matter. I was able to say the things I needed to say."
- Maria took a large, framed portrait of her father down from the wall and spoke to it. "I remember gazing in-

tently at every feature of his face," she said, "like I was trying to look into his soul." She did this a number of times over a period of months. Finally she was able to say, "Dad, I forgive you."

- Art went back to his childhood home, a rustic cottage in the woods. He explained to the current owners that he had lived there as a boy and wanted to see the place again. They gave him permission to stroll through the woods. As he walked, he talked to his long-dead parents.
- Felicia wrote a lengthy obituary about her parents. While she recalled the bad treatment she had received, she was also able to reflect on happy memories. That in itself was healing; in her days of pain, she had been able to remember nothing but the hurtful memories.
- Andrea asked a married couple in her church, a couple she knew well and respected deeply, to "sit in" as surrogate parents. Then she talked through with them some of what she had experienced from her real parents.

Does there seem to be an element of make-believe in these techniques? We are not contending that these exercises are the same as actual, concrete, face-to-face confrontation and reconciliation. But they *do* help bring to bear some of the same dynamics in a way that helps advance the process of forgiveness.

Our main need may not be to confront our parents as they are now, but to confront them as they were then.

Besides, in many cases what people really need to deal with is not so much their literal, flesh-and-blood, present-day parents, as it is the *memory picture* of our parents *as they once were*. Most of us carry around within us such a memory picture of those who hurt us. It may be that those people have changed in the intervening years—that the people who hurt us, in a sense, no longer exist. Our main need, in such a case, may not be to confront our parents *as they are now*, but to confront them *as they were then*. The kinds of exercises described above can be excellent tools for doing that.

THE GIRL WHO FOUND PEACE

When confrontation and other efforts at reconciliation are thoughtfully planned, and our attitudes and expectations are properly adjusted, such efforts can be a great help to the healing process.

Back in Chapter 1, we met Lydia, who had been molested by her stepfather with the full knowledge of her mother. She and her therapist decided it would be important for her to confront her parents with the truth about what had happened and how it had affected her.

Lydia spent several days writing out what she wanted to say and going over it with her therapist. She rehearsed it in her support group. Other members of the group even played the parts of her parents, giving Lydia a chance to practice handling different kinds of responses. When the day came, Lydia handled her part perfectly. She didn't get into blaming. She didn't lose control and get angry. She just told her parents, calmly and objectively, what she wanted them to know.

Neither parent responded. They just sat there and denied everything Lydia had said. They were quite pleasant and polite about it, but completely unyielding in their denial. When Lydia's therapist tried to talk to them about how they were responding, they shut that out as well.

But Lydia was prepared. She had gone into the session knowing they might deny everything. When it was over, she told the others in her group that she felt relieved, as if a tremendous weight had been lifted from her shoulders. "It was like I set the truth on the table and they were free to do whatever they wanted with it," she said. "If they wanted to ignore it, that was their business. But at least I wasn't lugging it around by myself anymore."

Lydia's story shows how we can be at peace even when reconciliation isn't possible. Lydia was at peace. She felt the need to test and see if reconciliation might be possible. When it turned out not to be, she wasn't thrown off. She knew that forgiveness was separate from reconciliation. And she knew that whether or not she ever reconciled with her parents, she *had* forgiven them. She had done everything that was in her power to do. She was released from the burden of the past.

Those of us who have worked through the process of forgiveness have the deep satisfaction of knowing that we can survive injury—and not only survive, but flourish. No matter how deep the wound, no matter how bitter the pain, once we forgive, we are no longer victims or mere survivors. We are victors! We have fought through to the ultimate triumph. We have learned to love.

12

*You and your parents may have been
"partners in crime" in perpetuating
harmful family dynamics.
You need to accept responsibility
for the ways you may have contributed
to your own pain—and then learn
to forgive yourself and go on.*

Forgiving My Parents, Forgiving Myself

"I DON'T THINK I'VE EVER met anyone who hated their parents," a colleague once said to me, "who didn't also hate themselves."

I think he was right. Our sense of self is derived so strongly from our parents that what we think about them, is inevitably going to shape what we think about ourselves. If we hate our parents, it is likely we will struggle with some degree of self-hatred. If we love our parents, it is likely we will feel better about ourselves.

Then it stands to reason that if we find ourselves needing to *forgive* our parents—and as adult children of dysfunctional families we do, almost by definition—we will also find that we need to forgive ourselves.

"HONOR THY FATHER...."

All of us recognize that there is no such thing as a perfect parent. All of us are descended from imperfect parents, and grew up in imperfect families. But to acknowledge this as an intellectual proposition is one thing. To actually admit that our parents have failed us is, for some of us, a very hard thing to do.

It may even seem like a *wrong* thing to do. Doesn't the Bible teach that we are supposed to honor our father and mother? (Exodus 20:12). Indeed we are. But what does it mean to *honor* our parents? Does it mean we should never acknowledge their weaknesses, limitations, and mistakes? Does it mean we should never acknowledge the pain they may have caused us? I don't think so.

To admit that our parents have failed us is,
for some of us, a very hard thing to do.

The original Hebrew word used in the passage literally means "assign weight to." It is as though someone told us something and we replied, "I want to carefully *weigh* what you've said." If we consider their words and decide that they are important, we are, in a sense "assigning weight" to them. Thus to "honor" our parents means to assign weight—value, importance, significance—to them.

When that original Hebrew word was translated into Greek for the New Testament, the Greek word had to do with "giving glory to" the thing being honored. Both the Greek and the Hebrew carried the sense of honoring people *because of the position they held*, not necessarily because of intrinsic value.

One way to understand this is to imagine that you are in a banquet hall. Part way through the banquet, your city mayor walks in. Now, let's suppose that you are not particularly fond of this mayor. You didn't vote for him in the last election, and you think he has made some bad decisions. Even so, when he walks into the room, you stand up along with everyone else to greet him.

Why? Because he is the mayor, and honoring him is the appropriate thing to do. You assign a certain value, or "weight," to him because of the position he holds. This does not mean you now have to start liking him, or even respecting him, as a person. It does not mean you have to start pretending that you agree with everything he has done as mayor. The honor is accorded to the position he holds, not so much to the individual.

In the same way, we can honor our parents—accord them an appropriate degree of "weight"—because of the position they hold in our lives as our parents. Similar to our example with the mayor, the fact that we honor them does not mean we have to pretend that they have never done anything wrong or hurtful to us.

It is *healthy*, not dishonoring, to acknowledge that our parents failed us, hurt us, damaged us in some way—especially if we are doing so *for the sake of forgiving them*. We do neither our parents nor ourselves any honor by denying reality, eliminating the possibility of forgiveness, and locking ourselves into dysfunctional patterns of thinking and acting.

DENYING THE PAST

There are a number of common ways in which we try to protect ourselves from truth about our past.

Denying Our Past

1. We deny that any injury ever occurred.
2. We make excuses for our parents.
3. We put the blame on ourselves.
4. We grant superficial forgiveness.
5. We attack those who suggest that we need to forgive.

---

1. We deny that any injury ever occurred. We often talk to people who are unable to remember anything about their early years. In many cases, this is a strong indication of childhood trauma. Without consciously realizing it, we substitute an idealized picture for the unpleasant reality.

We have a strong instinct to protect our parents (and often, other authority figures as well). We believe it is wrong to be angry with them, or to have any feelings toward them other than total love and devotion.

Some people honestly believe that if they are angry with their parents, something bad will happen to them. A woman named Shirley said to me, "I don't expect to live to old age." When I asked her why, she pointed to the biblical commandment about honoring parents, "that it may go well with you and that you may enjoy long life on the earth."

We have a strong instinct to protect our parents.
We believe it is wrong to be angry with them,
or to have any feelings toward them
other than total love and devotion.

"I gave my parents a lot of trouble," she said, "so I guess I'll have to pay the consequences." I had to point out to her that this is an exhortation given to an entire people, and has to do with societal welfare—not with punishment visited upon individuals.

2. We make excuses for our parents. We say things like, "Well, yes, my dad beat me a lot. But my folks were having financial troubles at the time." Or, "My parents never showed me affection—I don't remember them ever even hugging me. But they were doing the best they could under the circumstances."

3. We put the blame on ourselves. "I had a lot of bad times growing up. But I deserved everything I got. If I had been more thoughtful (or more helpful, or more obedient, or whatever), my parents wouldn't have had to treat me the way they did."

4. We grant superficial forgiveness. "Whatever they did to me, I forgive them." Or, "Sure, they made mistakes, just like everybody else. I don't hold anything against them."

5. We attack those who suggest that we need to forgive. "How could you even think such a thing?"

The traumatic memories of growing up in a dysfunctional family are not easy to live with. Before forgiveness can happen, however, we need to acknowledge and accept as much of the pain as we can. We need to feel the hurt, just as we felt it in childhood, in order to let it go. When we have progressed to the place where we can see our parents objectively, we can begin the forgiving process. Along the way, we will also see more clearly the ways *we* have failed. Then we must also begin the process of forgiving ourselves.

The traumatic memories of growing up
in a dysfunctional family are not easy to live with.
But before forgiveness can happen, we need to
acknowledge and accept as much of the pain as we can.

SHEDDING ILLUSIONS

Gaining freedom from the effects of growing up in a dysfunctional family is a learning process. We learn to accept ourselves, even with our limitations and vulnerabilities. We learn that life in this world entails the possibility of injury for all of us.

We also learn that some of our long-protected illusions about ourselves and others must change. Childhood expectations and idealizations of the way people should behave may wind up influencing us long into adulthood, with harmful results.

For example, it is a common childhood expectation that all families are happy: mom cheerfully takes care of the kids' every need; dad goes off to work each morning with a smile on his face, and returns each night for dinner; the family schedules all kinds of fun outings for the weekends; everyone is happy and fulfilled all the time. That picture of "normal" family life is reinforced in dozens of ways: in the storybooks we read in school, in the shows we watched on television, and so on.

As we grow older, we recognize that this rosy picture is an idealization, not the norm. We recognize that few—if any—families really look or act this way. We recognize that our own family does not look or act this way.

Or do we? In some cases, it is more accurate to say that part of us recognizes and accepts the unreality of this picture. But another part of us clings to it desperately, still believing it to be true, and ever more conscious of the ways in which our own situation falls short.

Once they are dead, we want our parents to be sheer light, with no darkness at all; and we feel a little foul if we allow shadows to darken our memory. We don't want them to need forgiving; because if we forgive them, we must have found fault with them first, maybe even hated them.

—Lewis B. Smedes, *Forgive and Forget:*
Healing the Hurts We Don't Deserve,
(New York, NY: Harper & Row, 1984)

In working through the process of forgiveness, we need to figure out how our own expectations may have set the stage for our being hurt. Part of maturity is accepting responsibility for our own outlook on life and relationships. If others have hurt us by failing to live up to our expectations, then one of the things we need to do is to examine whether those expectations may have been inappropriate and unrealistic.

If others have hurt us by failing to live up to our expectations, then one of the things we need to do is to examine whether those expectations may have been inappropriate and unrealistic.

If so, forgiveness for us will need to involve repentance (a fundamental change of our own minds and hearts about what we should rightly expect from others) as well as our working through our pain. The pain of unmet expectations is still very real, and still needs to be dealt with, even if those expectations *were* unrealistic.

THE MAN WHO WASN'T WORTH FORGIVING

Stephen had been physically abused by his father. His younger brother, the family favorite, was never punished and had always been allowed to do as he pleased. Stephen, understandably, needed to work through his feelings of anger toward his father. But he also found himself struggling with self-hatred and resentful feelings toward his brother, even though he knew it was not his brother's fault that he had been the favorite or that Stephen had been the whipping boy. Yet Stephen grew up believing that somehow he *deserved* punishment, while his brother deserved to be treated well.

Stephen was talking through his feelings with his pastor. At one point Stephen cried out, "My father loved my brother, and he hated me!"

His pastor asked in return, "Do you think you deserved your mistreatment?"

"That's how I feel," Stephen answered. He went on to catalog a number of ways in which he had let his father down.

"And you can forgive your father, but you can't forgive yourself because of your failures. Is that it?" the pastor questioned.

"I just keep thinking I'm not *worth* forgiving," Stephen replied. "I know things about myself that other people don't know."

The pastor sat quietly for a moment, thinking. Then he said, "Let's try something. I want you to imagine that you're another person, a different person, sitting in that chair over there, talking to 'Stephen.' Do you understand?"

"Yes."

"Now then, let's say 'Stephen' has offended you. Will you decide to forgive him?"

"Well... sure. Of course."

"Even if he doesn't ask you to forgive him?"

Stephen nodded.

"Why?" the pastor asked.

Stephen thought for a moment. "Whether he asks or not isn't the issue. The issue is whether or not I'm willing to forgive."

"Exactly!" the pastor exclaimed. "Now, think about it for a minute. You say you're willing to be compassionate and forgiving toward 'Stephen' for hurting you. But the fact of the matter is, 'Stephen' is *you*. You have been offended by *yourself*. Now you need to be willing to *forgive* yourself. Do you understand?"

Stephen took a long time to think before he responded. "I

never thought of it that way," he finally said. "But I see what you mean. Forgiving myself isn't really any different than forgiving anyone else. Even if I've done things wrong, even if I've caused myself a great deal of pain, I can still forgive myself. I don't need to go around blaming myself, being angry at myself, all the time. Right?"

Right!

> How unhappy is he who cannot forgive himself.
> —Publilius Syrus

THE MOST DIFFICULT PERSON TO FORGIVE

Freedom from the wounds of the past begins when we acknowledge to ourselves that others are in some way responsible for the hurt we have experienced. But we cannot stop there. We also need to face and forgive *ourselves.*

For many of us, the most difficult person to forgive is ourself. As hard as forgiveness is to learn, most of us have a much easier time learning to forgive others than we do learning to forgive ourselves. We are capable of feeling far more compassion toward others than toward ourselves.

If we have been raised in a dysfunctional home that encouraged blaming ourselves for anything bad that happened, it will be especially difficult to forgive ourselves. How many of us harbor such thoughts as the following deep inside us?

"Somehow I allowed all this to happen."

"I deserve this pain."

"It's all my fault."

"I could have stopped it from happening, but I didn't."

It is bad enough when self-blaming thoughts like these are untrue—when we are *not* really to blame but saddle ourselves with guilt anyway. But what about when they *are* true? What about when we *have* done wrong, when we *have* helped bring about our own suffering—and we know it?

Most of us have a much easier time learning to forgive others than we do learning to forgive ourselves. We are capable of feeling far more compassion toward others than toward ourselves.

We need to learn to accept ourselves, with all our limitations, failings, and vulnerabilities, just as we learn to accept others. Indeed, we need to learn how to work through the process of forgiveness with ourselves, just as we have learned to do it toward others.

Let's review briefly the process of forgiveness as we outlined it in Chapter 6—except this time, instead of looking at it in terms of forgiving someone else, let's look at it in terms of forgiving ourselves.

Forgiving Ourselves

1. Recognize the injury.
2. Identify the emotions involved.
3. Express the feelings.
4. Set boundaries to protect yourself.
5. Cancel the debt.

---

1. Recognize the injury. We need to answer the same kinds of questions we answered before. What happened? What role did I play in it? What did I do that was mistaken or wrong? We talked before about making up a list of "sins done to me." Here we are making a list of "sins done to me *by* me."

Again, the aim is not to heap scorn on ourselves, or to blame ourselves—we have done enough of that already! The aim is simply to get clear on what happened so that we can deal with it cleanly.

In taking this step, we need to be especially careful to take responsibility only for those things that *are* our responsibility. Adult children of dysfunctional families typically feel that everything that goes wrong in life is somehow their fault. But we can rightfully accept responsibility only for what we actually did. We cannot accept responsibility for what we could not have done, could not foresee, or could not have known about. We are responsible only for those things that are under our control, not for the entire world.

> That which we can excuse we need not forgive; only that which we cannot excuse is in need of forgiveness.
> —Dan Hamilton, *Forgiveness*, (Downers
> Grove, IL: Intervarsity Press, 1980) p. 145.

In other words, we may at times need to *excuse* ourselves rather than *forgive* ourselves. To excuse ourselves is simply to say, "Yes, I made a mistake there. But it wasn't my fault. There's no way I could have known to do it any differently." Or, "Yes, something did indeed go wrong there. But I didn't do it. Just because my parents always blamed me for everything doesn't mean that everything was actually my fault."

Once we have sorted out what actually happened, and what we ourselves actually did that was wrong, we are ready to take the next step.

2. Identify the emotions involved. As we clarify the ways we have been injured, a familiar set of emotions will rise to the surface. Earlier we identified them as fear, guilt, shame, and anger.

When we are looking into injuries we have inflicted upon ourselves, the predominant ones will probably be anger and shame. Self-directed anger and shame are often prime causes of depression.

3. Express the feelings. We need some way to get the poison of these negative emotions out of our systems. The same techniques we discussed before will work here:

- Talk it out with a friend.
- Write out what happened and how it felt in a journal.
- "Talk to yourself" about it, much as the pastor encouraged Stephen to do.

4. Set boundaries to protect yourself. Previously we talked about taking steps to protect ourselves from others. Now we must consider protecting ourselves from ourselves.

Many times our negative feelings about ourselves will prompt us to engage in self-destructive behavior:

- We overeat.
- We starve ourselves and become anorexic or bulimic.
- We abuse alcohol or drugs (including prescription drugs).
- We overdo our exercise program, staying at it until we're ready to collapse.
- We engage in unhealthy, illicit, or dangerous sexual behavior.
- We become antagonistic toward others, "hard to live with" or work with, in ways that trigger antagonistic responses in people around us. The onset of such destructive behaviors can alert us that there is a need for self-examination and self-forgiveness.

In addition, these behaviors themselves *cause* us injury and, as a result, further self-loathing. Thus, dealing with them is doubly important not only because of the direct damage they cause, but also because of the impact they have on our emotional health.

5. Cancel the debt. The emotional IOUs we hold against ourself are every bit as real—and every bit as damaging—as those we hold against others. We deal with them in precisely the same way—by canceling the debt.

Often, it can be helpful to have the act of forgiveness take some concrete, tangible form such as writing out a "bill of particulars" and then marking it "canceled," burning or burying it, etc.

The emotional IOUs we hold against ourself are every bit as real—and every bit as damaging— as those we hold against others.

WHY SELF-FORGIVENESS IS SO HARD

When we first talked about this process, we said that the forgiveness we show to others comes from the forgiveness God has shown to us; *our forgiveness flows from our forgiven-ness.* Nowhere is this more true than in forgiving ourselves.

No matter how grievously we may have injured ourselves, Jesus' death on the cross freed us. The grace of God is *always* sufficient. His forgiveness is *always* adequate. No matter how unloved or worthless we may feel, God loves us. Our feelings about ourselves do not change God's love for us. He gave each of us infinite worth and value by creating us, and by sending his son to die for us. If God himself is able to forgive us, how can we withhold forgiveness from ourselves? Because we have been forgiven, our obligation is to forgive those who do wrong to us, without exception—this includes ourselves.

One of the main reasons why we have difficulty with the notion of "forgiving ourselves" is simply that we have never seen forgiveness demonstrated. As with so many things in life, it is a great help to have seen forgiveness modeled by others if we are to understand and practice it ourselves. Adult children from dysfunctional families typically grew up in environments where forgiveness is not modeled.

If God himself is able to forgive us,
how can we withhold forgiveness from ourselves?

"No matter how hard I tried," Ralph told me, "nothing I ever did was good enough for my dad. Even when I told him how sorry I was and that I'd try harder next time, do you know what he said to me? He'd say, 'Do it right *this* time.' I never knew what it was like to have a mistake or a weakness *tolerated*, let alone accepted or forgiven."

"In our home, love was a manipulation device," recalls Allison. She came from a home where both parents were alcoholics. "When my mother said, 'I love you,' it only meant that she wanted something. She said it with a smile on her face, but she didn't really mean it. Even when she said something that sounded like she was forgiving me for making a mistake, I couldn't believe her. I knew she was just doing it to try to get something from me."

It's no wonder that people like Ralph and Allison find the notion of forgiveness hard to grasp—whether it is forgiveness of others or even more, forgiveness of self.

SELF-FORGIVENESS FOR ABUSE VICTIMS

Those who come from a background of physical abuse (and especially sexual abuse) often have to struggle with the belief that something is inherently wrong with them. They think that something about their very being made the bad things happen to them. They *deserved* the wounds they received. They see themselves as unworthy, unlovable, and unforgivable.

The fact that they came from a home where secrecy was so prevalent makes them feel even worse about themselves. "Don't talk" is always a cardinal rule in abusive homes. I have talked with women who actually hate their own bodies for causing their fathers (or uncles or brothers) to desire them. "I must have been inviting it somehow, or they wouldn't have kept doing it" is a familiar sentiment. They even blame themselves for the fact that no one protected or assisted them.

Often, incest victims experience a certain measure of physical pleasure even amid the emotional pain of being violated. This only intensifies their shame. If it "felt good," doesn't that prove that they secretly "wanted it to happen"? One of the things we work hard to teach incest survivors is that the body can respond to sexual stimuli even without the person's consent. Still, this apparent betrayal by their own bodies can be one of the hardest things for them to forgive—especially when it is compounded by the ingrained belief that if they tell anyone what happened, they will only receive more blame and condemnation.

For all those who have been victims or have suffered the pain of growing up in a dysfunctional family, one of the most important truths of life is summed up in this saying of Jesus: "'Love the Lord your God with all your heart and with all your soul and with all your mind.' This is the first and greatest commandment. And the second is like it: 'Love your neighbor as yourself.'" (Matthew 22:37-39).

Most of us are well aware that the Bible commands us to love God and to love our neighbor. But I want you to notice two little words in this passage. Jesus says, "Love your neighbor *as yourself.*"

Many people struggle with the idea that we are supposed to "love ourselves." It sounds so selfish. Actually, Jesus does not so much teach that we *should* love ourselves as he *assumes* that we *do* love ourselves. And why not? Are we not created in the very image and likeness of God? Is our welfare not of such importance to God that "even the hairs on our heads are all numbered?" Should we not love the things God loves, including ourselves?

We are not talking here about the kind of "self-love" that expresses itself in self-glorification, narcissism, despising others, and so on. Rather, we are talking about a self-love that acknowledges our worth and dignity as one of God's sons or daughters and acts accordingly. We have already seen that our duty to love our neighbors includes forgiving them when they do us wrong. Should we not likewise be able to forgive ourselves?

STOPPING THE ABUSE

If you are a man or woman who grew up in a dysfunctional family, and you are trying to break free from the wounds of your past by forgiving your parents and others, recognize that you will also need to work through the process of forgiveness with yourself. As you do, think about these statements:

- If I continue to accept blame, *the abuse is continuing.*
- If I accept guilt for what happened even when I was a helpless child, *the abuse is continuing.*

- If I continue to accept pain, guilt, and shame just because that's what I've always done, *the abuse is continuing.*
- If I refuse to be compassionate, loving, and forgiving toward myself, *the abuse is continuing.*

Why not put a stop to the abuse—to all of it—right now? Release yourself from the unhealthy burden of guilt you have placed upon yourself, even for such things as your depression, your withdrawal, your self-doubt, and your lack of trust. As you work through the process of forgiving yourself, looking back on times when you let yourself down, you might find it helpful to bear in mind this statement:

*I did the best I could
with the maturity, knowledge, and wisdom I had.
Now,
with more maturity, knowledge, and wisdom,
I can do better.*

Forgiveness is another way of saying, "I'm human. I make mistakes. I want to be granted that privilege, and so I grant you that privilege."
—Philip Yancey, "An Unnatural Act,"
Christianity Today, (April 8, 1991) p. 39.

Self-forgiveness is not a matter of assigning blame to someone else and letting yourself off the hook; it is not a license for irresponsibility. It is simply an acknowledgment that you are a human being like everybody else. It can be a celebration of survival, and of the fact that you've reached the stage where you are able to give yourself greater respect.

An interesting thing often happens when we work through

the process of forgiving ourselves. We find that for the first time we are able to say some important things to ourselves without feeling guilty or ashamed:

- I was, and still am, imperfect.
- I had, and still have, angry feelings.
- I held, and still hold, some unrealistic expectations.
- I have failed, and still fail, to live up to what I know is right.

We can comfortably say these things because we have also said, and believed, this:

- For all these things—and many more besides—*I forgive myself.* I forgive myself because God has already forgiven me. And with his help, I'm going to do better in the future.

Forgiveness and the Twelve Steps

FOR MORE THAN FIFTY YEARS—and especially in the last twenty years—millions of people have found help for problems relating to dependency and dysfunction through the programs based on the Twelve Steps of Alcoholics Anonymous. While originally written for those addicted to alcohol, the Twelve Steps have been modified for application to a wide range of problems, such as drug addiction, sex addiction, overeating, compulsive gambling, codependency relationships with addicted spouses, and—yes—adult children of dysfunctional families.

Although everything in this book is entirely compatible with a Twelve-Step approach to recovery, we have not specifically focused on the Twelve Steps. For the many readers who are familiar with this approach to recovery, however, it is worth considering the problems of adult children of dysfunctional families in the light of the Twelve Steps.

The Twelve Steps of Alcoholics Anonymous[1]

1. We admitted we were powerless over alcohol—that our lives had become unmanageable.
2. Came to believe that a power greater than ourselves could restore us to sanity.

3. Made a decision to turn our will and our lives over to the care of God *as we understood him.*

4. Made a searching and fearless moral inventory of ourselves.

5. Admitted to God, to ourselves, and to another human being the exact nature of our wrongs.

6. Were entirely ready to have God remove all these defects of character.

7. Humbly asked him to remove our shortcomings.

8. Made a list of all persons we had harmed, and became willing to make amends to them all.

9. Made direct amends to such people wherever possible, except when to do so would injure them or others.

10. Continued to take personal inventory and when we were wrong promptly admitted it.

11. Sought through prayer and meditation to improve our conscious contact with God *as we understood him,* praying only for knowledge of his will for us and for the power to carry that out.

12. Having had a spiritual awakening as a result of these steps, we tried to carry this message to other alcoholics, and to practice these principles in all our affairs.

In the most basic sense, the challenges of recovering from a dysfunctional family background are quite different from those of recovering from alcoholism. However, there are important similarities, especially those dealing with issues of blame, responsibility, and forgiveness, that make the use of the Twelve Steps effective in both realms.

Those addicted to alcohol and drugs typically start off blaming others for their troubles. They feel their problems are the fault of everyone but themselves. But these people also tend to be very self-condemning. They need to learn to take responsibility for their own lives, to forgive others—but also to forgive themselves.

Adult children from dysfunctional families, as we have seen, tend to start from the other end of the spectrum. They blame themselves for everything. As they come to grips with the realities of their past and discover ways in which they have been victimized, they can become quite bitter toward others. They need to learn to assign responsibility accurately for their problems, to forgive others, and also to forgive themselves. Thus the recovery needs of the two groups end up being quite similar, at least in certain respects.

Let's take a look at the Twelve Steps and see how they relate to those of us who were raised in dysfunctional homes.

1. We admitted we were powerless over our dependencies—that our lives had become unmanageable.

There is no question about it. As children of dysfunctional families, we were powerless indeed. This becomes evident as we work through the exercises in Part One of this book, where we looked at our families and how they operated. Those of us brought up in highly dysfunctional families have lived with craziness, both in our families and in ourselves. We have believed lies and myths, have helped maintain unhealthy secrets, and have lived as if all of it were normal.

We are powerless. What happened to us is all in the past, out of reach. We have no power to change the past. Yet many of us spend a lifetime trying to do precisely that. We think that if we act a certain way, the past will be magically resolved. We must accept that we are powerless. Our injuries are there—there is nothing we can do to change that fact.

Many of us talk of wanting to make certain that the sins of the past do not recur in our present families. We work like crazy to do things differently. Yet the harder we try, the more we seem to *repeat* the past—if not in precisely the same way, at least in very similar ways.

Recovery from wounds of the past always begins with accepting that we are *powerless* over the past.

2. Came to believe that a power greater than ourselves could restore us to sanity.

There is a subtle but important truth here. The power we believe in is "greater than ourselves," which means it must be *outside* ourselves. Many of us have become frustrated, trying to tap into a power *within* ourselves. We do not realize that any power that comes from within ourselves can be nothing more than an extension of ourselves, with all our evident weaknesses and limitations. The only power that can restore us to sanity is one that is greater than—and therefore outside of—ourselves.

When we ignore this reality and try to attain recovery in our own strength, we end up frustrated, depressed, guilt-ridden, and ashamed. It is the very futility that fuels our craziness and removes sanity ever further from our grasp.

3. Made a decision to turn our will and our lives over to the care of God *as we understood him.*

We begin to see how logical it is to turn our lives over to God. After all, we are dealing with issues of the past, and only God has the ability to deal with them.

Turning our will and our lives over to God is foreign to us. As adult children of dysfunctional families, our creed has always been, "I can do it myself—I always have, and I must continue to do so!" It requires great courage and trust to let go. But we must give to God our past with all its losses and shame, handing over every moment of disgrace, every disappointment, every tear, every dashed hope, every scar.

We turn our lives over to God with the knowledge that he has offered us a relationship with himself through his forgiveness of our failures. We find that God is able to make up for all we have lost. He can rid us of our shame and fill the empty places in our hearts.

From this we learn that resolution of problems rooted in the past can come only through forgiveness. When we make this third step, we begin down the pathway of forgiveness. First we *receive* God's forgiveness. In time, he will ask us to *extend* that forgiveness, both to others and to ourselves.

4. Made a searching and fearless moral inventory of ourselves.

Traditionally, this step has involved cataloging "the sins done *by* me," in recognition of the tendency of alcoholics and addicts to blame others for their problems. As adult children of dysfunctional families, we also need to own up to our wrong actions.

At the same time, we must recognize that, by and large, we have been out of balance in the opposite direction. Having been emotionally, sexually, or physically abused, or having been abandoned (or smothered) by family, we have spent years trying to figure out what *we* did to bring our pain upon ourselves.

For us, as for all those in recovery, it is important to make an inventory of the sins we have committed. But it is just as important to make an inventory of the sins done *to* us, the ways in which we have been victimized. We will need both inventories as we begin the process of forgiving others and ourselves.

5. Admitted to God, to ourselves, and to another human being the exact nature of our wrongs.

Again, we must confess both the wrongs we have done *and* the wrongs that have been done to us.

First, we must confess to God. Then we must take a step that for many of us is far more difficult: we must admit to *ourselves* the truth of our inventories. For years, we have lived in denial. Many of us have idealized our families of origin. It is hard for us to face the truth, but it is essential to our recovery and our healing.

Second, we must take further action by confessing the truth to another person. So much of what wholeness is about (both in the Bible and in psychology) has to do with the principle of openness toward others. Not because they can do anything to change our situations, but because confession to another person makes real and concrete our rejection of the myths and lies that have held us bound. It reinforces our decision to leave behind the darkness of denial and to live in the light of truth.

We must be careful who we choose for this step. A therapist, a trusted friend, a minister or priest—any of these might be a good choice. A sibling who is walking alongside us in the same process of discovery and healing may also be appropriate.

6. Were entirely ready to have God remove all these defects of character.

It is our *basic willingness* that matters here, not the perfection of our inventories or the absolute purity of our intentions. Many of us worry whether we are "entirely" ready—our very desire to "do it right" stops us from doing it at all! Others of us (concerned that we must unearth every last detail of our past) set off on impossible "archaeological digs" through our childhood years, trying to specify *every* injury, *every* wound, no matter how minute.

This is a dead end. What matters is that we understand our brokenness and hunger for wholeness. When we know enough about our past to throw ourselves wholeheartedly into a quest for recovery through forgiveness, we know enough to take this step.

Again, a subtle adjustment in interpretation is in order. We must indeed be ready to sacrifice our own defects of character. But we must also be ready to forgive the defects of those who have harmed us.

Even in this, however, the focus is on ourselves. Our goal is not to *change* others, but to *accept* and *forgive* them. This is something that happens in *us*. Nothing in our working of the Twelve Steps will make any change in any other person. But the changes that can occur in us will make all the difference in the world.

7. Humbly asked him to remove our shortcomings.

Asking for anything can be a very difficult task for adult children of dysfunctional families. We may have grown up in situations where we were refused whatever we asked for or even punished for asking in the first place. This experience may have caused us to wall ourselves off from others, to seek a self-sufficiency that will prevent us from being hurt or disappointed again.

Now, however, we must learn to ask. We give up our willfulness and our need to control. We allow God to begin working the changes in our lives that we have been unable to produce in our own strength. We ask him to remove not only our short*comings* but also what might be called our short*fallings*—the gaps in our development that are the result of our family's dysfunction.

8. Made a list of all persons we had harmed, and became willing to make amends to them all.

Again, this step will cut in two directions for us. We must first work through the step as written: taking responsibility for the wrong things we have done, working through the process of repentance, and taking responsibility for the consequences of our actions.

But we must also understand this step in another sense. We might restate it to read, "Made a list of all persons who had harmed us, and became willing to make peace with them all." In all cases, this willingness to make peace involves forgiving them, canceling the debt we hold against them. Whenever possible, it also involves seeking to be reconciled with them—bearing in mind that reconciliation is separate from forgiveness, and not under our control.

9. Made direct amends to such people wherever possible, except when to do so would injure them or others.

Here it is important to note that we must be careful not to add further injury to those who have hurt us. Our instincts may prompt us to confront those against whom we hold a grievance, without considering the consequences. But such behavior only makes our own pain worse.

We must come to see forgiveness as a process that takes time, so that we can patiently weigh each step and consider prayerfully how we ought to proceed. It is especially important at this point to have one or more "counselors" with whom we can discuss our plans.

We must also learn to discern our motives. Many times confrontation is motivated by a desire for vengeance, a desire to "get even." We must always bear in mind that forgiveness, not revenge, is our aim.

10. Continued to take personal inventory and when we were wrong promptly admitted it.

How many times a day do we stop to check our appearance? To see that our face is clean, our hair in place, our clothes neat? How natural it is, then, that our recovery—our growth toward wholeness—involve a regular check-up on ourselves.

Our check-up has two facets. First, we check to see that we are taking appropriate responsibility for our own behavior. Second, we check to see that our boundaries are intact—that we are not allowing harmful people or patterns to creep back into our lives in ways we have come to see as dangerous.

Forgiveness is often a process that must be repeated. Even when we have worked through our feelings and forgiven someone who has hurt us, we may find that pain from old wounds starts showing up again, signaling us that fresh forgiveness may be in order.

11. Sought through prayer and meditation to improve our concious contact with God as we understood him, praying only for knowledge of his will for us and for the power to carry that out.

As we work through this process of forgiveness, we are able to move beyond ourselves and our pain, to establishing a stronger, healthier relationship with God. Sometimes, as we are allowing ourselves to acknowledge and accept our pain, it feels as though God has forsaken us. The truth is that he is always walking alongside of us, helping us every step of the way.

One of the joys of forgiving is that we experience a wonderful freedom in our lives. Holding grudges keeps us focused on our pain—on ourselves. Forgiveness frees us to focus on God and on what his plan holds for us.

Recovery is a spiritual process. Our *forgiveness*, as we have seen, always flows from our *forgiven-ness*—from the mercy and grace that God has poured out upon us through his son Jesus. It builds on our relationship with God, as we come to know him better and to walk more squarely in the heart of his plan for our lives.

12. Having had a spiritual awakening as a result of these steps, we tried to carry this message to others, and to practice these principles in all our affairs.

Recovery can seem like a very self-focused exercise. But to be complete, it must focus on others as well. When we have been set free from the burden of a pain-filled past, it is only natural that we would want to share the freedom we have experienced with others. If we have included others in working these steps, it *will* be a natural part of the process to share our joy with others, especially with those who will benefit from walking the same path of forgiveness.

Having experienced forgiveness for our own wrongs and being able to extend forgiveness to others, we become new, free creatures. We move from codependency and dysfunctional behavior into genuine caring and love.

Worksheet for "My Forgiving"

1. Recognize the injury.

Whom do you need to forgive?

How have they hurt or injured you? Describe what happened:

2. Identify the emotions involved.

List some of the feelings you have about what happened:
"I am afraid to look at this because..."

"I feel guilty about…"

"I feel ashamed and humiliated by…"

"I am angry that…"

3. Express your hurt and anger.

If I could say what I wanted to this person (or persons), I would tell them…

4. Set boundaries to protect yourself.

List what you can do to protect yourself, both now and in the future:

Take the time—perhaps even before you fill out the worksheet—to talk with someone you trust about what you have written or will write. Ask them to help you to be thorough in steps 1-3, and realistic in step 4. Take your time before moving onto the next step.

5. Cancel the debt.

When you have released the other person from your own expectations, you are ready to forgive—to cancel the debt. Write down something you can do to symbolize your willingness to forgive.

6. Consider the possibility of reconciliation.

Why do you want reconciliation?

If you approach the other person, what do you think will be their response?

Can you accept the worst possible response?

How can you check to see if the other person (or persons) are open to working through their part of the reconciliation process?

A Guide to Twelve-Step Groups

Twelve-Step program offices are listed below. Most of them are staffed by volunteers who can direct you to local chapters of the national organizations.

Adult Children of Alcoholics
Central Service Board
Box 35623
Los Angeles, CA 90035

Al-Anon/Alateen Family Group Headquarters, Inc.
Box 182
Madison Square Station
New York, NY 10159
(800) 356-9996

Alcoholics Anonymous
Box 459
Grand Central Station
New York, NY 10163
(212) 686-1100

Co-Dependents Anonymous
Box 33577
Phoenix, AZ 85067
(602) 277-7991

Emotions Anonymous
Box 4245
St. Paul, MN 55104
(612) 647-9712

Families Anonymous
Box 528
Van Nuys, CA 91408
(818) 989-7841

Incest Survivors Anonymous
Box 5613
Long Beach, CA 90017

Overcomers Outreach
2290 W. Whittier Blvd.
Suite D
La Habra, CA 90631
(213) 697-3994

Sexaholics Anonymous
Box 300
Simi Valley, CA 93062

N O T E S

TWO
The Family System

1. Lynn Hoffman, *Foundations of Family Therapy* (New York, NY: Basic Books, 1981) p. 31.

THREE
My Family and Me

1. T.F. Fogerty, "Systems Concepts and the Dimensions of Self," in P.J. Guerin, ed., *Family Therapy: Theory and Practice,* (New York, NY: Gardner Press, 1976).
2. Ibid.
3. Based on work done by David H. Olsen, reported in David H. Olsen, Hamilton I. McCubbin and Associates, *Families: What Makes Them Work,* (Newbury Park, CA: Sage Publishing, 1989).
4. Murray Bowen, *The Family Therapy Networker,* (March/April 1991) p. 32.
5. The particular set of categories comes from H. Peter Laqueur, "Multiple Family Therapy," in P.J. Guerin, op. cit.

FOUR
The Sins of the Fathers

1. John and Linda Friel, *Adult Children: The Secrets of Dysfunctional Families,* (Deerfield Beach, FL: Health Communications, Inc., 1988) pp. 57-63.
2. Mel Roman, Ph.D., and Patricia Daley, *The Indelible Family,* (New York, NY: Rawson Associates, 1980) p. 34.
3. Monica McGoldrick and Randy Gerson, *Genograms in Family Assessment,* (New York, NY: W.W. Norton & Co., 1985) p. 6.

NINE
What's Anger Got to Do with It?

1. This formulation is taken from Dr. O. Carl Simonton, M.D., Stephanie Matthews-Simonton, and James L. Creighton, *Getting Well Again,* (New York, NY: Bantam Books, 1978).

TEN

The Blame Game

1. For a more complete discussion of codependency, see the following: Robert Hemfelt, M.D., Frank Minirth, M.D., Paul Meier, M.D., *Love Is a Choice*, (Nashville, TN: Thomas Nelson Publishers, 1989).

AFTERWORD

Forgiveness and the Twelve Steps

1. The Twelve Steps are reprinted with permission of Alcoholics Anonymous World Service, Incorporated. Permission to reprint and adapt the Twelve Steps does not mean that A.A. has reviewed or approved the contents of any publication that reprints the Twelve Steps, nor that A.A. agrees with the views expressed therein. A.A. is a program of recovery from alcoholism. Use of the Twelve Steps in connection with programs which are patterned after A.A. but which address other problems does not imply otherwise.

Study Guide

To GAIN THE FULL BENEFIT from the material contained in this book, it will be important for you to spend some time each day applying the things you have read to your own life and family situation.

If you will work through this study guide, with an openness and sense of discovery, you will find yourself enlightened about the origin of your parents' dysfunction (considering their childhood influences), about the person you present to others, and about the real you—the person who stares back at you from the mirror every day. You cannot change your past, but you can better understand its influences on you. This greater understanding will help you make choices to free you from the effects of the past, to make the most of your future, and to develop healthier family relationships.

CHAPTER ONE

Are you an adult child of a dysfunctional family?

For the purposes of this exercise, your "family" refers to the family in which you grew up. Answer the questions listed below truthfully and to the best of your recollection. Write your answers in a journal or notebook so that you can review them after you have completed the entire study guide.

1. Do the members of your family respect you and treat you like an adult when you are in their presence?
   a. If the answer is "No," who is the person(s) that refuses to give you respect?
   b. Has he or she always dealt with you in this manner?
   c. Why do you think that person cannot accept you as a mature adult?

2. Is there one family member who seems to have control over everyone else?
   a. If so, does this person control by manipulation (convenient weakness or crisis that causes other family members to resume familiar roles) or by intimidation?
   b. How do you react internally to this person's controlling behavior?
   c. How do you react outwardly?
   d. If your outward behavior is different from your true feelings, what makes you react falsely? What are you afraid would happen if you expressed your true feelings?

3. Was it OK for you to express your feelings and opinions as a child?
   a. If not, what did you do with those feelings and opinions?
   b. Are you able to express your feelings and opinions now that you are an adult?

4. How did alcohol or drug abuse impact your childhood?
   a. Who in your immediate family abused alcohol or drugs?
   b. What specific crises arose for you because of the alcohol and drug abuse?
   c. How did you feel in the midst of these situations?

5. Were you or any of your family members mentally, physically, or sexually abused?
   a. Was this abuse kept secret? If so, how did you deal with keeping such a secret?
   b. If you were abused, what have you done to seek help for yourself in resolving these issues and the emotional pain?
   c. If you were a witness to another's abuse, what have you done to deal with that?

6. What childhood memories do you carry that still bother you today?
   a. Do these memories, and any resulting inner turmoil, interfere with your ability to function normally in day-to-day life?
   b. Are you willing to look at those memories if necessary to get free of their negative influence?

7. What impact has growing up in a dysfunctional family had on your life?
   a. What is the negative impact?
   b. What positive impact has it had (as you have sought to overcome your past)?

Are you ready to break free from the bondage of your past?
Are you ready to make a commitment to yourself, your healing, and your future?

If your answer to both of these questions is yes—even a hesitant yes—complete the information on the following personal contract and sign it as your personal commitment. It will take commitment and tenacity to work through issues that may feel threatening or painful. You may want to share this contract with one supportive person who is not a member of your family system. You can then have someone to turn to for support as you make progress.

CONTRACTUAL AGREEMENT FOR PERSONAL HEALING

I _____, do commit myself, this _____ day of _____, in the year _____; that I will give of myself whatever is necessary to achieve the healing I need and deserve. I make the following commitment to myself, depending on God's help, to do all that is within my power to face the truth about my family, work through the unresolved issues from my childhood, and learn to forgive my parents and myself.

1. I will spend _____minutes each day reflecting on the teaching in this book and considering how these teachings apply to my life.
2. I will post a journal entry each day, making a full effort to be open and honest about the feelings that begin to surface. I will record memories that seem pertinent to my healing process.
3. I will work to identify my own areas of dysfunction and to see where these may fit into the pattern of our family system. I will look to identify persons whom I have not yet forgiven, and try to understand how my family relationships may connect with my own dysfunctional habit patterns.
4. I am willing to stop blaming others for the way I live my life, even while acknowledging their influence. I will take full responsibility for my own healing process, with or without the support of my family.
5. I will begin to allow my true feelings to surface, instead of pushing them down, and will note them in my journal as they come to mind.
6. If I find that I cannot work through these issues alone, I will seek the help of a support group or counselor.

Signed _____

Date _____

Witness (optional) _____

Chapter Two

You probably would not invest time reading this book if you didn't have family problems you are looking to solve. You may have tried—over and over again—to resolve these problems without making much headway. One reason may be that you have been taking a cause and effect (linear) approach to a problem that is a "family system" problem, requiring an interactive approach. If so, there's good news: you don't have to try harder! You may just need to take a fresh look at your baffling family problems from a new perspective. Once you see the problem clearly from an interactive view, the solution may follow.

You can learn to take an interactive perspective by analyzing one of your baffling family problems. Once you learn how to look at one problem from this perspective and test these theories to see how they work, you can follow the same approach to deal with other problems.

As you work through these exercises, keep note of your feelings. If you are coming close to uncovering family secrets (even in your own mind) or debunking family myths, you will feel uncomfortable. Take note of these feelings by writing them in a journal or in your notes here. Those feelings are part of your research; they don't mean you should stop, rather, they may signal that you are getting close to the truth.

1. Think of one problem in your family that you would like to better understand and resolve. State briefly what the problem is and how you would like to see it resolved. (The example from the book would be: "Tracy keeps running away. I want to know why she is doing this, and get her to stop.")

   _____

   _____

   _____

   _____

   _____

2. Describe your theory about what is causing the problem taking a linear perspective: Who is doing what; and what is his or her problem (apart from family issues). Using our example from the book you might say,

"Tracy keeps running away. She is rebellious and probably using drugs or running with the wrong crowd." Now write about YOUR problem from a linear perspective:

_____

_____

_____

_____

_____

3. How have you or other family members REACTED to this problem behavior?

_____

_____

_____

_____

_____

4. What positive results have you seen from your reactions that are based on a linear perspective?

_____

_____

_____

_____

_____

5. What have you tried—over and over—to solve the problem that has not worked?

_____

_____

_____

_____

_____

6. Consider the stories of Donna and Fred, or Joey and his parents in this chapter. Can you see any repeating patterns in your family that trouble you? _____ If so, describe the PATTERN of interaction and who is involved in doing the same things over and over?

_____

_____

_____

_____

_____

7. Are you willing to put aside your previous theory about this problem and break the pattern of reactions to consider it in light of the family system? _____ Are you willing to try to apply interactive thinking? _____ If so: Take the same problem you described above and try to describe it in the context of how that person connects with all the other players. Use the following questions to help you do so:

What is going on in family relationships just prior to the problem occurring?

- Is there a lifelong pattern of coping (like Fred's pattern of retreat under stress) that is repeated ?

- When the person (previously identified as having the problem) acts out, what typically happens? Does he or she get more attention, love, sympathy? Does it distract from something else that is going on?

- What do various family members do in reaction to the "problem" behavior?

- Is there a predictable payoff for the person who acts out? For instance, is stress relieved or pain averted or attention diverted from other problems in the family?

Considering all these angles, now describe the same problem in the context of family history and the family system:

_____

_____

_____

_____

_____

8. In Joey's case, how might the payoff fill a legitimate need that is otherwise unmet in healthy ways? For instance: Joey may have been neglected while Mother hurried around the kitchen and Dad ignored him to watch TV (page 58).

_____

_____

_____

_____

_____

9. Consider ways you might address any unmet needs directly or otherwise correct the family interaction to see what happens. What legitimate needs are not fully met that may play into this problem behavior?

_____

_____

_____

_____

_____

10. Sometimes other family members can adapt to meet these needs in legitimate ways. This is not to placate or appease a person for problem behavior; rather it is to accept the problem as a family, consider what may contribute to the problem, and work together to make the acting out unnecessary. How could other family members adapt to help meet unmet needs that may trigger the problem?

_____

_____

_____

_____

_____

11. Linear thinking locks you into few choices in response to problems; interactive thinking opens up a world of possibilities for positive change in your family system. Which has been your primary way of looking at this problem? _____

Are you willing to practice re-thinking every problem within your family as an interactive family problem? _____

How might this help you come up with new possibilities for dealing with problems? _____

FAMILY SECRETS:

12. Picture your extended family seated around a large dinner table. What is it that most everyone knows or certainly suspects that no one would dare mention out loud?

_____
_____
_____
_____
_____

13. What part may you be playing in maintaining the "conspiracy of silence" and why?

_____
_____
_____
_____
_____

14. What would happen if you dared to state the family secrets out in the open? (Who would faint, or have a heart attack, or be ruined, or "just die!" or not be able to bear it?)

_____
_____
_____
_____
_____

15. How has keeping the family secrets impacted your life? How does the fear and shame inhibit your life?

_____
_____
_____
_____
_____

16. What family myths have been created to cover up or compensate for the family secrets?

_____

_____

_____

_____

_____

17. How have they helped and hurt your family?

_____

_____

_____

_____

_____

18. What "family myths" do you still support today?

_____

_____

_____

_____

_____

19. What steps could you take to replace these myths with a healthy acceptance of the truth about your family?

_____

_____

a. How could you accept the truth?

_____

_____

b. How could you acknowledge the truth?

_____

_____

c. How could you express the truth?

_____

_____

20. Jesus Christ said, "You will know the truth and the truth will set you free." How could this apply to your family situation?

_____

_____

_____

_____

_____

1. The following are characteristics of a healthy family. Mark Y=yes S=somewhat or N=no to assess how healthy your family is now. For each one, cite an example to back up your assessment:

Adapts easily to change?
Y ~ S ~ N

_____

Handle problems as a unit?
Y ~ S ~ N

_____

Well defined boundaries?
Y ~ S ~ N

_____

Deal directly with each other?
Y ~ S ~ N

_____

Learn from one another
Y ~ S ~ N

_____

Encourage being individuals?
Y ~ S ~ N

_____

Considerate of other's feelings?
Y ~ S ~ N

_____

Tolerance for differences?
Y ~ S ~ N

_____

Individuals take responsibility
for own lives?
Y ~ S ~ N

_____

Expression of ups and downs OK?
Y ~ S ~ N

_____

All problems seen as family problems?
Y ~ S ~ N

_____

Respect between generations?
Y ~ S ~ N

_____

2. The following are characteristics of a "Rigid" family. Circle C if this is true of your current family, O if it was exhibited in your family of origin, or N/A if it is not applicable in either:

C ~ O ~ N/A Decisions are made quickly and arbitrarily

C ~ O ~ N/A Decisions imposed upon family members

C ~ O ~ N/A Members have a hard time dealing with emotions

C ~ O ~ N/A Expression of feelings–especially "bad" feelings–not allowed

C ~ O ~ N/A Anger typically expressed indirectly and manipulatively

C ~ O ~ N/A Rules are non-negotiable

C ~ O ~ N/A Punishment is swift and stern

3. The following are characteristics of a "Chaotic" family. Circle C if this is true of your current family, O if it was exhibited in your family of origin, or N/A if it is not applicable in either:

C ~ O ~ N/A Family member poorly equipped for problem solving

C ~ O ~ N/A Uncertainty; it takes forever to make a decision

C ~ O ~ N/A Excessive expression of emotions; little restraint

C ~ O ~ N/A Much confusion; it's hard to tell what's happening

C ~ O ~ N/A Children raised erratically

C ~ O ~ N/A Erratic discipline

4. A healthy family allows individual boundaries, while a dysfunctional family does not. The following are symptoms of a lack of healthy boundaries. Check those that characterize your response to life:

___ You find yourself saying "yes" when you want to say no.

___ You frequently become burdened with other people's problems, but resent it later.

___ You tend to take on the feelings of others and find that you are unable to remain objective.

___ You have trouble deciding what you want; opting to do what others want you to do.

If you checked any of the statements above, it may indicate you are tied into a somewhat dysfunctional family system. However, you can learn to develop healthy personal boundaries. Recognizing your need to do so is a step in the right direction!

5. If you had to classify your family as one of the following, which comes closest to describing your family?

ENMESHED: Rigid Boundaries, keeping family members in by controlling each others' lives, and locking "non-members" out.

DISENGAGED: Extreme lack of emotional support or bonding; very little togetherness in the family.

ATTACHED: A healthy balance between enmeshed and disengaged. Members enjoy doing things together but also function well as individuals, apart from the family.

6. The following are descriptions of dysfunctional types; does your family fit any of the following types?

ISOLATED ISLANDS: All members are isolated from one another.

GENERATIONAL SPLITS: Lacks significant interaction between generations.

GENDER SPLITS: Lack of significant emotional interaction across the gender lines.

FUSED PAIR: Two members of the family cut themselves off from the rest of the family.

QUEEN OF THE HILL: This family is openly dominated by one person.

QUIET DICTATOR: One member completely controls the family with subtlety and manipulation. This person will usually refuse to participate in counseling.

FAMILY SCAPEGOAT: One family member accepts blame for anything that goes wrong in the family.

If you recognize dysfunctional family patterns, don't get discouraged. These realizations will help you make wise choices about how to become healthier and encourage you to develop new patterns.

1. Create a genogram of your family, using the instructions found in this chapter (page 99). Go back at least two generations. You may not have all the information you need, but don't let that stop you. Start with what you do know and fill in as you gain more information.

2. After you have created your genogram, use it to answer the following questions:
    - What roles did you play in your family of origin?
    - Do you play the same roles now or have you taken on other familiar roles?
    - Who else played this role before you that you might be patterning yourself after— even unconsciously?
    - What unwritten rules are observed repeatedly in generation after generation?
    - What recurrent patterns do you see (consider those mentioned in the chapter: addiction, deception, codependency, adultery, divorce, desertion, abuse, playing favorites with children, and lying)?

3. Create a family timeline (p.110) describing the "horizontal axis" of your family life. Start with your marriage (or your birth if you are not married), then chart all the various stressful events that have happened to members of your family.

4. Identify anything from your past which still "bothers you, affects you, influences you, or hinders you."

_____
_____
_____
_____
_____

5. Using the definitions given and your genogram, identify the kind of boundaries you have in the following areas of your life. Circle the one that characterizes your typical behavior: R (rigid) ~ D (diffuse) ~ F (flexible)

Remember:
Rigid = too strong   Diffuse = too weak   Flexible = healthy

R ~ D ~ F   Individual Personal Boundaries

R ~ D ~ F   Inter-generational Boundaries

R ~ D ~ F   Family Boundaries

6. The following are unwritten rules which characterize dysfunctional families. Circle Y = yes, if this is characteristic of you, S = sometimes, if this is sometimes true of you; and N = no, if this is not true of you. If this is characteristic of other family member/s, write their name/s in the blank.

Y ~ S ~ N   Don't feel _____

Y ~ S ~ N   Always in control _____

Y ~ S ~ N   Deny what's going on _____

Y ~ S ~ N   Don't trust _____

Y ~ S ~ N   Keep family secrets _____

Y ~ S ~ N   Are ashamed _____

1. In which of your relationships do you and the other persons simply react to each other by habit, instead of interacting spontaneously?

   _____

   _____

   _____

   _____

   _____

2. Chart these relationships using the "triangle" method described in this chapter. Identify which type of triangle best represents each set of relationships:

   Ongoing continual patterns
   - All straight lines: Three people; solidly connected.
   - One straight and two wavy: Two people connect with one another against the third.

   Temporary, unstable patterns
   - All wavy lines: Three people who do not get along at all, or who cannot connect with each other.
   - Two straight and one wavy: One person, trying to hold together the other two, who don't get along.

3. Look at each of these triangle models; then identify any hurt or anger resulting from these relational patterns. Below, list anyone from your triangles toward whom you harbor such feelings and tell why:

   _____

   _____

   _____

   _____

   _____

4. In each of the instances above, list specific ways your lack of forgiveness hinders YOUR life today:

_____

_____

_____

_____

_____

5. How would you experience freedom if you could forgive each person on your list above?

_____

_____

_____

_____

_____

6. Page 133 refers to a how a new person can uncover hidden dynamics when they enter into your family relationships. How has a third person (from outside your original family system) entered a relationship with you and been able to "blow the cover" off your denial systems?

_____

_____

_____

_____

What fresh perspective on your family did this person bring to your attention?

_____

_____

_____

_____

_____

What reaction occurred within the family system that tried to return the relationships to the way they were before?

_____

_____

_____

_____

_____

Did you give in to the pressure of the family system to restore the denial, or form new relationships within the system? _____
Why or why not?

_____

_____

_____

_____

1. This chapter asserts that "Forgiveness is the only way to attain genuine freedom from the bad effects of the past." Before you can begin to forgive, you must recognize and acknowledge how you have been hurt by wrongs done to you. It is common in dysfunctional families to pretend not to be hurt.

    How have you felt pressured not to acknowledge the hurts that have injured you in your family?

    _____
    _____
    _____
    _____
    _____

2. Refer to your genogram and triangle models of your relationships. Use these to help you compile a list of wrongs done to you. This is a process that will take time. Use the space below to list any that come to mind immediately. Use a journal to list other memories as they surface. Wrongs done to me:

    1. _____
    2. _____
    3. _____

    (Start with the three most pressing incidents. Once you learn the process to forgive these, you can repeat the process for all the rest of the wrongs that remain to be forgiven.)

3. For each of the wrongs done to you (above) identify those people who hurt you and those who didn't protect you from hurt:

    THOSE WHO HURT ME   THOSE WHO DIDN'T
                               PROTECT ME FROM HURT

    Wrong #1 _____   _____

    _____   _____

Wrong #2 _____   _____

_____   _____

Wrong #3 _____   _____

_____   _____

4. Unforgiveness is characterized by feeling "as though they have taken away something that belonged to us—our peace, our joy, our happiness—and that they now owe it to us." This chapter used the analogy of holding an emotional IOU toward those who hurt you. Take a separate piece of paper for each of the persons you named above. Make out an IOU that represents what you are holding against them, what they did, how that robbed you of something and what you feel they owe you (if they had the power to give it back). Hold on to these, until you finish with them further on.

_____

_____

_____

_____

_____

5. Many people refuse to forgive because they think forgiveness means they must forget what happened, act as if it was OK or act as though it didn't hurt them. Does understanding that forgiveness includes acknowledging wrong and canceling the debt help you become willing to forgive? _____
    Why or why not?

_____

_____

_____

_____

_____

6. Forgiveness starts with a personal decision. If you are willing to begin the process of forgiveness toward those named on your emotional IOUs sign your commitment below: I choose to forgive. I commit myself to begin this process of forgiveness today:

Signature: _____

Date: _____

Remember, you will need to express the feelings associated with the injuries you have suffered. You may not FEEL like you are in the process of forgiveness. Whenever you doubt your commitment, look at your signature here and reaffirm your commitment to work through all the steps of forgiveness.

7. Look at each of the IOUs you have created to represent those you need to forgive. For each of these, identify the emotions stirred up when you dare to think about what happened and how it hurt you. In your journal, complete the following sentences to help you identify your emotions for each IOU you made:
   - I am afraid to look at this because...
   - I feel guilty about...
   - I feel ashamed and humiliated by...
   - I am angry that...
   - I feel sad because...

8. "Expressing your destructive emotions is important because it gets them "out of your system" so that they cannot poison you any longer." Choose how you will express your emotions related to each of the emotional IOUs you have created. I will:

___ Talk them out

___ Write them out

___ Talk to an empty chair

___ Other _____

Take time now to work on expressing your emotions associated with one of your IOUs. You can work through the others as you are able.

9. How have your boundaries been violated as you were growing up in your family?

_____

_____

_____

_____

_____

10. What new boundaries do you need to set to protect yourself?

_____

_____

_____

_____

_____

11. This is the time in the process to cancel the debt or transfer it to God. It may help you cancel the debt to know that you can transfer that person's account to God for him to settle as he sees fit. Even if the person has not repented or acknowledged how they have hurt you, you can let go of your demands that they make up to you what you feel they owe you. AFTER YOU HAVE WORKED THROUGH STEPS 1-4, as explained in this chapter, for any of the IOUs that represent what you were holding against someone, choose to cancel that debt or turn it over to God. Write CANCELED across the IOU and date it, to symbolize your release of that person's offenses against you.

12. Consider the possibilities of reconciliation. Answer the following questions for each person with whom you are considering reconciliation. Use your answers to help you decide where the relationship goes from here. Remember, to forgive someone does not mean you HAVE to reconcile the relationship.
    • Why do you want reconciliation?
    • If you approach the other person, what do you think their response will be?
    • Can you accept the worst possible response?
    • How can you check to see if the other person is open to working through their part of the reconciliation?

13. What is your next step to prepare yourself and move toward reconciliation?

_____

_____

_____

_____

_____

CHAPTER SEVEN

1. List two things you gain from remembering and accepting a past hurt, even though you've forgiven it.

   1. _____

   2. _____

2. Use these sentence starters to help you cite a specific example from your life: When I remembered...

   _____
   _____
   _____
   _____
   _____

   It helped me...

   _____
   _____
   _____
   _____
   _____

3. Your current problems may relate to past hurts that have not been fully resolved. List a few of your current problems below, then see if you can trace the problem back to a previous hurt.

CURRENT PROBLEM	PAST HURT
FOR EXAMPLE: I am insecure and suspicious	My spouse had an affair

CURRENT PROBLEM	PAST HURT
1. _____	_____
2. _____	_____
3. _____	_____

4. What past experiences have you had to try NOT to think about because they trouble you?

_____

_____

_____

_____

_____

5. What kind of emotions do you experience when you allow these repressed thoughts to surface?

_____

_____

_____

_____

_____

6. Are you willing to notice when you are trying NOT to think about something, face the feelings and deal with what happened so you can work through them? _____

7. Are there any periods of time during your childhood that are missing from your memory? _____

   Consider each of the time periods listed below. For each age range in your life, try to recall what life was like during these years—where you were living, what your room looked like, what was going on at home and at school. Circle any of these age ranges where you cannot remember details.

   Ages: 1-4   5-8   9-12   13-15   16-18

   These blank spots in your memory may give you clues to painful parts of your past you have not resolved.

8. Consider how you describe your father and mother to others. Do you tend to paint them as all good or all bad?

_____

_____

_____

_____

9. Try to write a description about your parents that includes at least three good characteristics and three bad characteristics.

_____

_____

_____

_____

_____

If you have trouble doing this, you may want to explore this further with the help of a counselor.

10. Which best describes your view of your parents:
    * Outright rejection
    * Unhealthy idealization
    * Healthy realization that they are only human—good and bad

11. Can you identify your mother in one of the following types:
    * INTRUSIVE: Very controlling; uses guilt trips; lacks respect for healthy boundaries in your life
    * ABANDONING: Either physically or emotionally absent
    * UNPREDICTABLE: Sometimes loving, sometimes cold and indifferent

12. Looking back over your childhood, can you now see where you may have thought that you were bad, because you could not conceive that your parents could be the ones at fault? How have you condemned yourself unjustly?

_____

_____

_____

_____

13. What crutches have you leaned on to cope with and escape the pain of your life?

_____

_____

_____

_____

_____

14. How have you used CONTROLLING behavior, living in DENIAL, AVOIDANCE of uncomfortable situations or memories, and existing in a state of emotional NUMBNESS to escape your inner pain?

_____
_____
_____
_____
_____

15. When have you been in hurtful situations, but were forbidden to acknowledge what was happening and express your anger?

_____
_____
_____
_____
_____

    How does this still influence your ability to express anger when anger is justified?

_____
_____
_____
_____
_____

16. What have you learned from the pain of the past that can help protect you from being "burned" again?

_____
_____
_____
_____

17. This chapter said, "We forgive—even as we remember!" Are you willing to do so? _____
    How are you actively doing this?

_____
_____
_____
_____

18. Are you willing to seek the help of a professional therapist, if necessary, to aid you in the process of remembering what happened, facing the feelings that arise and completing the process of forgiveness?_____

CHAPTER EIGHT

1. Think of a specific incident where you have been wronged (and still feel the sting, but where you have tried to brush it off, minimize what happened or avoid the issue because you feel uncomfortable going through the conflict. Describe that incident here (it may be one of the ones for which you had an IOU:

    _____
    _____
    _____
    _____
    _____

2. Have you offered superficial forgiveness? _____
    If so, did the superficial forgiveness resolve the issue? _____
    If not, how have you seen the issue raised again? _____

3. How would you define the following:
    *   Forgiveness as a decision: _____
        _____
    *   Superficial forgiveness: _____
        _____
    *   The process of forgiveness:_____
        _____

4. Quickly forgiving (superficially) will not mend a relationship for long; true forgiveness is a process. Will you commit to work through the issue at hand until it no longer controls you emotionally?_____

5. "Forgiveness is a journey of many steps." What steps have you taken so far?

    _____
    _____
    _____
    _____
    _____

What steps can you take next to work through your anger on the way to complete forgiveness?

1._____

2._____

3._____

6. Is there something you have done wrong toward another person that calls for repentance? _____

List the three steps of repentance from the chapter:

1._____

2._____

3._____

Where are you in this three-step process?

_____

_____

_____

_____

_____

7. Will you make a commitment to yourself, that you will no longer stop at superficial forgiveness, but rather will process and work through your feelings? _____

8. With whom can you share this commitment so that they can hold you accountable?

_____

_____

_____

_____

_____

CHAPTER NINE

1. Is it difficult for you to recognize, admit, or deal with your anger?
    _____

2. How does this show itself in your family relationships?

    _____

    _____

    _____

    _____

    _____

3. Do you accept what this chapter asserts: that it is not only OK, but necessary to recognize and accept your anger before you will be able to truly forgive? _____

4. If accepting anger as OK to feel is new for you, how can you remind yourself of this when you automatically try to ignore or stuff your angry feelings?

    _____

    _____

    _____

5. Resentment is the by-product of unexpressed anger. Toward whom do you hold resentment? (If you're not sure, it's those people who stir up anger or other repressed emotions when you see them or think about them.)

    _____

    _____

    _____

    _____

    _____

6. Unexpressed anger and the resentment it causes become a poison if they are not acknowledged and dealt with on a conscious level. Are you willing to do the work of expressing the anger and resentment you

currently have buried? If so, which of the methods listed below will you use:

- Write down exactly how you feel
- Share your feelings with a trusted friend
- Verbalize your feelings out loud to yourself
- Write a letter to the person (but DON'T send it)

7. When do you hide your angry feelings because you feel guilty? For example, you "have no right to feel angry."

_____

_____

_____

Who convinced you that you have no right to feel angry?

_____

_____

8. When do you hide your angry feelings because you are afraid to express them?

_____

_____

_____

What are you afraid will happen if your express your anger?

_____

_____

_____

9. Some people from dysfunctional families learn to negate their feelings. The "good" feelings are allowed to be acknowledged and expressed, but the emotions that are considered "bad" have to be squashed. Rate each of the following emotions on a scale of 1-10 (1=Not accepted at all, 10=Fully acceptable:

fear	1—2—3—4—5—6—7—8—9—10
frustration	1—2—3—4—5—6—7—8—9—10
hurt	1—2—3—4—5—6—7—8—9—10
sadness	1—2—3—4—5—6—7—8—9—10
anger	1—2—3—4—5—6—7—8—9—10
happiness	1—2—3—4—5—6—7—8—9—10

10. While all emotions are part of being human, there are acceptable and unacceptable ways of expressing them. What are some acceptable ways in which you can express the feelings you previously considered unacceptable?

_____

_____

_____

_____

_____

11. Will you make a commitment NOT to consciously repress your feelings of anger, but rather to face and express them in a constructive way? _____

12. It takes practice to learn to recognize your anger and express it in appropriate ways. One good guideline is to talk out your feelings with someone you trust, but wait before expressing your anger to the person to whom the anger is directed. Is there someone you trust with whom you could discuss your angry feelings prior to taking any further action? Who?

_____

_____

_____

13. There are four common ways people tend to deal with anger; which best describes you?

___ 1. You repress your anger until you explode.

___ 2. You immediately vent your anger to the person with whom you are angry.

___ 3. You realize and acknowledge your anger but opt to "count to ten" before reacting.

___ 4. You discuss your anger with someone that you trust, in an attempt to understand why you feel as you do, and how best to handle the anger.

Only numbers 3 and 4 are healthy ways of dealing with your anger. What can you do to begin reacting in a healthier way with regard to a specific incident about which you are angry?

1. When something bad happens in your life, do you have the tendency to blame someone else?_____

2. Blaming others is often a cover-up for fear. What are you afraid of that prompts you to look for someone to blame: punishment, embarrassment, responsibility, or what?

   _____
   _____
   _____
   _____
   _____
   _____
   _____
   _____
   _____
   _____

3. Do you accept that "stuff just happens" sometimes or do you always have to look for someone to blame when something goes wrong?

   _____
   _____
   _____
   _____
   _____

4. With whom do you need to break out of a "circular dance" of blaming?

   _____
   _____

5. God limited vengeance in the Old Testament to "an eye for an eye, and a tooth for a tooth." Are there limits to your desire for vengeance or does it seem insatiable? _____
   What limits do you put on your desire for vengeance?

_____

_____

_____

_____

_____

_____

_____

_____

6. What are some things you can do to put the bad or disappointing times in your life into the proper perspective?

_____

_____

_____

_____

_____

7. What is the difference between (a) blaming and (b) remembering a past offense while acknowledging the truth of what happened and blaming?

_____

_____

_____

_____

_____

8. Judging from past experience, has placing blame on someone else ever helped you move past the issue and away from bitterness?_____

9. Explain why it is good for YOU to begin the process of forgiveness, even when the offender may not deserve your forgiveness; include the benefits if you stop blaming someone else for your present condition:

_____

_____

_____

_____

_____

10. If you find yourself stuck in a pattern of blaming others, are you willing to seek professional help to help you stop blaming and start accepting responsibility for your own life? _____

11. Look at the model at the top of page 250; which path are you on and where along that path?_____

12. What tendencies of a "co-dependent" person described in this chapter do you exhibit?

_____

_____

_____

_____

_____

13. Is there anyone in your life who makes it easier for you to continue unhealthy patterns of living by their co-dependent behavior? _____

14. If you answered "YES" to the question above, what are you willing to do to bring your relationship with your enabling partner into a healthier pattern of relating? _____

15. Are you willing to practice speaking your feelings in "I" statements, rather than "You" statements? _____

    If yes, to whom will you make this commitment so they can help you monitor the way you speak and how you tend to place blame on others?

_____

_____

16. List the names of the people with whom you currently share your feelings and troubles:

    1. _____

    2. _____

    Do these people tend to join your pity party or help you move along the path of forgiveness and accepting responsibility for your life?

_____

_____

17. How does each of the persons listed above either help you move out of blaming or join you in blaming?

_____

_____

_____

_____

18. How can you change the nature of your relationships away from blaming and choose people who will not encourage you to blame others?

_____

_____

_____

_____

_____

1. Forgiveness and reconciliation are separate but closely related issues. Make a list here of all the people with whom you are somewhere in the process of forgiveness or reconciliation:

   _____

   _____

   _____

   _____

   _____

   - Draw a circle around any names on the list for those whom you have forgiven, but with whom you have not been reconciled.
   - Draw a box around any names of those with whom you have reconciled, without true forgiveness.
   - Put a star next to the names of those with whom you have reconciled and forgiven.
   - Draw a check next to the names of those you have forgiven and done all you can to reconcile (even if they have refused to reconcile.)

2. Have you been holding yourself responsible for a lack of reconciliation, in cases where you have done all you can? _____

   If yes, will you stop taking responsibility for the other person's decision? _____

3. Look at the names you drew a box around, those with whom you reconciled without going through the process of forgiveness. In each instance, did you:

   _____ Overlook the pain caused by someone else's actions

   _____ Deny that you were hurt

   _____ Excuse inexcusable behavior

   _____ Fear you would lose the relationship if you spoke up

   _____ Fear _____ if you spoke up

4. In situations where you are seeking reconciliation are you ready to bring forward the hidden things which need to be brought to light?

   _____

5. What are your motives in wanting to confront or deal with these issues:

___ Retaliation   ___ To bring the truth to light
___ Revenge   ___ To seek reconciliation
___ Retribution   ___ To restore relationship
___ Spitefulness   ___ To help me forgive completely

*If you answered yes to any of the reasons on the left, wait on any confrontation. When your motives move into the column on the right you are ready for a confrontation that can lead to reconciliation.

6. Confrontation calls for careful preparation. What will you do to prepare yourself to confront those you believe you need to confront?

_____

_____

_____

_____

_____

7. Can you go into a confrontation with no expectations about the outcome of the meeting? _____

What expectations do you have?

_____

_____

_____

_____

_____

What do you hope for, but don't necessarily expect?

_____

_____

_____

_____

_____

8. Are you prepared to handle the following reactions:

___ Denial (That isn't what happened.)
___ Counter-Charging (It's your fault.)
___ Minimizing the Issue (It wasn't that bad.)
___ Ambiguity (I don't remember it like that.)

Practice how you would handle each of these reactions if you were to confront the issue.

9. Do you need to work through forgiveness and reconciliation with someone who is dead? _____

   If so, what technique will you use to help you do so?

   _____

   _____

   _____

   _____

   _____

10. Are you in a situation where the person who hurt you as a child, has changed and is no longer the type of person who would still hurt you?_____

    If yes, can you acknowledge and forgive what they did in the past while dealing with the person as they are now?_____

Chapter Twelve

1. Are you willing to consider how your attitudes and choices (about how to deal with what happened to you) contributed to your pain?

   _____

2. List the ways (if any) in which you have added to your own pain:

   1._____

   2._____

   3._____

3. Are you ready and willing to forgive yourself for the things you have listed above? _____

4. You will need to work through the steps listed below, to be ready to forgive yourself:

   a. Recognize the injury...

   What happened?

   _____

   _____

   _____

   What role did you play?

   _____

   _____

   _____

   Did you do anything wrong?

   _____

   _____

   _____

   b. Identify the emotions involved. Do you feel:

   ___ Fear

   ___ Guilt

   ___ Shame

   ___ Anger

   ___ Sadness

   ___ Other _____

5. Which of the following techniques will you use to express your feelings about how you have contributed to your own pain:

___ Talk them over with a friend

___ Write out what happened

___ Talk to yourself about it

6. Are any of the following conditions a sign that you lack boundaries:

___ Compulsive overeating

___ Starving yourself

___ Abuse of alcohol or drugs

___ Overdoing exercise

___ Engaging in dangerous behavior

___ Become antagonistic

___ Other

A "YES" answer to any of these conditions will lead to further injury and self-loathing, if left unchecked. What will you do to deal with any of these problem areas?

_____

_____

_____

_____

_____

7. Are you ready to cancel the debt you hold against yourself?_____

8. Which of the following statements of self-forgiveness can you agree with:

___ I am no longer willing to blame myself.

___ I am no longer willing to accept guilt over what happened.

___ I did the best I could with the knowledge I had.

___ I will be compassionate toward myself.

___ I am human. I will make mistakes.

9. Are you willing to pray and ask God to forgive you all your sins and shortcomings, and to accept the payment Jesus Christ made on the cross to pay for all your sins? _____

If so, giving consideration to everything listed above, can you and do you choose to forgive yourself? _____

10. Make a replica of the emotional IOU you have held against yourself. Write CANCELED across it when you have CHOSEN to forgive yourself, and date it.

You have shown your determination to forgive and find healthier patterns of relating by conscientiously working through this study guide. Remember, it's OK to seek help. When you are dealing with patterns of life that have molded your thinking from childhood, you may need the help of a counselor to work through these issues. Don't be afraid or embarrassed to ask for help. If you find yourself stuck on any of the exercises given here, please seek help from a qualified professional you can trust.